LIGHTS FOR THE PATH

LIGHTS FOR THE PATH

JOHN SULLIVAN

VERITAS

Published 2022 by
Veritas Publications
7–8 Lower Abbey Street
Dublin 1
Ireland
www.veritas.ie

ISBN 978 1 80097 026 7

10 9 8 7 6 5 4 3 2 1

A catalogue record for this book is available from the British Library.

Designed by Jeannie Swan, Veritas Publications
Printed in the Republic of Ireland by SPRINT-print Ltd, Dublin

Veritas books are printed on paper made from the wood pulp of
managed forests. For every tree felled, at least one tree is planted,
thereby renewing natural resources.

This book is dedicated to Jean, who has lightened my burdens and been a light for our journey of life together.

Contents

Acknowledgements

Many people exert an influence on the writing of a book and only some of them can be recalled by authors since they are not always aware of how they have been touched by others. When this book was originally conceived as a project, it was to be co-written with Mario D'Souza, CSB. Sadly, he was struck down suddenly by cancer before he could even begin work on his chapters and he died very soon after. I am grateful for the enthusiasm he shared with me when we talked about this book immediately prior to his falling ill and I am indebted to him for his encouragement with regard to the need for it. His own magisterial volume, *A Catholic Philosophy of Education: The Church and Two Philosophers* (McGill-Queens University Press, 2016), which offers a penetrating and authoritative critical retrieval of the thought of Jacques Maritain and Bernard Lonergan, demonstrating their relevance for an authentically grounded understanding of Catholic education, was a major stimulus for embarking on *Lights for the Path*.

I am greatly indebted to Carol Devine, librarian at Liverpool Hope University. I have always considered librarians as unsung heroes, a hidden power, behind teachers, in schools and especially in universities. With her prompt, reliable and cheerful service, Carol enabled me to access many articles over the past few years which have fed into my research and writing.

Richard Wilkin, Raymond Friel and André Gushurst-Moore, each of whom has vast experience of teaching and leadership in Catholic education, kindly read and offered feedback on draft chapters. While I was not always able to incorporate all their advice, their affirmation of the project certainly helped me to remain motivated and I very much appreciated their wise insights.

Margaret Buck generously read and offered feedback on every chapter, giving close attention to content, relevance and presentation. Her wide-raging experience of educational leadership in schools, local education authorities, as a government inspector and as a Director of Education for the Catholic schools in her archdiocese, apart from the quality of her deep faith and her innate personal wisdom, together with her encouragement from start to finish – all made a huge difference to my morale and gave me reason to believe that the book is addressing a real need and she gave me grounds to hope that it does so in a relevant and worthwhile manner.

Thanks are due to Gareth Byrne in Dublin and to Patricia Kieran in Limerick for their unflagging support and encouragement for my work as well as for their own creative initiatives for Catholic education. Both are models, in their integration of intellect, Christian faith and accomplished professionalism, of how to blend imagination, strong conviction and gentleness with others.

Tony Slingo, my parish priest and brother in faith, has been alongside me as this book was being written, constantly in dialogue with me about the deeper meaning and demands of our shared commitments and we have enjoyed frequent lighter moments of theological ping-pong.

My thinking about what is missing in and what is needed for the healthy flourishing of Catholic education has been clarified, challenged and reinforced by countless teachers in Catholic primary and secondary schools, through their responses to the professional development days that I have led on aspects of mission into practice, and by many university colleagues in their conversations with me over the years. Whether those in-service sessions were met with welcome, warmth and wonderful affirmation, or with suspicion, confusion and resistance, I learned more from them than they realised at the time and more than I can now recall.

Paul, my youngest son, is always my refuge and rescuer whenever I run into difficulties in managing the computer and I am constantly grateful for – and somewhat in awe of – the speed with which he solves problems that seem inexplicable and which feel insuperable to me.

There are many hands at work in the process of moving a book from the author's computer through all stages of publication and onwards into the public domain. I am grateful for all the staff at Veritas, including Pamela McLoughlin, Síne Quinn, Fiona Dunne, Mags Gargan, Greg Daly and others. They have been encouraging, supportive and highly competent throughout.

Finally, I must thank Jean, my loving wife of the past fifty-one years (long may this continue). She has unselfishly supported me in in my vocation as a teacher and writer, warmly looked after me, and forgiven my foibles and failings. Her high standards in all she does, her intelligence and multiple skills as well as her resilience in the face of a series of health challenges, all call forth my admiration. Always willing to give me the time and space I need to concentrate on research and writing, she is stimulating and enjoyable company and I could not ask for a better friend and loving companion.

Introduction

The path that Catholic educators walk is a challenging one. It can seem highly demanding and perplexing, calling for personal qualities and types of knowledge that are often misunderstood and subject to criticism in the wider culture. Academic norms, legislative frameworks, cultural assumptions and institutional requirements can sometimes threaten to crowd out the attention, time and energy needed for teachers to become familiar with and confident about the intellectual and spiritual underpinning of a Catholic approach to education. The immediately urgent can get in the way of what is ultimately more important. Pressure to address current issues, even when these are important, can easily colonise our minds and direct our thinking away from eternal truths. Being open to and ready to address new questions, circumstances and challenges in no way requires us to disavow what we have received and can still learn from the past. In the living tradition of the Church, the faithful have always drawn upon and deployed as vital resources what have been handed on to them from their predecessors. While it is possible to so venerate the insights and practices from the past that we are reluctant to be flexible and creative in developing this legacy in changing contexts, there is also the danger that we so exaggerate the newness of our current situation that we neglect the wisdom – gathered by generations of Christian disciples – about what leads to human flourishing, social harmony and care for creation. Far too few teachers in Catholic universities and schools, even those with a vibrant personal faith, are confident about drawing upon, or even simply being familiar with, essential features of a Catholic worldview. This book is intended to remind readers that there is a wealth of vitally important spiritual, intellectual and pedagogical wisdom conveyed across the centuries by major thinkers in the living tradition of Catholic Christianity. Each chapter (with the exception of Chapter 7, which combines the treatment of two scholars) emphasises key insights of one major exemplar of that wisdom and then demonstrates the enduring relevance of that scholar's thought and example for today's teachers in Catholic schools and universities.

My goal in writing this book is to provide an introduction to and an exploration of major witnesses from the Catholic intellectual and spiritual tradition who provide inspiration and guidance to Catholic educators today. I hope to make key insights from these witnesses (or 'lights') accessible to Catholic educators and to indicate how their writings provide valuable perspectives on the philosophy and practice of Catholic education. Put succinctly, my intention is to nurture a Catholic consciousness among educators and to introduce them to important elements of a Catholic worldview.

Romano Guardini, on taking up a post at the University of Berlin as Professor in the Philosophy of Religion and Catholic *Weltanschauung* ('worldview') in 1923, gave his inaugural lecture, 'The Essence of a Catholic *Weltanschauung*', which explored how a Catholic way of reading and responding to the world has a bearing on education in particular and, more generally, on life itself. Such reading and response continues in an endless cycle: the way we read the world influences how we respond in our choices, actions and priorities; in turn, that response reinforces, challenges or modifies our reading. In sharing a Catholic worldview with others, we can achieve two things simultaneously. First, we show what the world and everything in it looks like from where we are standing; this includes how we see that everything holds together in an integrated way. Second, we reveal to others (as transparently as possible) the position from which we are looking: our starting points for investigation, our foundational assumptions and bedrock principles, our deepest values, and how we see the source or author of the meaning and purpose of life.

All people, consciously or unconsciously, possess a worldview that makes a real difference in how the world appears to them and how they engage with that world. Embracing a worldview involves more than holding a set of concepts. American missiologist Paul Hiebert defines a worldview as 'the foundational cognitive, affective, and evaluative assumptions and frameworks a group of people makes about the nature of reality which they use to order their lives'.[1] Worldview is about configuration, inter-connectedness and mutual reinforcement in those leading perspectives we have that function as the keys to our main perceptions of reality and our judgements, but our ideas and viewpoints neither emerge on strictly logical lines nor do they get deployed on purely logical grounds. Rather they are embedded in a pattern of behaving and belonging that 'carries' whatever reasoning they contain beyond any strict remit that flows from reason alone. That is, people are formed (and sustained) in a worldview largely through the company they keep, the practices they engage in, and the lives they lead, as well as by what and who they love. Their worldview gives them some kind of rationale and picture of the whole, and a sense of meaning within the flux and ambiguities of life. This worldview is rough and ready rather than sharply shaped; it is often not reflected upon, nor articulated; in many cases it operates clandestinely rather than explicitly. It can contain irreconcilable elements. Worldviews function partly as ways of framing the world, giving us a handle on it; they filter the world for us, so we can cope with parts of it without being overwhelmed by the sheer buzzing confusion of it all; they also help us to order it in terms of how we channel our attention, energy and effort and they help us to prioritise certain values without having to agonise about each one.

Our worldview influences what we notice, take in and accept. It shapes how we perceive messages that we receive from various individuals and groups and from life's experience and then how we relate what we have filtered and sifted into what we already hold, know and are committed to. It guides what we do with what we have learned. It manifests itself in those things we care about and to which we give our energy.

David Foote highlights several helpful insights from Guardini's worldview lecture.[2] After noting that 'a worldview "gazes" upon the concrete things in existence from the perspective of totality, or the whole', Foote makes four observations. First is the need for context in making sense of anything: 'For example, we can make no sense of a hand until we understand it as part of a body. If we continue in this direction, we reach that ultimate context or whole – the worldview.' Our intuitive assumption about the whole 'allows us to place the concrete objects of experience in context so that we can begin to understand them in their particularity'. Second, he acknowledges that, for each of us, our worldviews are necessarily limited and incomplete because they are conditioned by the historical, sociological and cultural circumstances that frame what we learn and what we do with that learning. Third, Foote clarifies the relationship between a worldview and academic disciplines: 'A worldview begins with the whole; academic disciplines begin with the parts. A worldview contextualizes the object; then, an academic discipline studies the object intensively.' Finally, and with special reference to a Christian worldview, Foote points out that such an outlook cannot adequately be described as a view of the whole from within the world because it is illuminated and transformed by divine revelation, an encounter with the Living Word of God, Jesus Christ, and it is awakened, galvanised and extended by the enduring presence of God's Holy Spirit.

Thus a Christian worldview is more than a merely natural, human achievement (although reaching some degree of clarity about it does require much human effort); it is supernaturally graced. That divine underpinning, however, does not guarantee that, on our side, we always grasp the fullness of truth in all its ramifications. For that we need the guidance of the Church, constant prayer, openness to God's promptings, humility, a virtuous life and earnest searching. Only by that path will we learn how to internalise the message of Christ, enter into communion with him, participate in his work, come to see the world with his gaze and respond to it with his loving touch.

Imagine Christian faith as a constantly bubbling stream that is permanently energised and replenished by the non-stop rain of God's grace. The waters of this stream have been used over the centuries to quench many different kinds of thirst and to douse many different types of fire. Witchcraft, warfare, famine, persecution, plague, drought, floods, as well as addiction and abusive relationships – the waters of Christian faith are called upon in diverse ways. These experiences exert important influences on which aspect of the faith is given priority, which feature is partly neglected or treated as less urgent at this moment, and which dimension is rethought in the process of being applied to specific contexts.

In a similar fashion, the individuals who are the focus of the following chapters can be considered as rivulets that pour into the great ocean of Christian tradition, renewing, enlivening and extending its flow, making sure that the waters of faith continue to be available, wherever they are needed. We can claim that Catholic education is constantly being replenished by ordinary and extraordinary individuals from the great chain of witnesses who simultaneously draw from, and contribute to, our living tradition. Teaching is one of those vocations where one person's life (in this case, that of the teacher) touches and lights up another's in significant, enriching and enduring ways. Our task as teachers is not so much to 'win' people for Christ or to get them 'into' the Church (although both are legitimate aspirations) as it is to share our knowledge and our very self with our students, with a view to releasing, fostering and reinforcing the giftedness already latent within them. I hope that, through your encounter with the men and women in the following chapters, one or more of them will catch your interest and stimulate you to explore more deeply what is implied in a Catholic worldview, so that, in turn, you will impact on your students in life-giving and faith-filled ways.

Towering figures who have contributed significantly over the centuries to the development of Catholic education, such as St Augustine of Hippo, St Benedict, St Thomas Aquinas, St John Henry Newman, Jacques Maritain or Bernard Lonergan, do not receive attention here. This is not because I question their importance, but they are not examined here for two reasons. First, I have already written about some of these figures elsewhere[3] and, second, such leading figures have been extensively covered by many other scholars.[4]

This book aims to draw attention to some lesser-known representatives of the tradition than the eminent (and still vitally important) thinkers just named. To that end, I have selected three figures from the earlier history of the Church (the seventh, twelfth and thirteenth centuries): St Maximus the Confessor, a Greek monk who is revered in both the Eastern and the Western Church, St Hildegard of Bingen, a Benedictine nun, and St Bonaventure, a Franciscan friar, each of whom has been canonised as a saint and both Hildegard and Bonaventure having the accolade of being named as official Doctors of the Church. Their life and work, together with major themes in their writing that remain relevant for Catholic educators today, are treated in Part One, under the broad heading of 'Christ and Creation'. These three writers exemplify what it means to read the world and human beings in the light of Christian faith. After examining central elements of their Christian worldview, I highlight a handful of key points from each of their worldviews that can offer guidance for Catholic educators in the twenty-first century.

In Part Two, 'Interiority and Engagement', the focus is on six twentieth-century thinkers, most of whom dealt more explicitly with educational issues than was the case with the authors reviewed in Part One. The first of these is the German Jewish philosopher Edith Stein, who converted to Catholicism and several years afterwards became a Carmelite; more recently, she has been canonised as Saint Teresa Benedicta of the Cross. Then there is the English poet Elizabeth Jennings, followed by the Brazilian expert on adult literacy who later became an international adviser on educational policy, Paulo Freire. The next chapter combines an examination of two North American scholars, both specialists in English literature and cultural analysis, the Canadian Marshall McLuhan, and a Jesuit from the United States, Walter Ong. The last figure whose relevance for Catholic educators is explored here is the French lay philosopher and historian Étienne Gilson. These six writers have in common their sensitivity to the needs of the inner life and the development of personhood, and their vision of how Christian anthropology could be preserved and communicated in the modern world. Once again, I explore how teachers in Catholic schools and universities can build on their insights and take these forward into their classrooms. Encountering the life and thought of these witnesses opens up different aspects of the Catholic tradition and their bearing on teaching and learning: theological and spiritual, philosophical and cultural, political and social, moral and aesthetic.

No prior knowledge of these key witnesses is assumed; nor do I seek to provide a comprehensive overview of their teaching. I limit myself to highlighting a few key insights that offer inspiration and guidance for Catholic educators and that may have a bearing on the overarching purposes of Catholic education, Christian anthropology, a theological foundation for the curriculum, the practice of pedagogy, relationships with students and the spirituality of teachers. The underlying tone and ethos of this book might be summarised as follows: 'Here are some treasures from our tradition; you might find it helpful to draw upon their example and relate their insights to your own work context in order to help you to appreciate more deeply the resources available in the Catholic educational tradition and then to participate more effectively in that tradition with your own vitally important contribution.' My hope is that a reading of these chapters might both afford entry points into aspects of the tradition that might otherwise be unknown or inaccessible, thereby expanding teachers' horizons, and offer stimulus for teachers' own reflections on the role they play in Catholic education and how that might be enhanced. There is no attempt to develop a cumulative or systematic argument that encapsulates all the essential elements comprising Catholic education.

In my lengthy experience of working with teachers in Catholic schools and universities, in the United Kingdom, Ireland, Australia, and in the USA, what they most frequently request is help in reigniting enthusiasm for their mission and roles, as they face personal doubts, professional challenges and cultural obstacles. They are seeking something more substantial and enduring than 'tips for tomorrow', and they yearn for something that transcends current policy requirements and practical imperatives for productivity and assessment that threaten to render them cogs in a machine or human resources enlisted in service of a bureaucracy. They hunger for the kind of nourishment that offers a positive and attractive vision of the lofty purposes that should drive and direct Catholic education; they want affirmation of their own role and appreciation of the good they are already doing; and they hope to become more confident in the ongoing task of integrating the intellectual, educational and spiritual dimensions of life. The writers whose work is explored in this book may be especially helpful in demonstrating how to envisage that integrative process.

In the period since the late-eighteenth-century Enlightenment, we have seen how technological progress, increasing personal autonomy, a strict separation between faith and reason, and the fragmentation of knowledge have replaced salvation, aspiring to sanctity, the complementarity of and harmony between faith and reason, and trust in the unity of all knowledge (as derived from the authorship of God). However, as was pointed out in the encyclical *Spe Salvi*, 'If technical progress is not matched by corresponding progress in man's ethical formation, in man's inner growth (Eph 3:16; 2 Cor 4:16) then it is not progress at all, but a threat for man and for the world.'[5] A reductionist construction of human persons has prevailed, which increasingly sees them as producers and consumers rather than as bearers of inherent dignity, made in the image of God, and called upon to grow into their potential for divine likeness. People are distracted from questioning transcendence and, even when aware of such questions, are sometimes prevented from raising them in the public domain.

A critical appreciation and creative appropriation of the living tradition of Catholic Christianity could help to rejuvenate education in Catholic schools and universities by countering a cultural tendency towards 'presentism', that is, an over-emphasis on the assumptions, concerns and achievements of the current age coupled with a lack of awareness, let alone any serious appreciation, of our predecessors' wisdom in the faith. 'Presentism' tempts us to believe that we have nothing to learn from the past. As the teacher and scholar Roy Peachey pertinently observes, 'one of our main challenges in a secular age is convincing our own people that what we have inherited is worth fighting for'.[6] He goes on to point out that 'Cut off from premodern ways of thinking, cut off from ways of thinking that were shaped by our religion, it is no wonder that our children accept secularized notions of what it means to be human.'[7] The lack of a historical perspective among teachers can only undermine the development of a Catholic consciousness. Unfortunately, it is not just the absence of an appreciation of the rich history of their intellectual and spiritual tradition among teachers that hampers the potential transformative power of Catholic education but also the fact that 'many who enter teacher education programmes to work in Catholic schools may not have a strong cognitive grasp of Catholicism'.[8] Individual teachers and Catholic educational institutions need to invest in strengthening that cognitive grasp of the Catholic worldview and how this relates to the human and divine endeavour of education. Here an understanding of Christian anthropology is pivotal for teachers in Catholic schools and universities. If the faith that is witnessed to in such institutions is not pervaded by a rigorous intellectual component, it may slip into sentimentality and superficiality, lacking the capacity to engage robustly and credibly with countervailing perspectives.

The image or metaphor of light is often linked in the Bible to the working of God in the world and also to our need for guidance as to how to discern that work and to participate in it. 'Your word is a lamp for my feet and a light for my path' (Ps 119:105). Jesus is described in John's Gospel as 'the light of the world' (Jn 8:12). Those who follow him are assured that they too are to be a light for the world (Mt 5:14). And St Paul echoes this: We are to 'shine like lights in the world' (Phil. 2:15). 'Faith is not a light which scatters all our darkness, but a lamp which guides our steps in the night and suffices for the journey', claims Pope Francis.[9] In *The Prayer of the Church* we can read the following: 'You gave wonderful guidance to your Church through her holy and distinguished teachers. May Christians rejoice in the splendid legacy these teachers have given to your Church.'[10] God speaks to us through Holy Scripture, in the preaching of his Word, in the liturgy, through the living tradition of the Church, in our own experience and through the witness of the saints (whether recognised as such or not). I hope that God speaks to you through the witness of the people whose lives and teachings are presented in the following chapters.

Two temptations can come knocking on the door of Christians charged with teaching truth, beauty and goodness in their multiple forms and expressions, and as communicated in different areas of the curriculum. The first is the temptation to hide some of the realities and truths about individual and community practice, in aid of what is thought to be the greater good that the educational community seeks to serve. Such a temptation is partly fostered by the understandable desire of one's school or university to promote a positive image of itself in the eyes of its potential benefactors and supporters and its prospective students (and their parents), and to protect itself against negative evaluations and damaging publicity. This leads to a tendency to close ranks against possible hostility, to be selective in presenting information about the institution, and to try to cover up shortcomings that reflect badly on the institution's public image. This is reflected in the individuals who comprise that community. Each of us wants others to think the best of us; we fear exposure of our weaknesses; we become skilled in hiding the gap between our aspirations and our actual practice; we are prey to self-delusion; we come to believe the picture of ourselves that we present to others; we protect ourselves against criticism by wearing a mask that eventually warps who we become and leads to hypocrisy, a vice that Jesus vehemently castigated.

The second temptation facing teachers, whose role is to advocate and to model ideals, is to allow themselves to be overwhelmed by the enormity of their task, which often feels impossible. Too much is asked of me; the gap between what I am supposed to stand for and my personal limitations and inadequacies in living out the ideals seems ridiculously huge. As a result, I might suffer burnout or breakdown, depression and defeat, or I might slip into cynicism: it is all a game; nobody lives up the claims they make; if you don't look after yourself, no one else will; don't let them get you down; the trick is to go through the motions, do the minimum you can get away with and switch off. Yet this is to ignore the way that God can make miraculous use of earthen vessels that are cracked and leaking. God can lift up the puny efforts of our apparently insignificant actions, and through God's grace our feeble attempts to represent his Word can be empowered to communicate to others more than we dared to think possible. The very mediocrity of our witness, if offered with honesty, authenticity, perseverance, humility, courage and compassion for others, can make a difference for good in their lives. The game of Catholic education *is* worth playing: we must allow God to work in us and through us and let our light shine (even if at times it is barely flickering). And the light given off by others can help show us the way. Let me end this introduction with some exultant words from Theodore H. Kitching:

> How wonderful it is to walk with God
> along the road that holy men have trod.
> How wonderful it is to hear Him say:
> Fear not, have faith
> 'tis I who lead the way.[11]

ENDNOTES

1 Hiebert, quoted by Jim and Therese D'Orsa, *Explorers, Guides and Meaning-Makers*, Mulgrave, Victoria, Australia: John Garratt Publishing, 2010, pp. 57–8.

2 David Foote, 'Romano Guardini: The Essence of a Catholic Worldview', *Crisis Magazine*, 2013. Available from: https://www.crisismagazine.com/2013/romano-guardini-the-essence-of-a-catholic-worldview (accessed on 14 January 2021).

3 See (on Newman) John Sullivan, 'Newman and interconnectedness: Integration and university education', *Journal of Religious Education*, Vol. 60, No. 1, (2012), pp. 48– 58; John Sullivan, 'Newman's Circle of Knowledge and Curriculum Wholeness in *The Idea of a University*' in Frederick D. Aquino and Benjamin J. King (eds), *The Oxford Handbook of John Henry Newman*, Oxford: Oxford University Press, 2018, pp. 538-56; and John Sullivan, 'The University', in Frederick D. Aquino and Benjamin J. King (eds), *The Oxford Handbook of John Henry Newman*, Oxford: Oxford University Press, 2018, pp. 538–556. On St Augustine, see John Sullivan, 'St Augustine, Maurice Blondel and Christian Education', in Stephen J. McKinney and John Sullivan (eds), *Education in a Catholic Perspective*, Farnham, UK: Ashgate, 2013, pp. 31–48.

4 For example, on St Augustine, see Ryan S. Topping, *St Augustine*, London and New York: Continuum, 2010. André Gushurst-Moore has written on St Benedict in *Glory in All Things: Saint Benedict & Catholic Education Today*, Brooklyn, NY: Angelico Press, 2020. For Aquinas, see Vivian Boland, *St Thomas Aquinas*, London and New York: Continuum, 2007. On Newman, see Miguel Martin-Sánchez and Jorge Cáceres-Muñoz, 'Cardinal Newman: his importance for Catholic education', *International Studies in Catholic Education*, Vol. 8, No. 1, (March 2016), pp. 29–43. On Lonergan, see Brendan Carmody, 'Towards a contemporary Catholic philosophy of education', *International Studies in Catholic Education*, Vol. 3, No. 2, (October 2011), pp. 106–19 and also Paddy Walsh, 'From philosophy to theology of education, with Bernard Lonergan and Karl Rahner', *International Studies in Catholic Education*, Vol. 10. No. 2, October, 2018, pp. 132–55. On both Maritain and Lonergan, see Mario D'Souza, *A Catholic Philosophy of Education. The Church and Two Philosophers*, Montreal and Kingston: McGill-Queens University Press, 2016.

5 Pope Benedict XVI, *Spe Salvi*, Rome: Libreria Editrice Vaticana, 2007, #22.

6 Roy Peachey, *Out of the Classroom and Into the World*, New York: Second Spring/Angelico Press, 2017, p. 12.

7 Ibid., p. 38.

8 Leonardo Franchi and Richard Rymarz, 'The education and formation of teachers for Catholic schools: responding to changed cultural contexts', *International Studies in Catholic Education*, Vol. 9, No. 1, (March 2017), pp. 2–16, at p. 5.

9 Pope Francis, *Lumen Vitae*, Rome: Libreria Editrice Vaticana, 2013, #57.

10   *The Prayer of the Church* (for the feast of St Barnabas), Nairobi: Pauline
        Publications Africa, 2009, p. 1357.

11   Theodore H. Kitching, quoted in Northumbria Community Trust, *Celtic Daily
        Prayer*, London: Collins, 2005, p. 468.

PART ONE

CHRIST AND CREATION

CHAPTER ONE

Maximus the Confessor:
The Symphony of Creation

Maximus the Confessor (580–662 CE) offers a Christ-centred and holistic vision of creation that is complex, magnificent in scope, and strongly marked by its interconnectedness and sense of coherence.[1] He provides us with a remarkable feat of synthesis, integrating Christology, cosmology, the Eucharist, ecclesiology and eschatology. He also supplies a substantial and penetrating Christian anthropology integrating the intellectual, emotional, moral, spiritual and volitional aspects of our nature, showing connections between how we manage ourselves, read the world and make our way in it, and relate to God. His writings may justly be considered to constitute a symphony of creation and to display many of the features one finds in a symphony.

What are the features of a symphony? It is composed of various strands and multidimensional elements. It displays a certain complexity, holding together with shape, coherence and unity, despite inner variations of tone and tempo. It unfolds in time, conveying dynamic movement and directionality. Proper appreciation of it depends on the listener avoiding distractions and applying disciplined attention. It fully reveals itself only at the end. It also reveals the composer. It is to be enjoyed and received more than it is to be analysed and used; one needs to allow oneself to be carried by it. In the symphony of life, each of us is given an instrument and notes to play, but we can refuse to play, play badly/carelessly, or learn to play well. The symphony can benefit from and be enriched by our part being played, no matter how humble that part might seem to us. The symphony is deficient, incomplete, if any instrument or note is omitted. A symphony is orchestrated; the parts are pulled together according to a certain order. Without suppressing individual expression by instrumentalists, their contribution has to be coordinated, under regulation. This notion may be compared to James Fowler's definition of our vocation: 'The orchestration of our leisure, our relationships, our work, our private life, our public life, of the resources we steward, so as to put it at the disposal of God's purposes, in the service of God and our neighbour.'[2] Finally, a symphony needs an integrating thread or theme to give it its identity. In the symphony of creation, this integrating theme is that of love – of God for creation and humanity, and of human beings for God, each other and creation. 'Love is the golden key that unlocks all the doors in the Maximian castle.'[3] This love is revealed and expressed in the twin movements of descent by God and ascent by humanity: the first movement being shown by God's reaching out to humanity in the incarnation, when the divine took on human form; the second movement being shown when humankind responds to God's prevenient love by embracing and doing their best to live out the new life offered in Christ.

This chapter has four sections. First is a brief outline of Maximus' life, context and works. The second section focuses on his teaching about Christ and creation. In the third part, 'Humanity', I highlight key features of Maximus' Christian anthropology, and the final section explores the educational significance of Maximus' teaching and identifies seven implications for Christian educators.

Life and work

Maximus was raised and educated in Constantinople, where he served for a while in the imperial court. He left to become a monk in what is now Turkey, then in Crete, and later, briefly, in Cyprus, before a much longer stay in Carthage, the largest city in North Africa. He had a leading role in the Lateran Council in Rome in 649, supporting Pope Martin I against the imperial authorities in the Monothelite dispute (about whether Christ had a human as well as a divine will). This was the first council convened without the cooperation of the Emperor, Constans II, who believed that failure to follow his ruling on religious matters constituted a threat to the political unity of his realm. Maximus paid the penalty for opposing such a powerful figure: he was captured, tried, exiled, then tried again, and publicly mutilated (by having his tongue and his right hand cut off) before a final exile. He died in 662 in disgrace in what is now Georgia, by the Black Sea. He was vindicated (too late) at the Sixth Ecumenical Council at Constantinople in 681.

He lived on the frontier between the Church of the East and the West while they still constituted an undivided Church – although, just as is the case today, the Church was riven by disputes over matters both major and minor. This was the period after the fall of the Roman Empire and before the emergence of medieval Christendom, between the patristic age and the flourishing of the Carolingian Empire in Western Europe and the Byzantine Empire in the east. He wrote at a time whose culture 'was rocked by the emergence of a whole new religious and political entity on its immediate horizon: Islam'.[4] The forces of Islam captured three of the five patriarchates of the Church – Jerusalem and Antioch in 638 and Alexandria in 642. At the same time the Byzantine empire faced the threat from Arab Muslims in the south, and a series of invasions from Persia in the east. In such circumstances of military aggression, religious competition, and the efforts of emperors and secular rulers to control doctrine in an effort to maintain political stability, arguments about theological orthodoxy had political implications of life or death.

Although Maximus remained a monk who was never ordained as a priest nor became an abbot, he developed a reputation as a wise spiritual guide and was sought out for advice. He communicated (at great length) with friends as their spiritual advisor, as well as corresponding with civil authorities and leading churchmen (for example, debating with a former Patriarch of Constantinople) about the interpretation of Christian doctrine.

His writings fall into the following categories. First, he assembled collections (sometimes called centuries) of 100 paragraphs (called chapters) of his reflections about different aspects of the spiritual life to be read slowly as food for contemplation. There were four centuries on charity[5] and two centuries on theology.[6] Second, he produced extensive responses to questions raised by others about obscure or confusing statements in Scripture or in earlier theologians. These were more complex and demanding works, synthesising different strands of thought. There are two formidable works in this category: the *Ambigua* or *Difficulties in the Church Fathers*[7] and *On Difficulties in Sacred Scripture: Responses to Thalassius*.[8] Although he did not write about 'education', Maximus explicitly thought of himself as teaching when he addressed individuals. Other writings in this category include letters and commentaries on Psalm 59, the Lord's Prayer and a small, but highly compressed, masterpiece on the Eucharistic liturgy, the *Mystagogia*.[9] He wrote most of these important works in Carthage between 628 and 633. The editors of *The Oxford Handbook of Maximus the Confessor* summarise the principal themes pervading his writings as being on 'the operation of human and divine will, the mediating role of Christ, the ascetic life and divinization or *theosis*, the relationship between knowledge and virtue, and the place of the liturgy in the life of the church'.[10] In these writings he displayed knowledge of philosophy, mathematics, astronomy, natural sciences, classical literature and patristic writings.

Maximus begins with Scripture and builds on tradition (which for him means Scripture, the Early Church Fathers and the Councils of the Church, the witness of the saints, and the sacraments). He responds to issues raised by theologians such as Origen, Pseudo-Dionysius, John Chrysostom and Gregory Nazianzen. He also had great regard for Cyril of Alexandria and drew upon such major religious writers as Gregory of Nyssa, Philo and Evagrius Ponticus. His reading was filtered through his life of prayer, his liturgical and mystical experience, the sharing of community with fellow monks, and his personal asceticism, as well as the influence of his spiritual elder, Sophronius of Jerusalem. In 645, aged sixty-five, he debated with a deposed bishop of Constantinople, Pyrrhus, on the question of whether Christ had one will or two, coming down firmly on the side of Christ possessing both a divine and a human will; otherwise he would be either incompletely divine or incompletely human – and thus unable to save us.[11] It was his stance on this issue, which to twenty-first-century minds might appear unduly technical and abstruse, that caused him suffering, torture and exile. He would not compromise salvific truth for the sake of political expediency or personal safety.

Despite his condemnation, only a few years after his death a council acknowledged that he had been right and his reputation and influence have remained strong in the Eastern Church ever since. Two modern commentators, Paul Blowers and Robert Wilken, refer to 'his decisive work in the shaping of Eastern Orthodoxy' and describe him as 'one of the few genuinely ecumenical theologians of the patristic era'.[12] Although he was neglected in the West for many centuries, in recent years there has been a revival of interest, as displayed both in an exponentially increasing flow of publications in many different languages and also through recent international conferences devoted to his work. A major catalyst for the renewed interest in Maximus among Catholic thinkers was the powerful and penetrating synthesis of Maximus' thought by Hans Urs von Balthasar in *Cosmic Liturgy*, a work first published in 1941. Balthasar describes Maximus as:

> a contemplative biblical theologian, a philosopher of Aristotelian training, a mystic in the great Neoplatonic tradition of Gregory of Nyssa and Pseudo-Dionysius the Areopagite, an enthusiastic theologian of the Word along the lines of Origen, a strict monk of the Evagrian tradition, and – finally and before all else – a man of the Church, who fought and who gave his life in witness for the orthodox Christology of Chalcedon and for a Church centred in Rome.[13]

Although these different strands can be identified and distinguished in Maximus' writings, it is important to note that he believed they should not be separated; what stands out is the interconnected and holistic nature of his vision. For him, the intellectual, moral, spiritual and practical dimensions of life should nourish, complement, correct and express each other. More recently, the Greek scholar Sotiris Mitralexis has pointed out that, despite not setting out to be original, and seeing himself merely as clarifying the tradition he had received, Maximus constructed 'the most complete, most consistent, and more markedly philosophical synthesis of the whole of the patristic *Weltanshauung*' (worldview or outlook).[14]

Christ and creation

Christ is at the centre of Maximus' worldview, not just as personal saviour, but also as the one who holds the cosmos together, and in whom all philosophical problems can ultimately be resolved. For Maximus, the world of scripture and the worlds of nature, history and experience all constitute the theatre where God is implementing his purpose over time and in every dimension of existence – and the key actor in this cosmic drama is Christ. Christ, for Maximus, is the key to understanding both God and humanity. Thus the doctrinal statements made by the Church about Christ have a direct bearing on moral and spiritual life; they are not just an intellectual account of Christ.

Maximus provides an extended commentary on key passages from the New Testament. Two vital texts for him are 'He has made known to us the mystery of his purpose … which he set forth in Christ … to gather up everything under Christ' (Eph 1:9–10); and 'in him were created all things … in him all things hold together … and through him to reconcile all things in him' (Col 1:16–19). These texts touch upon the mystery of salvation, God's plan for creation, which is to bring all things into harmony and communion with him, through the work of human beings whose lives are patterned after Christ.

According to Maximus, the face of Christ shines everywhere, giving life and purpose, holding everything together and drawing it into unity. In Maximus' theocentric view, creation, incarnation and resurrection are all aspects of God's work, planned from the beginning. Maximus holds to a view that once was the default position of many, but which is now rare: that God is the originating source of life, and endows every creature with a purpose; that every person has a part to play in God's plan; and that our life is teleological, directed towards an end or goal, this purpose being that we share in his life. God is the reason for our being and the goal of our being. As Vincent Rossi puts it, 'the Logos is the constituting and hence unifying principle of all things, the true inspiration of all their activity and the source of the aspiration that moves and impels all toward completion, fulfilment, consummation.'[15] Maximus viewed the coming of Christ as God's original intention, not an afterthought to rectify a first draft of creation that went wrong. Thus, he believes, it is vital that we understand the nature and role of Christ, who is the ultimate and definitive expression of God's intentions for us and who comes to us in creation (if we have the eyes to see), in sacred scripture, in humanity, in the liturgy and via the sacraments. This means that we can legitimately speak of multiple incarnations, embodiments or expressions of God's word or logos: most obviously in the flesh of Jesus, but also in the words of scripture, in the life, sacraments and work of the Church, and in the virtues of human beings when their lives are aligned with God's purposes and insofar as they embrace God's will. The incarnation of Christ was the culmination of God's intention for creation, but it was not limited to a one-off event; it is ongoing.

On the grandest scale, Maximus' Christ has a cosmic dimension. The cosmos is a sacred text, as is scripture. God's word is present everywhere, in all creatures, as much as in Holy Scripture. As the contemporary Orthodox scholar Maximos Constas notes in his introduction to Maximus' *Responses to Thalassius*, 'each is a "spelling out" of the Word, who makes himself "legible" by "inscribing" himself in the multi-layered parchments of creation, Scripture, and the human nature he assumed when he became flesh'.[16] If Christ is the centre of the cosmos, the key to its meaning and purpose, the original goal of God for creation, the one who holds together the two phases of the divine economy – creation and salvation – we could call him the centre of the circle of existence, around which everything radiates and through whom everything is connected – but without confusion, division, or separation.[17]

Thomas Cattoi explains the significance of this for Maximus: 'If everything is patterned after Christ, clearly the inner dynamics of the hypostatic union are analogous to the inner dynamics of the created order as a whole.'[18] Therefore, Maximus teases out the implications of the Chalcedonian definition of Christ that had been agreed in 451, that in Christ there were two natures: human and divine. These were united without confusion, change, division or separation. The definition implies, as Lars Thunberg observes, that this double feature of inseparable union and preserved identity (whereby neither nature is suppressed) 'is equally characteristic both of the relationship of God to all creation and of the different entities of creation in relation to one another.'[19] How this relates to human beings will be explored in the third part of this chapter, 'Humanity'.

One of the most valuable works of Maximus, in my view, is his remarkable set of reflections on the Eucharistic liturgy in the *Mystagogy*. First, it shows how important the liturgy was for his view of the world, colouring all aspects of his experience and philosophy. Second, consideration of his liturgical outlook highlights one of the major challenges he poses to our modern mentality, which is so deeply influenced by perspectives untouched by a liturgical sensibility: our tendency to isolate our 'reading' of the world from the worldview we are being inducted into in the liturgy.

The term 'mystagogy' commonly refers to an initiation into the mysteries of faith; for Maximus it specifically meant the Divine Liturgy. By comparison with earlier examples of mystagogical writings – intended to engage a live audience – Maximus' book *On the Ecclesiastical Mystagogy* was much more rigorous, marked by 'philosophical sophistication, terminological precision, and intricacy of argument'.[20] This book begins with a reflection on the nature of the Church, which represents for Maximus both the image of

God and the entire created order. Maximus explains the symbolic significance of the various elements of the liturgy, for example, the entrance of the bishop into the church; then that of the people; the reading of scripture; the singing of hymns; the closing of the holy doors; the kiss of peace; the recitation of the Creed and other prayers. He relates these to the soul's journey to God and to the moral transformation brought about by each part of the liturgy. He weaves together the cosmic and the mundane, the eternal and the present, the intellectual and the material. In his introduction to the 2019 edition, Armstrong summarises Maximus' purpose in showing how 'the Church is the community in and by which God accomplishes his mission of reconciling the world to himself'.[21] 'The elements of the liturgy are both parts of material reality and functions of divine grace.'[22] For each element or action in the liturgy, Maximus refers to its significance, its symbolic meaning, what it points to or indicates. Symbolic action leads to real spiritual participation, one might say immersion, in divine realities and an authentic anticipation of heaven. We are used to the idea that the liturgy – across the Church's seasons – invites us to internalise and assimilate ourselves to the history of salvation. In his *Mystagogy*, Maximus extends this to include not only the life and teaching of Jesus, but everything from the cosmos as a whole to the divinisation of each individual soul.

In the final chapter, Maximus observes of the grace made available by liturgical participation:

> This grace remakes, reshapes – and to speak truly – transforms each one found there [in the liturgy] into something more divine in a way that is proportionate to him. And this grace leads each one to that which is signified by the mysteries performed during the holy synaxis [liturgical assembly], even if he does not perceive it with his senses because he is still an 'infant in Christ' and he is unable to see into the depth of what is occurring.[23]

The Eucharist is a locus for celebration, commemoration, and self-offering; for receiving Jesus as Word and Life, bringing unity out of diversity, anticipating God's kingdom and mutual participation in God's life for the deification of persons and the transformation of communities and creation. It is the event or occasion when the incarnation of Christ opens up anew in the myriad lives of his disciples today when they explicitly enter into his life, commit themselves to sharing in and living out the pattern he laid down for his followers – first by receiving Word and Sacrament, and then by being sent into the world to convey and embody his love in their lives. Maximus teaches that the liturgy is a link between individual and world transformation. If Christ is the (divinely given) code by which all the diversity and plurality of creation is brought into a harmonious symphony, then the liturgy provides a compressed and symbolic rehearsal of the working out of God's providential plan for creation. Having received Christ in the Eucharist, we are given the code that enables us to interpret creation and the cosmos as the theatre of God's work. Could one speak of receiving the Word (in Scripture) as enlightening the mind in its search for truth and receiving the Bread of Life as feeding the body so that it is ready to be active in a virtuous life?

Maximus proposes that the different parts of the church building represent the different parts of the human person. In *Mystagogy*, Chapters 3–5, he also describes the Church as an image of the sensible cosmos considered on its own terms (sanctuary as heaven; nave as earth); of a human being (sanctuary as mind; nave as body); and of the soul alone (sanctuary as intellectual power for contemplation; nave as its animating power for praxis).[24] In chapters 6–7, he draws analogies between Scripture and a human being (New Testament as mind and Old Testament as body; or spiritual sense as mind and literal sense as body) and between a human being and the cosmos (soul as intelligible world; body as sensible world).

Chapters 8–24 demonstrate how each action assists in the process of deification, rendering those who participate worthily and with the help of grace, similar to God in their manner of living (see 'Humanity', below, for more on deification). Maximus lists the various stages on the journey marked out in the liturgy, including entrance into the church (leaving behind a corrupt world and entering a haven for contemplation), scriptural readings, which guide self-discipline and growth in virtue, chanting to arouse desire, closing of the door into the holy of holies and moving into a more intense phase where the faithful are invited to receive the Eucharist, the holy kiss as a sign of all those joined with the Word.

Thus, for Maximus, Christ is the intended culmination and explanation for all things in the cosmos, and at the same time the centre of our personal lives, the pattern of our calling and the source of our salvation. And through the Eucharistic liturgy Christ brings together two levels, the macro and the micro, with the intention that human beings should reflect the true image of their creator, bring harmony out of the divisions in creation, and offer the world back to God in praise and thanksgiving. No education that aspires to be Christian can be constructed without putting Christ at the centre; he will constitute its focus, its foundation, its form (or pattern), and its motivating and integrating force. Maximus offers us a picture of Christ as the manifestation of God who can be found in all situations, in the personal story and struggles of our salvation, in the context of liturgical worship and in a cosmic vision in which he is the key to the meaning and purpose of all creation.

Humanity

Our human nature is what we have in common: our souls, our reason, our capacity to act and to exercise free will. Our personhood relates to the unique configuration of the way we realise or actualise our nature. Maximus teaches that, through a life of disciplined self-renunciation, human beings who have fallen away from God and obscured their true nature through weakness, sin and disordered passions can be brought back into proper harmony and relationship with God.[25] Furthermore, as their real nature is revealed and restored by a life of self-discipline and virtue aided by grace, the great variety and many differences evident in humanity will be brought into unity via the Church.[26] He refers to differences of language, nationality, customs, opinions, skills, levels of learning and types of character. It is not that these differences will disappear, but they can be reconciled and brought into harmony in the context of the Church where regeneration by the Spirit takes place: 'To all [God] gives equally and grants freely one divine form and designation, that is to be and to be called from Christ.'[27]

According to Maximus, humans are rational, unique, relational and teleological. He gives particular emphasis to this last feature: as teleological beings they are given a direction, a route to follow, a purpose and role in creation; they are created with an end in view – union with God. This purpose can be obstructed by a misuse of our powers and in our mode of living, but it remains as our ultimate calling. Maximus speaks of a movement between three types of being in us. The first is the nature we are given from birth. The second he calls 'well-being', which we achieve (if we do achieve it) through our choices (and the choices of others). The third is eternal being, which is not at our command but occurs as a result of grace. Situated within this movement there is the creative tension between the image of God we are given and the likeness to God that we are invited to grow into. Strictly speaking, Christ is *the* Image of God, while human beings are images of this Image. The image of God in us is ineradicable and, although it can be defaced, it cannot be effaced. Likeness to God is a fruit of our becoming; it is the fruit of grace empowering and sublating our attempt to grow in virtue. In his 'Centuries on Charity' (3.25), Maximus writes: 'God has imparted to rational beings four divine characteristics by which he "supports, guards, and preserves" them. These are being, eternal being, goodness and wisdom.'[28] The first two characteristics pertain to the image of God in us, while the second two are given for the sake of will and judgement and pertain to our likeness to God. We share the image with others; we differ from others in how we actualise the likeness. Maximus has a rule of 'proportion' whereby God engages with human beings 'in proportion' to the degree to which that they display likeness to God.[29] This likeness is 'related to the use of power of self-determination'[30] and therefore relies on the exercise of our free will, although this will always depend on an alignment between our will and God's.

If the notion that human beings are made in the image of God and are called to grow into the likeness of God is central to a Christian anthropology (and therefore an essential building block for Christian education), Maximus also articulates a striking account of the role that humanity is to play in the world as both microcosm and mediator. As microcosm, a man or woman constitutes a world in miniature, a world that mirrors the wider world, in that the human person comes from God, is given a derived autonomy to cooperate with God's plan for creation, with a range of powers allotted to him or her, and is invited to develop his or her life in a unique way that authentically expresses individuality while remaining within God's providence. There is a certain unfinishedness about the set of potentialities latent in each person; otherwise there would be no scope for the exercise of free will and humans would be so 'pre-packaged' as to render them impotent to cooperate willingly with God. Furthermore, these potentialities need to be harmonised and integrated; otherwise they threaten to spin off in different directions and work against each other. Each human being is called to overcome the divisions within his or her own self and within the world in order to bring all to God. The notion of a human being as a microcosm is not original to Maximus but he develops and connects it specifically to the notion that man is called to be a mediator.[31] As microcosm, humanity stands in both the material world, the world of the senses, and the intelligible world, the world accessible by mind and spirit; as mediator, human beings are able to hold these two worlds together in unity. As mediator, humanity can, by virtuous living and with the assistance of grace, bridge the various differences that exist between creatures, connect together all levels of reality, bring harmony out of cacophony, and, in a priestly role, offer in praise all things back to God as their fulfilment.

When people live up to this vocation, playing the part intended for them by God, their capacity for communion with God reaches fulfilment in a state of deification, being made God-like. Thunberg claims that 'man's deification is from another point of view God's continuing incarnation'.[32] This does not mean that God and man are identical because a gulf in their being remains but that a real communication can develop between them. Analogously, if one says of an adult that he or she seems childlike, one is not claiming that they have reverted to being a child, but rather that that person shares in and displays some of the qualities of a child. Blowers and Wilken explain how deification is an outcome of a transformation of human appetites and desires; it entails 'the ultimate alignment of the whole array of human affections with the soul's natural desire for God'.[33] This reorientation of human powers and passions depends on self-discipline, practising the virtues, willingly receiving grace and living lovingly in imitation of Christ and the saints. The cumulative effect of such deification is right relation with God, neighbours and all creation. When God is left out of the equation, all other relationships are fatally distorted and undermined.

Maximus constantly emphasises that the presence of God in us, which increases the more closely we come to deification, does not preclude or diminish human involvement. He uses the term *theandric* to refer to the joint action of the divine and human. To help explain how the divine and human can become united in us – theandric union – Maximus uses the metaphor of a red-hot sword.[34] The nature of a sword's edge is to cut, while the nature of a fire's heat is to burn. When plunged into fire, the sword becomes burning hot and the heat acquires a cutting edge. Maximus compares this exchange of attributes between the cutting edge of a sword and the burning heat of a fire with that of Christ's divine and human natures. Both the sword and the fire remain unchanged in their own nature even though each acquires the property of its partner in union.

Three comments may be made here about deification. First, 'such participation and deification imply a union with God that avoids pantheism, a union with God in which personal distinctions are fully maintained'.[35] The more I allow God into my life and seek to participate in God's life, far from suppressing my own identity, the more it is enhanced and reinforced: I become ever more uniquely *me*. I am not swallowed up in the relationship; my receptivity remains active; my responsibility for my development is not lost. Second, through deification, 'the human person achieves, not simply union with God, but also fulfils what is the essentially human role of being the natural bond of all being, drawing the whole created order into harmony with itself, and into union with God.'[36] This is the mediating role referred to earlier. Third, the more we become like God, we also become revelatory of God in the experience of others and thus a source of grace for them.

Apart from the capacity for participating in God's life, Maximus writes about other important human faculties including passion, free will and the ability to imitate. He frequently classified human faculties in three categories, rational, irascible (or incensive) and concupiscible: first, the capacity to seek what is according to reason, second, the ability to resist, fight or move against something seen as threatening, and third, the inbuilt tendency to desire and to move towards something seen as attractive. Each capacity can be deceived, distorted and misused or misdirected, and each one can also be directed towards good: the rational seeks out truth, the irascible or incensive arouses courage in defending truth and goodness, and the concupiscible tendency moves us towards pure love.[37] Human beings often feel divided by internal conflict between these tendencies.

Human passions, for Maximus, are double-edged: on the one hand, they threaten to turn us away from truth and goodness, to rob us of freedom, to undermine our flourishing and to put our salvation at risk; on the other hand, they can assist us in the path towards deification. Demetrios Bathrellos lists many of the passions identified by Maximus, including gluttony, fornication, avarice, grief, anger, listlessness, vainglory, pride, rapacity, resentfulness, envy, slander, laziness and carelessness.[38] Bathrellos shows how Maximus distinguished the objects of our passions, which are innocent in themselves, from an immoderate or unbalanced attitude towards them.[39] He points out that Maximus observed that: 'food is not evil, but gluttony; nor is the begetting of children, but fornication; nor money, but avarice; nor glory, but vainglory … Scripture takes away nothing that God has given us for use, but chastises immoderation and corrects unreasonableness.'[40]

The challenge is to harness the passions and direct them towards the good. Maximus says that 'The mind is like a sparrow that is bound to the earth when it is ruled by the passions, but when it is free of these, it flies to God in contemplation.'[41] To which, Nevena Dimitrova responds, 'The human task is not to reject the inferior faculties, but to bring about a unity of the diverse elements that we call human.'[42] Maximus explains that 'The passions become good among the spiritually diligent, when they wisely separate them from corporeal objects and use them to acquire the things of heaven.'[43] The passions have a tendency to focus on the surface of things and to prevent us from seeing deeper, taking a long-term view, or from detecting either the implications of our actions or the interconnectedness of our decisions. But, as Blowers reminds us, 'the passions become good when they are *used* by those who "*take every thought captive in order to obey Christ*" (2 Cor. 10:5).'[44] Furthermore, when under our control and directed towards the good, these same passions have the power to offer valuable assistance in the moral life. Adam Cooper wisely points out that 'A stable disposition to perform good acts relies upon the impetus provided by the affections and desires.'[45]

Maximus presents twenty-first-century readers with an understanding of freedom and free will that differs significantly from today's. He works this out in the context of his dispute with Pyrrhus, the former patriarch of Constantinople, about whether Christ had a human as well as a divine will. The episode in the Garden of Gethsemane shows how Christ willingly struggled before subordinating his human will (to avoid suffering and death) to God's will so that he fulfil his mission, whatever the cost. Maximus distinguishes between the natural power of the will (which is neutral in itself) and the objects towards which it is directed. Then he links very closely the deployment of the will to careful consideration: 'when we are willing we also inquire, examine, deliberate, judge, are inclined toward, elect.'[46] A most helpful analysis of Maximus' understanding of the will is given by Ian McFarland, who notes that the point of human freedom is not radical self-determination. Because we are *creatures* whose life and movement depend at every moment on the Creator, the quest for self-determination can only lead to self-destruction. Our proper goal is rather to do what God wills, since it is only as we conform to the will of the One who brought us into being that we can flourish as the creatures that we are.[47]

When we follow God's will, we are taken to a level beyond our normal capacities that we could not have thought was possible. McFarland argues that 'when it is operating properly, the will does not lead, but follows. And as it follows, it fulfils its role as the feature of our nature that gives us the opportunity "to obey the commands of God voluntarily."'[48] For Maximus, 'the fulfilment of human freedom is not a matter of self-mastery, but a surrender of the self to God.' Although we remain free to deny or to ignore God's call, this does not mean that following his will (as we understand it) is experienced by us as merely one option among many possibilities from which we can pick or choose. McFarland offers an illuminating analogy to help us understand the experience of 'I can't not do something' or 'This is something that I – while doing so freely – *must* do.'

> One day I meet a person; later I fall in love with and marry her. While it is common to speak of not being able to help loving a person, it is nevertheless not accurate to speak of this process as a matter of compulsion, as though I exercised no agency in the matter and could therefore not truly say that I loved. But neither does it make sense to speak of it as a choice, as though my loving a certain person were a matter of conscious decision, such that I might equally well have chosen to refrain from loving. And yet precisely because it properly leads to a lifelong commitment, love is arguably the highest expression of my freedom as a human being, the act where the integrity of my agency is most in view and at stake. It is undeniably something I do – and therefore will – but it is not a matter of choosing between various options.[49]

Another respect in which Maximus poses a challenge to modern self-perceptions is his emphasis on imitation as a vital element in human development and growth towards Christian maturity. For many people, the advocacy of imitation seems an affront, first, to their understanding of rationality and critical thinking, second, to their acute, even insistent and radical, individualism, and third, to their sense that the inevitable march of progress means that we do not need to rely on or be restricted by models of behaviour that were held to be important (and even binding) in the past. Imitation can arise from a variety of motives, not all of which are good. It can be a sign, for example, of 'flattery, mockery, humility, worship, or dependency.'[50] In educational literature, imitation rarely receives a positive press with regard to children older than primary school age. There are, of course, some advocates of imitation today, for example, Bryan Warnick in philosophy of education; Gabor Csepregi in philosophy, who provides some of the most pertinent comments I have found on the important and potentially positive role played by imitating models, not only in our youth but throughout life; and Fiona Murden in psychology.[51]

Paul Blowers summarises the importance of imitation for Maximus: 'Whether monk, non-monastic layperson, or cleric, every Christian had to look to exemplars, icons of the virtuous life, and time-tested templates of moral and spiritual growth reinforced through catechesis, preaching, worship, and the sacraments.'[52] Most obviously, the primary example is that of Jesus Christ, the preeminent model for Christians, but it was also appropriate and salutary to follow the example of the saints who have adopted the mindset of Christ. Indeed, imitation makes the Christian 'another Christ.'[53] And, as Daniel Haynes explains, 'It is thus our vocation to be transformed into "living icons" of the Lord.'[54]

For Maximus, it is important to acknowledge, first, that imitation of Christ holds the promise of enhancing human capacities, rather than of undermining them; second, that such imitation opens the inner door, allowing Christ to be incarnated in us; and third, that any serious entering into the Christian mysteries is conditional upon a readiness to imitate Christ. St Paul says that: 'Those who are unspiritual do not receive the gifts of God's Spirit, for they are foolishness to them, and they are unable to understand them because they are discerned spiritually' (1 Cor. 2: 14). Maximus claims that having the mind of Christ 'comes about not by virtue of a privation of the intellectual faculty in us, ... but rather, as enlightening by his own quality the faculty of our kind and taking it toward the same activity that is in him.'[55]

Maximus sees an intimate connection between the inner work of self-discipline and personal integration that each person is called to carry out and the outer work of playing their part in healing, shepherding and exercising stewardship in creation. Without order within the person, there can be no external order in the world, for our personal disorders have a drastic and ever-widening impact on the world around us. This brings us to three further aspects of Maximus' understanding of humanity: the necessity for asceticism, the role played by virtues, and the intimate link between goodness and knowledge. Maximus holds to that assumption held for centuries before the modern age, that knowledge is the fruit of a combination of an ethical life and contemplative practice. Asceticism helps to free us from desires, habits and patterns of behaviour and attachment that turn us to less worthy attractions and away from our Godward orientation – which, when followed, opens us up ecstatically to the other, to reality, to grace and to true fulfilment. Maximus mentions the following ascetic practices: 'temperance, fasting, the distribution of wealth, hospitality, chanting, reading, sleeping on the ground, keeping vigil', disciplines that contribute to self-mastery and that must be accompanied by both prayer and love.[56] 'Love tames anger; self-mastery quenches concupiscence; prayer withdraws the mind from all thoughts and presents it, stripped, to God Himself.'[57] A final extract from Maximus illustrates how asceticism works:

> The aim of ascetic labour is to extract the nails of desire, which fasten us to sensual pleasure (for it was through these that the soul ... lost its longing and inclination for God) ... and thus to wrest free those caught in the grip of vice, so that they might be genuine disciples of virtue, with souls unshakeable in the face of whatever might hinder them in the devotion to the Beautiful.'[58]

If asceticism describes the restraining aspects of self-discipline, the eradication of damaging tendencies within us, practice of the virtues represents the good qualities that should replace these tendencies. 'The virtues aid in that character state the Confessor terms "dispassion," which is not apathy or lack of emotion, but rather the absence of contrary forces at work in the human mind to divide it on the level of mode of existence.'[59] Growth in virtue is the fruit of both personal effort and participation in divine life through imitating Christ. Building on faith, fear of God, and the self-mastery assisted by asceticism, combined with patience and trust in the mercy of God, the virtues still the voices of temptation and distraction and grant us the gift of detachment, which enables us to love wisely. In one of the earliest surviving works of Maximus, a letter he sent from a monastery to a group in Constantinople looking to him for advice, he refers to 'those qualities that will assure your passage to love's goal. I mean: love of humankind, brotherly and sisterly love, hospitality, love of the poor, compassion, mercy, humility, meekness, gentleness, patience, freedom from anger, long-suffering, perseverance, kindness, forbearance, goodwill, peace towards all.'[60]

Maximus divides virtues into two main categories: those of the body and those of the soul. 'Those of the body include fasting, vigils, sleeping on the ground, service of others, manual work, done in order not to burden anybody or else to have something to share, and so on. The virtues of the soul are charity, long-suffering, meekness, self-mastery, prayer, and so on.'[61] Maximus uses an image that was frequently deployed by writers about Christian formation for many centuries, that of receiving an 'imprint':

> The soul by its natural capacity becomes in character either wax when God-loving or clay when matter-loving. ... Every matter-loving and world-loving soul ... is hardened ... towards destruction. But every God-loving soul is softened as wax, and letting it both the impressions and characteristics of divine traits, it becomes 'by the Spirit the dwelling place of God' (Eph 2:22).[62]

Contrary to the modern notion that acquiring knowledge depends on the appropriate and systematic application of an academic discipline's particular methodology, and that one's personal moral life is irrelevant to this process, for Maximus, truth and goodness belong together and cannot be separated. Our contemplative side searches for, and gazes upon, truth. Our active side searches for, and lives out, goodness. The former puts us in touch with the source of the image of God in us; the latter moves us closer to expressing that image, to developing our likeness to it. Knowledge is a fruit that ripens after a process of purification involving displacing distractions and replacing our sinful habits and inclinations with virtues. Knowledge also requires imitation of the good (in others, and in Christ pre-eminently), faithful practice and participation, contemplation, and cultivating love (which brings about intimacy with the object of our affection), together with prayer that opens us up to accepting God's teaching. Only with the deeper part of us can the deeper truths be accessed ('Deep cries out to deep', Ps 41:8). There must be an emptying – a letting go – before there can be a filling. This raises the question for the person wanting to know: am I ready to receive what is being offered? And, if not, what is required of me in order to become ready? Our wanting has to be rightly oriented and ordered, so that we can 'see' properly. Our longing must become a divine longing to enter into communion with God.

Educational significance

Education, of whatever kind or inspiration, is founded on a metaphysics, an ethics and a spirituality; that is, an understanding of reality, of how we should act in light of that reality, and how we should relate to that reality. Christian education must include these elements but also goes further. It relates these three foundations to a theology of creation, a Christology, an anthropology, an ethic and an eschatology. These tell us where we come from, who Christ is, who we are and the nature of our condition, how we should respond and where we are going. Maximus addressed each of these. He provides a vision that is complex and demanding, comprehensive, coherent and inspiring, of how we hold together the multiple dimensions of our lives. These are composed of our relationship to God through Christ, our place and role in the universe, self-knowledge, our hopes and how to achieve our best selves in dealing with the world and with others, ourselves and God. His vision presents an ultimate goal of all learning – how to love. Where we have come from, where we are headed, and how God is present in everything around us (as well as within us) – no real understanding of life is possible without awareness of these three concepts, which are integral to education in the deepest sense. Maximus supplies a sound philosophical and theological foundation on which to develop a realistic, wise, coherent and comprehensive approach to education, though it was not his specific aim to devise educational principles.

Many alternative worldviews and visions for education are possible. For some, our primary role as human beings is as a subject of the State or other secular authorities. For others, it is to contribute to the market economy. For some, we are self-made and autonomous individuals who should aim at maximising our freedom, perhaps at the expense of our communal nature. For others, it is our nature to be masters of the world, to exercise dominion, not in the sense of shepherding creation or acting as stewards, preparing to hand it back to God, but as sole owners who can put it to whatever use we think fit. Some emphasise our intellectual dimension at the expense of other aspects of our nature; others focus on our sinfulness and fallen nature at the expense of our giftedness and destiny. In contrast, some neglect our proneness to sin and selfishness, exaggerate our capacity to succeed, and foster unrealistic and utopian expectations of ourselves and society.

There are seven respects in which one can claim that Maximus offers a valuable starting point for thinking about Christian education. First, he displays a vision that counters the tendency to fragmentation that we see in education and in life, where, too often, there is no sense of the whole into which the parts fit. Doru Costache notes that the most prominent feature of modern culture 'is the propensity towards separating culture and life, information and wisdom, external context and the inner experience. ... The challenge addressed to our generation is to restore the link between *to know* and *to be*, between knowing and living.'[63] Maximus goes some way towards remedying this situation.

Second, even when the religious dimension is foregrounded by some Christian educators, it is possible to ignore the cosmic dimension of faith. This makes Christian faith seem separated from secular and scientific insights into human nature and the universe and thus insufficiently comprehensive in coverage and scope and insufficiently coherent through lack of connectedness. Maximus succeeds in embracing the mundane and the heavenly: the micro and the macro levels of existence.

Third, he identifies the importance of detachment, for instance, freedom from passions, as a condition for right seeing. This is often neglected in educational literature. Maximus reconfigures our understanding of freedom, away from simply being a matter of unfettered and spontaneous choices that are disconnected from one another, to set freedom in the context of living in tune with ultimate reality and authentically living out the person God calls us to be.

Fourth is his ecumenical potential as a bridge between the Eastern and Western branches of the Christian Church. It seems to me that the spilt between these two branches, which become hardened and irrevocable by the eleventh century, must be healed before there is any chance of healing those divisions that occurred at and after the Reformation of the sixteenth century. We have known since Pope John Paul II's 1995 encyclical on Christian unity, *Ut Unum Sint*, that Catholic education must embrace the ecumenical imperative and that ecumenism must be an integral feature of the outlook promoted in Catholic communities. Maximus offers great potential for this task because of the high regard in which he is held among both Orthodox and Catholic Christians.

Fifth, he is a relevant source for a theology that equips Christians to respond to the ecological crisis. He finds a way to speak about God's presence in the created world that avoids damaging misinterpretations. The Romanian Orthodox theologian Radu Bordeianu, in an article that explores Maximus' relevance for the current ecological crisis, claims that Maximus 'both safeguards God's transcendence without falling into deism, and asserts the sanctity of creation ... without affirming pantheism'. Furthermore, Bordeianu continues, 'while rejecting anthropocentrism, Maximus still affirms that God has placed the human being as the centre of creation. ... As God's agent, created with a mixed nature of spirit and body, [the human person is] thus a being capable of uniting the spiritual and material realms ... as servant or priest.'[64] Maximus is shown by Bordeianu as teaching that creation is the context in which our spiritual growth occurs, that our lives exert an influence, for good or evil, on our environment and that our task is sanctify creation, even as creation assists us in our salvation.[65] Bordeianu draws from Maximus three principles relevant for developing an ecological sensibility that is theologically based: first, that no created reality can be a purpose in itself; second, that we ought to see how all creation reveals God; third, that we need to listen to creation, learn from it, and join in its praise of God.[66] Bordeianu's linking of Maximus to the task of addressing our ecological crisis echoes Pope Francis' urgent appeal in 2015's *Laudato si'* for human beings to change their wasteful, careless, abusive and consumerist attitudes, which have caused and continue to perpetuate the present ecological crisis. Like Maximus, Pope Francis calls for a Eucharistic attitude to creation.

Sixth, Maximus combines three essential aspects of Christian faith that should be reflected in Christian education – the intellectual, the moral and the spiritual; concern for truth, for right living and for union with God. When these are kept apart, as if each were entirely autonomous and could operate without being reinforced, enlightened, complemented and corrected by the other, none of these aspects of our humanity function properly.

Seventh, Maximus wrote at the culmination of the patristic era, yet this patristic source rarely receives attention in the formation of Catholic teachers in schools and universities. An engagement with Maximus' thought opens up for us not only the high level of argument of his predecessors, the learned fathers and mothers of Christian faith from whom he drew and derived great benefit, but also the depth, sophistication, scope and symphonic coherence of his own vision – from which educators today have much to learn.

* * *

Maximus offers a vision of life that is realistic rather than utopian or pessimistic. He links our earthly weaknesses and strengths to our openness to, desire for, and capacity to become Godlike. He maps out a path towards spiritual transformation that does not require either denial of, or hostility towards, the positive (although incomplete) role of worldly affairs or civilisation. If, as Costache claims,

> civilisation, understood as an external accomplishment, needs a soul, a spirit, which could bring it to life and meaning, wisdom and coherence, then the point is to learn how to live spiritually ... beyond addictions and necessity – within our civilisation. Maximus teaches us to pursue our upward journey with everything we are and represent; soul and body, male and female, spirituality and technology, wisdom and science.[67]

Maximus' careful attention to the physical, moral, intellectual and spiritual dimensions of human life and how these are interrelated makes him a valuable source for underpinning and illuminating Christian education. I give the final word to the scholar who first alerted me to the value of engaging with the synthetic and symphonic thought of Maximus, the Dominican Aidan Nichols:

> Maximus couples the Fathers with the Bible and uses for both the same vocabulary of divine origination. For, like the biblical writers, the Church's Fathers were God-inspired; approved by God; carried away by God; God-carriers; made wise by God; and given eloquence by him.[68]

One might also attribute these gifts and qualities to Maximus.

ENDNOTES

1 For consistency and brevity, I have referred in the text and notes simply to Maximus (rather than the alternative spelling Maximos) and omitted 'the Confessor'.

2 James W. Fowler, *Becoming Adult, Becoming Christian: Adult Development and Christian Faith*, San Francisco: Harper & Row, 1984, p. 95.

3 Kallistos (Timothy) Ware, 'The Imitation of Christ According to Saint Maximus the Confessor', in Daniel Haynes, *A Saint for East and West*, Eugene, OR: Cascade Books, 2019, p. 83.

4 Maximus, *On the Cosmic Mystery of Jesus Christ*, translated by Paul M. Blowers and Robert Louis Wilken, Crestwood, New York: St Vladimir's Seminary Press, 2003, p. 19.

5 Maximus, *The Ascetic Life. The Four Centuries on Charity*, translated and edited by Polycarp Sherwood, New York: Newman Press, 1955.

6 Maximus, *Two Hundred Chapters on Theology*, edited by Luis Joshua Salés, Yonkers, New York: St Vladimirs Seminary Press, 2015.

7 Maximus, *On Difficulties in the Church Fathers. The Ambigua*. Volumes 1 and 2, edited and translated by Nicholas Constas, Cambridge, MA: Harvard University Press, 2014.

8 Maximus, *On Difficulties in Sacred Scripture: The Responses to Thalassios*, translated by Maximos Constas, Washington, DC: The Catholic University of America Press, 2018. As with Maximos/Maximus, the Romanised 'Thalassius' spelling is used in the text.

9 Maximus, *On the Ecclesiastical Mystagogy*, Introduction & translation by Jonathan J. Armstrong, Yonkers, New York: St Vladimir's Seminary Press, 2019.

10 Pauline Allen and Neil Bronwen (eds), *The Oxford Handbook of Maximus the Confessor*, Oxford: Oxford University Press, 2015, p. vii.

11 Maximus, *Disputation with Pyrrhus*, translated by Joseph P. Farrell, Waymart, PA: St Tikhon's Monastery Press, 2014.

12 Maximus, *Cosmic Mystery*, p. 16.

13 Hans Urs Von Balthasar, *Cosmic Liturgy*, translated by Brian E. Daley, San Francisco: Ignatius Press, 2003, p. 57.

14 Sotiris Mitralexis, *Ever-Moving Repose*, Eugene, OR: Cascade Books, 2017, p. 9.

15 Vincent Rossi, 'Clash of Paradigms: The Doctrine of Evolution in the Light of the Cosmological Vision of St Maximos the Confessor', *Orthodox Christianity*, 26 August 2015, p. 15. http://orthochristian.com/81599.html; accessed 14 March 2022.

16 Maximus, *On Difficulties in Sacred Scripture*, p. 31.

17   See Ambigua to John 7 in Maximus, *On Difficulties in the Church Fathers*; Maximus, *On Ecclesiastical Mystagogy*, chapter 1; and Maximus, *Two Hundred Chapters on Theology*, chapters 2–4.

18   Thomas Cattoi, 'Liturgy as Cosmic Transformation' in Allen and Bronwen, Oxford Handbook, p. 416.

19   Lars Thunberg, *Microcosm and Mediator*, Chicago and La Salle, IL: Open Court Publishing, 1995, p. 49.

20   Armstrong, Introduction to Maximus, *Mystagogy*, p. 23.

21   Ibid., p. 35.

22   Ibid., p. 40.

23   Maximus, *Mystagogy*, pp. 85–6.

24   Paul M. Blowers, *Maximus the Confessor: Jesus Christ and the Transfiguration of the World*, Oxford: Oxford University Press, 2016, p. 177.

25   Maximus, *Disputations with Pyrrhus*, p. 46.

26   Ibid., p. 48.

27   Maximus, *Mystagogy*, p. 53.

28   Maximus, *Four Centuries on Charity*, p. 177.

29   Luke Steven, *Imitation, Knowledge and the Task of Christology in Maximus the Confessor*, Eugene, OR: Cascade Books, 2020, p. 8.

30   Thunberg, *Microcosm and Mediator*, p. 127.

31   Maximus, *Mystagogy*, chapters 5 and 7; Maximus, *Difficulties in Church Fathers*, chapters 10 and 41; Maximus, *Difficulties in Sacred Scripture*, chapter 32.

32   Thunberg, *Microcosm and Mediator*, p. 59.

33   Maximus, *Cosmic Mystery*, p. 43.

34   Maximus, *Difficulties in Church Fathers*, pp.55–7.

35   Clement Yung Wen, 'Maximus the Confessor and the Problem of Participation', *Heythrop Journal*, Vol. 58, No. 1 (2017), p. 4.

36   Andrew Louth, *Maximus the Confessor*, London and New York: Routledge, 1996, p. 73.

37   Maximus, *Difficulties in Sacred Scripture*, chapter 39.

38   Demetrios Bathrellos, 'Passions, Ascesis, and the Virtues' in Allen & Bronwen, op. cit., p. 293.

39   Ibid., p. 292.

40   Maximus, *Centuries on Charity*, pp. 173, 202.

41   Ibid., 1: 85. I have used here the translation given by Nevena Dimitrova, *Human Knowledge According to Saint Maximus the Confessor*, Eugene, OR: Wipf & Stock, Resource Publications, 2016, p. 43.

42   Dimitrova, *Human Knowledge*, p. 68.

43   Maximus, *Difficulties in Sacred Scripture*, p. 95.

44   Blowers, *Maximus the Confessor*, p. 270.

45   Adam Cooper, 'Freedom and Heteronomy' in Allen and Bronwen, p. 99.

46   Maximus, *Disputations with Pyrrhus,* p. 63.

47   Ian McFarland, 'The Theology of the Will' in Allen and Bronwen, p. 517.

48   Ibid. p. 528.

49   Ibid. p. 530.

50   Bryan R. Warnick, *Imitation and Education*, Albany, New York: State University of New York, 2008, p. 11.

51   Warnick, op. cit; Gabor Csepregi, *In Vivo*, Montreal and Kingston: McGill-Queens University Press, 2019, pp.67 –86; Fiona Murden, *Mirror Thinking: How Role Models Make Us Human*, London: Bloomsbury, 2020.

52   Blowers, *Maximus the Confessor*, p. 280.

53   *Difficulties in Sacred Scripture,* chapter 29.

54   Kallistos Ware, 'The Imitation of Christ' p. 72. Ware is quoting from Maximus, *Difficulties in Church Fathers*, chapter 21.

55   Maximus, *Two Hundred Chapters on Theology*, p. 165.

56   Maximus, *Difficulties in Sacred Scripture*, p. 392.

57   Maximus, *Centuries on Charity*, p. 114.

58   Maximus, *Difficulties in Church Fathers*, Vol. 1, p. 351.

59   Salés in Maximus, *Two Hundred Chapters on Theology*, p. 33.

60   Louth, *Maximus the Confessor*, pp. 91–2.

61   Maximus, *Four Centuries on Charity*, p. 164.

62   Maximus, *Two Hundred Chapters on Theology*, pp. 49–50.

63   Doru Costache, 'Going Upwards with Everything You Are'. This is a revised version of the same article originally published in Basarab Nicolescu and Magda Stavinschi (eds), *Science and Orthodoxy: a Necessary Dialogue,* Bucharest: Curtea Veche, 2006, pp. 135–44. Available from: https://www.academia.edu/1077440/The_Unifying_Ladder_of_St_Maximus_the_Confessor_Going_Upwards_With_Everything_You_Area; accessed 14 March 2022.

64   Radu Bordeianu, 'Maximus and Ecology: The Relevance of Maximus the Confessor's Theology of Creation for the Present Ecological Crisis', *The Downside Review*, Vol. 127, No. 447 (April 2009), pp. 106, 111.

65   Ibid. pp.115–16.

66   Ibid. p. 116.

67   Costache, 'Going Upwards', p. 143.

68   Aidan Nichols, *Byzantine Gospel*, Edinburgh: T & T Clark, 1993, p. 50.

CHAPTER TWO

Hildegard of Bingen:
Polyphonic Prophet

A prophet, mystic and visionary, as well as being a scientist and creative artist (in poetry, music and drama), Hildegard of Bingen lived from *c.*1098 to 1179, born in Bermersheim and dying in Bingen, both in the Rhineland-Palatinate area of what is now modern Germany. This was an age of overlapping secular and religious jurisdictions, of crusades and pilgrimages. There were Church–State struggles in every country, but her lifetime was especially marked by clashes between the Pope and the Holy Roman Emperor. Hildegard lived through a seventeen-year schism in the Church, with several antipopes competing for office at the same time. It was an era of cathedral building and the flourishing of monasticism, but it was also a period overshadowed by a rise in heresy.

The subtitle of this chapter, 'polyphonic prophet', is intended to underline two features of Hildegard's vocation and spirit. As a prophet, she considered herself the mouthpiece of God, driven by a force outside herself; she felt called by God to speak on his behalf with a social message against the evils of the day and to challenge people to embrace more faithfully God's will for their lives and for the right ordering of creation and society. As it says in the Benedictus, the role of the prophet is to 'go ahead of the Lord to prepare his ways before him, to make known his salvation through forgiveness of their sins, the loving-kindness of our God' (Lk 1:76–77). This Sibyl of the Rhine, as she was known both during and after her lifetime, was a prophet with many different talents and sides to her character: spiritual, pastoral, musical, medical, even political. But she harmonised these diverse aspects of her life, just as polyphony involves multiple voices cooperating with one another to make a rich, intricate and beautiful sound. Not only did she condemn the greed, arrogance, corruption, cowardice and hypocrisy of her age, she did this while winsomely conveying a complex yet astonishingly integrated worldview. Kathryn Kerby-Fulton describes the essence of Hildegard's self-image as prophet: 'charismatic, self-effacing, inspirational and evangelical'.[1] She was disclosing God's hidden purpose in creation and in history and then calling on people to align themselves with this divine plan.

As a woman in a male-dominated age, she stands out not only for her prophecy, but also for her wisdom, spiritual insight, pastoral leadership and interventions in Church politics. She is famous today for her music, her knowledge of herbal medicine, the inspiration she has given to New Age thinking, her positive appreciation of creation, stressing the need for humanity to live with respect for, and in harmony with, all of nature, and for her positive approach to the nature and gifts of women (which anticipated modern feminism by many centuries). Several aspects of her life and her writings deserve attention from, and provide inspiration for, Catholic educators today. In order to bring to light these features of her example and teaching, this chapter is divided into four parts. First, I provide an overview of her life and work. Second, I explain the peculiar – and potentially off-putting – style of Hildegard's writings and some of the principal assumptions that frame and govern her output. Third is a brief introduction to key themes in her teaching. These include the role of the Holy Spirit in enlivening and connecting creation, her special (and highly distinctive) emphasis on *viriditas* ('greenness', i.e. vitality) or humanity as a microcosm that mirrors God's broader work in the macrocosm, cooperation between body and soul and how this plays out in both medicine and music, and her treatment of the virtues. Finally, I tease out the educational significance of Hildegard's worldview, indicating how it might both challenge and inspire those working in Catholic education in the twenty-first century.

Life and work

The youngest of ten children, at eight years old Hildegard was entrusted as maid and apprentice to Jutta, an anchoress. Later, they together oversaw the building of a Benedictine convent attached to a monastery at Disibodenberg in the western German state of Rhineland-Palatinate where, after Jutta's death, Hildegard, aged thirty-eight, became abbess in 1136. Around 1147, she moved away with eighteen sisters to found Mount St Rupert Monastery near Bingen and, in 1165, she established a daughter community at Ebingen, continuing as abbess for both communities. Under her lengthy leadership, she attracted many new members to her community – while maintaining an uneasy relationship with the host monastic community. Thus steeped in the lifestyle of the Benedictine tradition, like the monks, Hildegard and her fellow sisters were formed by a disciplined regime that allocated regular times for sleep, worship, study and manual labour. In this environment the emphasis was on silence, stability, obedience, community life and ongoing conversion.

Hildegard suffered from ill-health throughout her life, troubled by severe migraines that might well have contributed to her visions. One of her biographers, Fiona Maddocks, refers to similarities between Oliver Sacks' studies of migraine and Hildegard's experience: 'The visual disturbances, nausea, rushing and roaring sensation, abdominal pain, trance-like drowsiness, muscular weakness, epileptic-like attacks and pallor.'[2] The vulnerability she experienced because of constant illness was compounded by her awareness that her informal schooling as a woman left her lacking many linguistic and conceptual skills and by her ambivalence about her lifelong experience of receiving visions. For many years, she kept these visions to herself until, eventually, she felt compelled by God to share them with others and to explain the divine messages conveyed in them. An essential element in her capacity to communicate was her combination of profound self-doubt and complete certainty that God was speaking to her, and through her, for others.

She may have been vulnerable in health, but as Pope Benedict XVI has noted, she was also 'vigorous in spirit'.[3] Benedict also praises 'the power of penetration and comprehensiveness of her contemplation of revelation, theology, humanity and creation'.[4] The combination of her vulnerability and her vigorous spirit enabled her to plumb great spiritual depths and to exert a powerful influence on those who knew her or who heard her works read aloud. Despite canon law forbidding women to preach, Hildegard went on four major preaching tours between 1158 and 1171, visiting Cologne, Trier, Liège, Mainz, Metz, Bamberg and Würzburg, and lamenting abuses in the Church. Such activity was unheard of and would not have been possible if her authenticity as an orthodox visionary had not been recognised by Pope Eugenius III and Bernard of Clairvaux. Even so, she encountered fierce opposition as well as acclaim.

Hildegard wrote three major theological books. The first of these is *Scivias* (written 1141–51), whose title is an abbreviation for *Scito vias Domini*: 'Know the ways of the Lord', and which dealt with the creation and fall, the redemption of humanity through Christ's incarnation and his continuing presence through the sacraments, and the history of salvation and the development of virtues in the journey towards God. Her second is *The Book of Life's Merits* (1158–63). This book is a form of *psychomachia* or 'battle of the soul', a struggle between virtues and their corresponding vices. Her third and most mature book is *The Book of Divine Works* (1163–73/74), which covers the Trinity, creation, salvation history, and the human response required.

Hildegard was consulted by, and corresponded with, a wide range of people – popes, bishops, kings, princes, monks and nuns. Her letters often combine castigation of faults with encouragement and offering a path towards amendment and renewal. She was unafraid to remind her readers of their duty towards God and the practical implications of following the divine purposes they were put on earth to fulfil. She urges people to exercise their spiritual muscles, to follow their conscience, to resist temptations, to put themselves in God's hands, and to trust in God's providence and grace. Furthermore, they should foster virtue in themselves, be honest in their self-examination, take care to ignore the false voices that might tempt them into immorality and remain ready to answer for their lives before divine judgement. She urged people to attend to what is truly life- and light-giving within themselves, to bring forth fruits from the seeds divinely planted in them and to be faithful to the role and tasks that God has given them – despite tiredness, lack of success, and opposition.

She could be vehement and petulant, for example, in her resistance to two nuns leaving her convent to become abbesses elsewhere. In her letters to various popes and to the Emperor, she veered between being pretentious and prophetic, or oscillated between being intemperate and insightful, sometimes offering encouragement and advice and at other times conveying either challenge or admonishment. Her writing could be ferocious, intense, pictorial and prophetic. It was suffused in symbolism and scriptural references, which were mingled in ways that were obscure yet striking. For example, in deploying the traditional images of the man, the lion, the bull and the eagle from Ezechiel 1:10, often linked to the Four Evangelists, she relates these images to aspects of God's qualities, in this case his goodness, power, sacrifice and knowledge. She did not pull her punches, but castigated her targets for their various shortcomings. Yet the recipients of such letters often cherished her admonishment and claimed to return to her letters as a powerful reminder to mend their ways.

Clerical behaviour that attracted her anger and called forth her criticism included neglect of preaching, taking concubines, selling ecclesiastical offices (simony), laxity in performing duties, and inattention to pastoral care. She accused secular authorities of interference in appointments to Church offices, of promoting schism in the Church and of undermining the work of religious leaders.

She fiercely opposed heresy and promoted orthodoxy. Much of her correspondence entailed supporting, encouraging and advising (and occasionally chiding) fellow religious in other monasteries and convents, often in response to requests for help. Her wisdom and realism about religious communities showed in her understanding of the conflicting motivations, personality types and foibles, and the particular temptations and causes of disruption that pervaded monastic houses. John Van Engen illustrates how she balanced correction and mercy when guiding those who sought her help:

> If your daughters weep, she advised one abbess, console them; if they rise up in anger, set them straight; if they act madly, subject them to the discipline of the Rule; if they turn away from you, recall them in person with stories and Gospel words; and if they still do not obey, act firmly in obedience to your supreme teacher. Those who exercise religious authority should love the good and right-minded, reproach the vain and delinquent, and bear patiently with those as hard as stone.[5]

These sisters should respond in moderation rather than in anger or with harshness. Moderation (and, thereby, balance and harmony within each person) was a key prescription for Hildegard that she applied to food, clothing, discipline and celebration. As abbess, she saw herself as a gardener, nurturing the flowers, for instance the virtues, of those entrusted to her, with a view to bringing them to full bloom in godly and human flourishing. It should be noted that she was subject to criticism herself for the unusual way that she allowed members of her religious community to wear bright clothing, crowns, and jewellery when in celebration mode.

Hildegard faced a final crisis in the last year of her life.[6] Her community was put under interdict for allowing the burial in consecrated ground of someone who, it was alleged, had been excommunicated as a heretic. The nuns were forbidden not only from having Mass celebrated but even from singing the Divine Office (a defining monastic activity for Hildegard). Hildegard refused the order to disinter and remove the body and she vigorously contested the judgement against her community. She claimed that the person in question had confessed his sins, received absolution and extreme unction, and had been buried without objection; thus he had died in good standing with the Church. She complained bitterly to the relevant Church authorities about the injustice done to her community; the interdict was lifted a few months later. Her strength of character, her reputation, and the forcefulness of her appeal (also perhaps her venerable age – then eighty) prevailed.

Canonisation proceedings began only a few years after her death in 1179 but were discontinued for lack of sufficient evidence. It was only in 2012 that Pope Benedict XVI canonised Hildegard, and then named her a Doctor of the Church. She is only the fourth woman, along with Saints Catherine of Siena, Teresa of Ávila and Thérèse of Lisieux, given this designation, which acknowledged her outstanding contribution to the understanding and interpretation of the Christian faith. The eminent scholar of medieval spirituality Bernard McGinn calls Hildegard 'the first great woman theologian in Christian history'.[7]

I end this section by quoting the assessment of Hildegard given by a leading scholar of her work:

> Hildegard was the only woman of her age to be accepted as an authoritative voice on Christian doctrine; the first woman who received express permission from a pope to write theological books; the only medieval woman who preached openly, before mixed audiences of clergy and laity, with the full approval of church authorities; the author of the first known morality play and the only twelfth-century playwright who is not anonymous; the only composer of her era (not to mention the only medieval woman) known both by name and by a large corpus of surviving music; the first scientific writer to discuss sexuality and gynaecology from a female perspective; and the first saint whose official biography includes a first-person memoir.[8]

Signature style

Modern readers of Hildegard's work face a challenge with regard to determining the genre of her writing. We expect differences between a poem, a history book, a newspaper editorial, an academic journal article and a personal email and we interpret each of these in the light of our expectations and the weight we attribute to these forms of communication. We also learn how to take into account differences of approach between various academic disciplines: thus sociology, history, philosophy, science and theology all have different modes of investigation, canons and checks for accuracy and truth, prevailing concerns, modes of evaluation and styles of communication.

Hildegard's writing, like that of her contemporary, Bernard of Clairvaux, was steeped in biblical language and allusions, moving back and forth between Old and New Testaments in a manner that is disconcerting to us today. Her scriptural literacy provides the lens through which she 'reads' the world and her own life. Such familiarity with scripture, assumed by both Bernard and Hildegard, is not a feature of our contemporary culture and modern readers cannot detect the allusions and associations picked up by twelfth-century men and women. Furthermore, we can easily be confused by how Hildegard mixes (as it may seem to us, indiscriminately) cosmological and biological observation, scriptural commentary, moral exhortation, social and ecclesial critique, and spiritual insight and warnings about future calamities and trials for secular rulers and for Church leaders (if they continued to fail to live up to the responsibilities of their offices).

Her writing is symbolic, dramatic and idiosyncratic; it conjures up images that are esoteric, coded, and which have a strong reformist goal; Hildegard can seem a heavy-going and complex writer for readers today. Filled with immensely sophisticated and intertextual allegories, her prophetic writing both castigates failings that are unfamiliar to us and at the same time offers hopes and consolations that are not immediately relevant to us today. Her apocalyptical visions were both entrancing and terrifying for her readers, in a similar way to how some viewers enjoy being frightened by horror movies. In her deployment of images of winds, rivers, fires, animals, the sun, moon and planets, Hildegard links physical objects in the universe to scriptural teaching, salvation history, moral and spiritual life, and the events of secular history, moving back and forth between multiple levels of meaning and interpretation in a manner than can be disconcerting for readers today.

She meticulously maps all parts of creation and the role each part plays within God's overarching purpose in a complex and glorious amalgamation of cosmology, biology, psychology, theology, scripture, morality, symbolism and imagination, blurring the boundaries of disciplines. In our contemporary context, specialisation, separation and fragmentation of areas of study prevail in higher education and, to a lesser extent, in secondary schools. Hildegard weaves together aspects of life that we tend now to treat in isolation: the physical structure of the universe and an appreciation of cosmology; the laws of biology and embodiment; human psychology; moral virtues, spiritual practices; social harmony; biblical knowledge; the working of the Holy Spirit. Her boldness in doing this can appear outrageous to those concerned with upholding their particular disciplinary norms.

Underlying all her works two pervasive assumptions were at work, neither of which relates to our contemporary mindset. These assumptions frame her vision, control her fears and hopes, direct her interpretations and motivate her recommendations for action by those who read or listen to what she has to proclaim. The first of these assumptions is that a contest between good and evil takes place in our individual lives and in the affairs of society and the Church. For Hildegard, this contest is real, urgent, demanding and unavoidable; it should never be lost sight of and it requires constant vigilance in order to protect ourselves from making self-destructive choices. The second assumption is that, in all things, and whatever it looks like to us, God's purposes will be fulfilled, with or without human cooperation. If the first assumption should make us rightly anxious, the second should prevent us from despairing. More positively, Hildegard is convinced that discipline and devotion open doors to both the discernment of truth and to delight, that virtue leads to 'viridity' (a term we return to in the next section), and that faithfulness enables our efforts to be fruitful.

Emphases that seem strange or even alien in light of assumptions commonly held today pervade all her work, for example, the need for constant spiritual struggle, testing, chastisement and admonishment. The fear of the Lord is a central pillar of her thinking, just as it has been for most of Christian history. In common with much of Christian tradition, she accepts that sin has a noetic effect; sin clouds our vision, misdirects our desires, causes us to develop damaging habits, and undermines our capacity to recognise, pursue and embrace truth. She values patience and humility, virtues that are not esteemed so highly today. Far from envisaging discipline as something restrictive, for Hildegard, as for so many spiritual writers across the centuries, discipline opens the door to delight by enabling us to discern the divine ordering of all things and to live in rhythm with, rather than against, the grain of reality. This divine ordering is what was meant by 'hierarchy', a notion as powerful in the medieval period as evolution has been over the past two centuries.

Key themes

Five aspects of Hildegard's thinking are presented here in order to illustrate the breadth, coherence and practical outworking of her vision. First, I refer to her understanding of the intricate and interconnected nature of creation and the ongoing effect of the Incarnation and the role of the Holy Spirit in that creation. Second, as an outworking of her understanding of the effect of the Spirit's operation, I concentrate on her distinctive emphasis on *viriditas* or 'greenness'. Third, I examine her view of human beings as a microcosm, mirroring God's actions in the macrocosm. Fourth, I show the importance she attributed to medicine and to music, both of which display how body and soul cooperate and need each other, and finally, I survey her treatment of the virtues.

Hildegard sees all of creation, and human beings within this creation, as the work of God, with all creatures dependent on God for their existence and powers, their operation and purpose. The task of human beings is to recognise their relationship with God and to cooperate with God's will in bringing creation to fruition and fulfilment. Hildegard teaches us that God reveals himself to us in our experience, if we open ourselves to receive such revelation and are willing to embrace what it conveys. For her, the mystery of the Trinity is not something removed from the mystery of our own lives, although we do not appreciate this unless we also see how God is at work in creation as a whole and in the Incarnation in particular; for her, the Incarnation transformed the world. If humanity is to imitate Christ, this, too, will have a transformative effect on everything touched by men and women. Her understanding of how Christ's Incarnation can be continued, reflected or echoed in an ongoing way by human beings influenced her appreciation of the positive and creative effects of any kind of human labour because such labour has the potential to develop and to bring something new into and, indeed, out of, the world. In this way, 'not only is humanity saved through the Incarnation, but all of creation is too'.[9] This view of humanity's participation in the transformative effects of the Incarnation was played out in the importance she attributed to medicine and to music. The historian Constant Mews notes of Hildegard that 'She sees the Incarnation not as an external intervention in the world but as the full manifestation of an inherently natural process',[10] while theologian Elizabeth Dreyer underlines how Hildegard attributes a powerful role to the Holy Spirit, both in bringing life to creation and to the souls of believers. Dreyer illustrates Hildegard's appreciation of the operation of Holy Spirit by quoting from her *Symphonia*:

Holy Spirit, making life alive,
moving in all things, root of all creation,
cleansing the cosmos of every impurity,
effacing sin, anointing wounds.
You are glistening and praiseworthy life,
you awaken and re-awaken everything that is.[11]

Here we see the Holy Spirit continually at work, both on a grand scale in the cosmos and also personally within the moral life of each individual. Barbara Newman also quotes Hildegard on the animating and unitive role of the Holy Spirit:

> O current of power permeating all –
> in the heights, upon the earth,
> and in all deeps:
> you bind and gather
> all people together.
> From you clouds overflow, winds
> take wing, stones store up moisture,
> waters well forth in streams –
> and earth swells with living green.[12]

In the light of this all-surrounding presence and power of the Spirit, Hildegard challenges those who read or hear her words to put aside their fears, to pray for courage, and to be ready to open themselves to the divine grace with freedom and boldness. She tells us that God not only speaks *to* us through nature and in our experience but also *through* us to other people and on behalf of the rest of creation. Hildegard felt called, through her visions, to unlock the mysteries that are obscurely hidden within the world and to share what had been divinely disclosed to her: 'For the one who rules his creation with mercy and power pours out the brightness of heavenly enlightenment on those who fear him and serve him with love in a spirit of humility.'[13]

Referring to forces in nature such as winds and fire, and to creatures such as animals, Hildegard is concerned that 'Humankind ought to understand how all these things relate to the soul's salvation.'[14] For her, through observing nature we can detect God's power and judgement and learn how we should take these into account as we try to align ourselves with God's will. Furthermore, all parts of creation exist in mutual dependence. Thus, she observed, 'one part of creation is restrained by another part of creation, and likewise each is sustained by the other'.[15] In her worldview,

God strengthened Man with the powers of all creation and clothed him with them as with a complete suit of armour, so that through sight he might come to know creation, through hearing understand it, through smell make distinctions, through taste be fed by it, and through touch master it. ... God crafted the human form according to the constitution of the firmament and of each and every part of the rest of creation, as a foundryman uses the form according to which he will make his vessel.[16]

I have already referred to Hildegard's celebration of 'greenness', the Spirit's power to bring vitality and fertility to creatures. Her understanding of the role of the Holy Spirit leads her to an original and distinctive emphasis on *viriditas* or 'greenness'. Such greenness refers to the fruits, or the outworking, of the divine spirit working within humanity, as with the rest of creation. If, in the physical world, greenness refers to life and renewal in nature, in a religious sense she intended the term to refer to the power of God's Spirit at work in history and in human lives, a power that shows itself in virtuous life, love and holy devotion.

Alternative words for *viriditas*, as used by Hildegard, include verdant, fragrance, blossoming, fruitfulness, fertility, and fecundity. One might contrast such greenness to dryness, desiccation, sterility, even depression. If Hildegard had been a school principal – and serving as an abbess is a similar role in many respects – then she might have adopted as her motto, 'Grow into greenness'. This phrase evokes the notion that one should unlock all the channels that might get in the way of bringing to fruition the potential God has injected into each creature; when applied to the educator's task, it implies that one should nourish, support, reinforce and strengthen the goodness within, so that this goodness can emerge in all its possible splendour. The injunction to 'grow into greenness' is, for Hildegard, the 'principle of all life'.[17]

Hildegard believed that God's 'goodness and love charge the whole world with life, beauty, and renewal'.[18] And creatures, consciously or not, are charged with bearing fruit, just as Christ speaks of bearing good fruit in Matthew 7:17–20 and St Paul refers to the fruit of the Holy Spirit in Galatians 5:22–23. Activating inbuilt potential requires God's help. 'A man can sow a field, but it is divine power that sends the moisture of fresh greenness and the warmth of sunlight', which cause the crop to bear fruit. In the same way, she continues, a person can 'sow a word' in another's ear, but only God can send irrigation and 'bring forth the fruit of holiness'.[19] But God's prior initiating force does not excuse us from the part we are called to play: the continuing and unfinished effort to align ourselves to God's will, to strive for internal integration and to promote harmony outside ourselves insofar as this lies within our power.

One can usefully compare Hildegard's emphasis with Pope Francis' stress on fruitfulness. In talks he gave to teachers as Archbishop of Buenos Aires, before he became Pope, Jorge Bergoglio pressed his listeners to direct their work towards fruitfulness, distinguishing this from a concern for results. He suggested that:

> A teacher who wisely aims to make his task *yield fruits* will never limit himself to hoping for something predetermined. ... *The metaphor of the 'production of results'* belongs to the field of industry, of serial and calculable effectiveness. A result can be foreseen, planned, and measured. It implies a control over the steps that are being taken. A set of perfectly determined actions will have a *predictable* effect.[20]

Knowing that educational encounters are essentially unpredictable and dynamic and, rather than being capable of being measured purely objectively, are filtered through the fine mesh of subjective experience and personal circumstances, he encouraged teachers to resist being colonised by the machinery of measurement, advocating a long-term view of the vocation of teaching, where outcomes may take years to appear and where the personal appropriation of healthy ways of living takes priority over regurgitation of objective knowledge. This kind of fruitfulness is an echo of Hildegard's emphasis on greenness.

Nevertheless, the then Archbishop also asked his listeners to maintain an awareness of the importance for their pupils of more tangible results. Here the effectiveness of education in equipping pupils for taking their place in society is foregrounded, rather than the more personal and inner transformational influence of teaching: '*Many times we Christians have dissociated "fruits" from "results"*'.[21] While a concern for results is significantly different from a concern for fruitfulness, and while fruitfulness must never be sacrificed on the altar of results, true education demands that we attend to both. Bergoglio describes this twofold task as follows: 'It is a question of resolving the polarities, integrating them with each other: "to educate for fruits" while providing all the possible tools so that this fruit becomes more concrete in every moment in an effective way, "*producing results*"'.[22] The danger of over-relying on results rather than fruitfulness might be said to have two aspects, the first of which is only implied by Bergoglio, while the second is made explicit. On the one hand, the personal humanisation and transformation of the learner (that is, what fruitfulness is about) can only truly be judged over a lifetime and is unlikely to be seen unless viewed through the eyes of love. On the other hand, as pointed out by Bergoglio:

> A standard of efficiency left to itself would lead us *to invest more where we have the greatest guarantee of success.* ... What is the proportion between the *investment* made by God and the object of this expenditure? We could say without being irreverent: there is nothing more inefficient than God. ... The logic of the history of salvation is a *logic of disinterested generosity.*[23]

Here Hildegard's stress on greenness and Bergoglio's on fruitfulness coalesce and become one.

Just as the enlivening and capacitating energy of God's Spirit is constantly at work in creation, bringing all things to fruition, on the smaller scale of humanity, men and women are similarly called to serve as catalysts for this life-giving force. As Helen John points out, in Hildegard's worldview, 'each human being is a microcosm, a little world through whom the great world, the universe as macrocosm, comes to self-awareness'.[24] In her visions she saw a vast number of parallels between 'the relationships between each macrocosmic component of the universe and humankind as its physical, spiritual and moral microcosm'.[25] She maps out the different paths people can take and the ends these paths will lead them to: either to the fullness of light and of beatification or to darkness, diminishment and destruction. She places great emphasis on the human task of discerning God's work in creation as a necessary prerequisite to aligning ourselves with that work and committing ourselves to enacting it in our own lives. In her treatment of the symbiotic relationship between the physical world and human actions, she anticipated by some centuries today's ecological concerns about our detrimental impact on the environment.

All things only live within the power and with the permission of God. No part of creation exists by its own power; none is self-sufficient. It is God's wisdom that 'fixes the functions of creaturely existence.'[26] The eye of God sees all things and God provides the order in which all things exercise their being and in which all things hold together.

Within this order, the lives of human beings should unfold in such a way as to mirror and function as a microcosm of the way God's purposes are worked out in the macrocosm, a microcosm that reflects, and is influenced by, the macrocosm in which those purposes are set.[27] Here Hildegard anticipates the teaching of Pope Francis in his 2015 encyclical *Laudato si'* – that everything is interconnected as part of God's providential plan for creation and as serving God's purposes. Thus, all aspects of creation impinge on human salvation, and human actions either impede or facilitate the harmony and fruitfulness of creation. Hildegard, as was common among medieval people, reads creation as a book written in code, which we must decipher.[28] Moral lessons can be learned from a right interpretation of creation; from this we see for which qualities and virtues God intends us to strive.

Unlike one of the important heretical groups of her time, the Cathars, who considered that everything connected to the material world and to the body was evil, Hildegard regarded the body as blessed and the material world as a source of health and well-being, if used rightly. She orients her listeners and readers towards heaven while taking full measure of their material and mundane nature. Her view of the human person holds together both our material grounding and our spiritual potential, our proneness to sin and our capacity for glory. 'I'm a living breath God placed in mud,' she observes, 'I'm merely a too-sensitive, frail rib with mystical lungs, who saw a living blazing fire that couldn't be put out.'[29] Hildegard pointed out the divine mandate for human beings to the Abbess of Bamberg: 'In the same way that the stars illuminate the sky at night, God made humanity to sparkle. We're created for maturity. We're made to give out light like the sun, the moon, and the stars.'[30] To meet this purpose, body and soul need each other and must learn to work together. Thus, 'the body is also the garment of the soul, and the soul functions by working with the flesh. Yet the body would be nothing without the soul, and the soul could do nothing without the body.'[31]

In an earlier work she had claimed that

The soul provides the body with life like fire flooding the darkness with light; it has two major powers like two arms: the understanding and the will. ... Understanding is in the soul like the shoulders in the body, acting as the moving force behind the other powers of the soul, giving them strength like the shoulders give strength to the body.[32]

In contrast, 'The will is like a fire baking every action in an oven. ... The will is the force behind the whole of the action. ... [Our action is] like a loaf of bread which the will bakes to perfection in the heat of its zeal.'[33]

Hildegard wrote some scientific works in the 1150s that continued to enjoy a wide readership for a long time after her death. The first of these was her *Physica*, on the healing qualities of plants, trees, precious stones, fish and animals. The second was *Causes and Cures*, a book that describes a range of human temperaments and their physiological foundations, prescribes treatment of common ailments, and comments on menstruation and pregnancy. She thought that certain stones could be used to treat various ailments because the basic elements in them of fire and water could serve to restore balance among the humours of the body. She was greatly interested in healing, partly, perhaps, due to her own frequent bouts of ill-health and partly because of the suffering she encountered in the infirmary that was an important part of her monastery. Nuns often acted as midwives and they tended herb gardens to provide for their diet as well as for medicinal purposes.

Her medical knowledge was closely linked to her theological vision of creation and the cosmos. This led her to discern reciprocal influences between the material both of the universe and of the human body, on the one hand, and the spiritual dimensions of life on the other:

> As body and soul are one and support each other, in the same way the planets with the firmament confirm each other and strengthen each other. And like the soul that enlivens and strengthens the body, the sun, moon and stars are the eyes; the air is our sense of hearing, the winds our sense of smell, the dew our taste; the sides of the cosmos are like our arms and our sense of touch.[34]

Furthermore, for Hildegard, physical and spiritual wellbeing cannot easily be separated. 'Medical knowledge and practice can be used to ameliorate the bodily consequences of the Fall, much as theology and right faith ameliorate the spiritual ones.'[35] Although the body can cause us to turn away from God, Hildegard did not denigrate the body; rather she emphasised how important it is to take care of the body because it is with the body that we do God's work and this body of ours is a temple of the Holy Spirit.

Physical and spiritual aspects of reality are fully integrated, according to Hildegard. All the biological aspects in our lives are assumed to be thoroughly suffused with spiritual significance and every spiritual aspect is rooted in, and affected by, one's biology. Here the physical or natural is never isolated from the spiritual or supernatural, and the supernatural is always incarnate or embodied, rather than ethereal. Cosmology, biology, psychology, morality and spirituality form a continuum, with every aspect interacting and being mutually implicated. It is a marked feature of her writing that Hildegard moves back and forth between the forces of nature, the stars, winds, plants and animals, the various parts of the body, the virtues and the struggle with temptations, the text of scripture and the teaching of the Church. The world of science is inextricably linked by her to the story of sin and salvation, not kept separate from it. The five senses, the seasons of the year, spiritual gifts, the functioning of the body, moral virtues (and their corresponding sins) form a unified whole when they are rightly ordered.

In addition to being greatly interested in medicine, Hildegard attributed huge importance to music. In 1158, she completed a cycle of liturgical songs, *Symphony of the Harmony of Celestial Revelations*, also known as *Symphonia*. Butcher describes Hildegard's songs, most of which honoured Mary and the saints, as passionate, inventive, exuberant, original and dramatic, with soaring melodies and powerful metaphors.[36] Here are two examples, in Butcher's translation:

> Life-Altering Love
> And Your Word dressed Himself
> in flesh …
> His sinlessness breathed life into compassion,
> cleaning that sad smudge from the bony outfit every human
> wears.

> To Sophia
> You soar, sustain, and animate,
> climb, dive, and sing
> Your way through this world,
> giving life to every beating
> heart.[37]

For Hildegard, singing was of vital importance for the physical and spiritual health of monastic communities; it was 'an incarnational act, basic to the regeneration of life which takes place within the monastic community'.[38] Singing not only contributed to the formation and education of nuns by introducing them to, and reinforcing in their hearts, the story of salvation and the teaching of scripture, it also played 'a major role in promoting *conversio*, the turning point from sin to God, the ongoing process of change and betterment which is the vocation of monastic life'.[39]

Music for Hildegard provides an experience that brings about a union of body and soul. It is a healing activity that assists personal wellness and aligns one with the divine ordering of creation. Music is not merely an expression and an embellishment of spiritual life, it is integral to the healthy development of spirituality. Music opens us up to beauty and harmony both within and beyond us. 'The symphony manifests itself whenever the community assemble their instruments and voices to project them heavenward, but also inwardly, in the accord of each soul with its body, orchestrated by the divine law.'[40] According to Hildegard, music tunes participants to the heavenly voice. She gloried in her experience of pattern and improvisation in music, in the body, in movement, and in relationships. Her conviction as to the physical and spiritual benefits that music can bring explains why she was so vehement in resisting the interdict on her community imposed in the final year of life by the Church leaders in Mainz, as referred to earlier in the chapter. She claimed that 'Music stirs our hearts and engages our souls in ways we can't describe. When this happens, we are taken beyond our earthly banishment back to the divine melody. ... Remember that singing is our best hope to hear divine harmony again.'[41]

Also essential for discerning the divine harmony is a life attuned to the virtues. Hildegard wrote two books that addressed the virtues, although she also examined these extensively in several other works, especially in *The Book of Divine Works*. Apart from *The Book of Life's Merits*, referred to earlier, also included among her publications there is a play, *Ordo Virtutem* ('The Play of the Virtues'), written *c*.1150, one of the earliest surviving morality plays. This depicts the human soul struggling with the opposing forces of its own potential for virtue and the temptations of the devil. The virtues dealt with include humility ('queen of virtues'), charity, obedience, faith, hope, chastity, innocence, discipline, modesty, compassion, discernment and patience, fairly standard spiritual concepts at the time of her writing.[42] However, certain virtues stand out in Hildegard's overall treatment and receive an emphasis that seems distinctive to her. She constantly stresses the need for moderation, balance and discretion as qualities to watch for and to cultivate.[43]

The following extracts from *The Book of Divine Works*, her last major book, illustrate how she underlines the vital importance of discretion in the moral and spiritual life.

For when a person sometimes tackles the path of righteousness without discretion, the lack of moderation in his course turns him aside into unsuitable behaviours and leads his abstinence into the wrongful excess of conscience. Thus, when he immoderately chooses to abstain even from permissible things, he discovers a loathsome weariness among his other virtues; and when he thinks that having an over-scrupulous conscience can return him to the way of justice, he prepares for himself only the trap of fatigue. For through such foolhardy and improper abstinence, he gives little heed to the rashness of presumption, only then to doubt whether he can persevere in such a way; and from there he falls into the trap of despair. ... if a person's thoughts are neither too hard and ferocious nor too slick and easy-going, but are arranged decently and well in an honest morality in regard to both humankind and God, they lead that person with a gentleness that is restful for the body and refined in the conscience. ... [When we act without discretion] the powers of the soul are torn apart. ... God hates overindulgence and condemns irrational abstinence, and so the faithful person imposes upon himself a just measure in both.[44]

Moderation and discretion are closely linked in her understanding. She knew well the Rule of St Benedict's statement that 'Yet all things are to be done in moderation on account of the fainthearted' and 'drawing on examples of discretion, the mother of virtues, the abbot must so arrange everything that the strong have something to yearn for and the weak nothing to run from.'[45] We can justly claim that there is nothing naive or fanatical about her account of the journey towards God. She maps out not only the sources of help but also the many obstacles to be met along the way and she displays an acute awareness of our multiple vulnerabilities.

Hildegard's description of the virtues is fully integrated into her comprehensive worldview in a way that holds together cosmology, scripture, physiology and morality. For example, she links the seven gifts of the Holy Spirit (as listed in Is 11:23) to the seven celestial bodies known in her time. Thus wisdom corresponds to Saturn, understanding to Jupiter, counsel to Mars, fortitude to the Sun, knowledge to Mercury, piety to Venus, and fear of the Lord to the moon.[46] For Hildegard, the virtues (which she personifies and endows with characteristics based on aspects of human, animal, plant, demonic or angelic spheres of life) are antidotes to sin; they convert whatever they touch into something good.

The sins she lists are not so obvious to a modern sensibility: love of the world, shallowness, showiness, hardheartedness, laziness, anger and lusting after pleasure.[47] In *The Book of Life's Merits*, she presents conversations between various sins and corresponding virtues, for example, between love of the world and Christian love (*agape*), between shallowness and self-control, between showiness and modesty, between hardheartedness and mercy, between anger and patience, and between lusting-after pleasure and desire for God.[48] For all the apparent strangeness of Hildegard's account of the virtues, the most important point to take from her writings is both simple and profound: right relationship with God leads to right relationship with creation at the same time as it enables entry into our humanity: we become who we were made to be.

Educational significance

What lessons can educators learn from Hildegard? Four fundamental contributions may be drawn from her example and her teaching. First, in a world where, despite the progress made, women still face discrimination and encounter obstacles to full equality with men – in education, in the world of work, in the Church and in political leadership – Hildegard provides an example of a woman exercising authority and influence in her society and can serve as a role model to inspire others. Her use of feminine images of God's power (as nurturing, fecund and fresh) and the way that she 'presents an all-encompassing vision of reality pervaded by the imagery and the experience of her own womanly existence' could prompt a more inclusive deployment of language in the Church.[49] This would not only affirm women's perspective and insights but would also enrich the liturgical and spiritual life of men, by making sure that the full range of human experience is drawn upon in the language used in and by the Church. Furthermore, Hildegard's forthright and bold, yet always orthodox and faithful, interventions in Church affairs demonstrate how it is possible to display critical fidelity in such a way as to avoid the extremes of a supine passivity in the face of the shortcomings of Church leaders when they fail to proclaim and promote the Gospel, or a carping and corrosive, self-righteous and unduly negative critique. Catholic educators should assist their students in learning how to combine a committed and humble faith with the capacity to apply critical questioning to the Church as well as to the wider world.

Second, perhaps Hildegard's most significant legacy for Christian educators lies in her holistic outlook and the powerful manner in which she emphasised the interconnectedness of all creation. Two aspects of her holistic vision deserve mention here. One of these is Hildegard's remarkable refusal to separate secular wisdom and divine revelation; she saw these as being inextricably linked, since God is the author and source of all truth. Thus, there is no intellectual justification for separating the consideration of salvific truth from worldly wisdom. Keeping religious truth and other kinds of knowledge strictly separate is likely to make our knowledge of Christian faith seem less rational and more subjective (and therefore merely optional) in the eyes of many, and can reduce the impact of discipleship on secular decision-making, everyday life and our role as citizens. At the same time, the separation of secular learning and religious teaching is likely to invite various academic disciplines to assume a mandate and authority that exceeds their scope and thereby distorts what they legitimately have to offer. The other aspect is that Hildegard's holistic vision also serves as a strong stimulus for the development of an integrated curriculum that is framed and illuminated by a Christian theology of creation. Even in Christian educational institutions, it is far too often the case that a theology of creation (with Christ at its heart) is not brought to bear on how the disciplines of the curriculum might work coherently together in harmony. Such a task remains at best an aspiration and rarely is attempted seriously.

Third, Hildegard's moral teaching displays the creative tension that educators need to maintain between challenging their students and offering support, between demanding high standards and the asceticism and self-discipline required to attain virtue while also providing encouragement for faltering steps along the way. At the heart of Hildegard's moral teaching was the importance of discretion, of knowing how far to push people to do better and when to lighten up and loosen the reins. Affirmation and approval, holidays and celebrations, play and relaxation – all play as vital a role in directing people towards responsible maturity, dedicated self-giving and a life of virtue as do self-denial, communal discipline and the curbing of individual preferences in order to serve the good of all. In her role as abbess, Hildegard modelled as well as taught the need for moderation, balance and discretion. This is not an easy path for educators to walk because what one person experiences as challenging and prompting them to grow, another finds intimidating and causes them to withdraw from the struggle. What one person experiences as supportive, another rejects as paternalistic or infantilising.

Fourth, Hildegard strongly emphasises the providential value of experiencing vulnerability as it teaches us the wonder of God's power at work in the world and in ourselves; it reminds us of our creatureliness and our need for grace; and it prompts us to adopt a humble realism about our limitations and our dependency. When educators today stress competence, mastery and the measurement of performance and success, it may cause them to pay too little attention to the multiple vulnerabilities people can experience.

In reality, all of us are vulnerable and we all have special needs as well as special gifts. As Hildegard teaches, we cannot adequately appreciate Christ as physician, as healer, if we are unrealistic about our common need for healing and help in our different kinds of vulnerability. In a society that deludes itself into believing that we are safe, secure and self-made, entitled to success and comfort, it is little wonder that many people feel they can get along perfectly well without Christ as Saviour. Have we been living in a bubble of self-delusion? Will the COVID-19 pandemic serve as a wake-up call, alerting us to our false self-assurance, our radical individualism, our neglect of the climate, the environment, and the social fabric and health of our communities? Have we been blind to the radical mutual interdependence between humanity and our environment that Hildegard so powerfully highlights?

If Christian educators were to focus on the range of human vulnerabilities in the curriculum, this could help reduce the gap between academic priorities and everyday life, thereby making educational experience more relevant to all students. To offer a curriculum theme such as vulnerability, which could be revisited at different educational levels (primary, secondary, tertiary and adult), from multiple perspectives and drawing upon many different academic disciplines, could also serve to give a more inclusive tone to the classroom, laboratory, lecture theatre or seminar room. It would significantly increase the chances of learners appreciating how some feature of their own experience of vulnerability was receiving recognition in the curriculum, whether this vulnerability was caused by physical, medical, psychological, intellectual or social difficulties or discrimination; it also would help learners to become more familiar with, and more sensitive to, the vulnerabilities suffered by other people. From a more explicitly Christian perspective, giving attention to vulnerability in the curriculum would be one way to establish closer links between the kinds of learning that takes place in educational institutions and the teaching of Jesus in the Gospels. There is something counter-intuitive in teaching about Jesus and his healing (of the body and the spirit) in one small component of the curriculum, such as religious education, and ignoring the areas of life in which we need healing and help in the rest of the curriculum. Attending to vulnerability can serve to moderate emphases on absolute freedom and radical individualism in our culture by reminding us of two kinds of dependency: what may be called our vertical dependence, as created beings, on God for our very existence as well as for our salvation; and what we may think of as our horizontal interdependency with the rest of creation, since every aspect of this creation is interconnected; and our need for the support and contribution of other people if our humanity is to flourish.

* * *

The purpose of Christian education is to encourage people to understand, appreciate, internalise, embrace, embody and communicate the Gospel of Jesus Christ by cultivating a Christian lifestyle based on the values of the Kingdom of God. Christian education includes activities and experiences that elicit the awakening, nurturing, maturing, expression, sharing and practice of Christian faith. Hildegard drew upon imagery, metaphors and mythology familiar in her time to explain and invite others into Christian faith. Responding to her example today, Christian educators can honour her vision, not by repeating her approach and style – which would be unlikely to receive a hearing because of its strangeness and unfamiliarity – but by emulating her holistic, multidimensional and imaginative spirit.

ENDNOTES

1   Kathryn Kerby-Fulton, 'Prophet and Reformer: "Smoke in the Vineyard"', in
     Barbara Newman (ed.), *Voice of the Living Light: Hildegard of Bingen and Her
     World*, Berkeley: University of California Press, 1998, pp. 70–90, at p. 72.

2   Fiona Maddocks, *Hildegard of Bingen*, London: Faber and Faber, 2013, p. 63.

3   Benedict XVI, *Proclaiming Saint Hildegard of Bingen, professed nun of the Order
     of Saint Benedict, a Doctor of the Universal Church*, Rome: Libreria Editrice
     Vaticana, 2012, p. 1.

4   Ibid. p. 2.

5   John Van Engen, 'Abbess: "Mother and Teacher"', in Barbara Newman (ed.),
     Voice of the Living Light: Hildegard of Bingen and Her World, Berkeley:
     University of California Press, 1998, pp. 30–51, at p. 44.

6   Maddocks, *Hildegard*, pp. 244-5.

7   McGinn, cited in Elizabeth A. Dreyer, *Holy Power, Holy Presence*, New York:
     Paulist Press, 2007, p. 80.

8   Newman, *Voice of the Living Light*, p. 98.

9   Patricia Ranft, *How the Doctrine of the Incarnation Shaped Western Culture*,
     Lanham, MD: Lexington Books, 2013, p. 178.

10   Constant Mews, 'Religious Thinker: "A Frail Human Being"', in Barbara
     Newman (ed.), *Voice of the Living Light: Hildegard of Bingen and Her World*,
     Berkeley: University of California Press, 1998, pp. 52–69, at p. 66.

11   Dreyer, *Holy Power, Holy Presence*, p. 65

12   Newman, *Voice of the Living Light*, p. 187.

13   Hildegard of Bingen, *Selected Writings*, translation and introduction by Mark
     Atherton, London: Penguin, 2001, p. 132. This quotation comes from *Scivias*.

14   Hildegard of Bingen, *The Book of Divine Works*, translated by Nathaniel M.
     Campbell, Washington, DC: Catholic University of America Press, 2018, p. 75.

15   Ibid. p. 84.

16   Ibid. p. 225.

17   Helen J. John, 'Hildegard of Bingen: A New Twelfth-Century Woman
     Philosopher?', *Hypatia*, Vol. 7, No 1 (1992), pp. 115–23, at p. 117.

18   Carmen Acevedo Butcher, *St Hildegard of Bingen: Doctor of the Church*,
     Brewster, MA: Paraclete Press, 2018, p. 18.

19   Hildegard, *Selected Writings*, pp. xxviii –xxix.

20   Jorge Mario Bergoglio, *Education For Choosing Life*, San Francisco: Ignatius
     Press, 2014, p. 64.

21   Ibid. p. 5; emphasis in original.

22   Ibid. p. 66; emphasis in original.

23   Ibid. p. 68; emphasis in original.

24   John, 'Hildegard of Bingen', p. 18.

25   Hildegard, *Divine Works*, p. 6.

26   Hildegard, *Selected Writings*, p. 154; from *The Book of Life's Merits*.

27   Hildegard, *Divine Works*, pp. 244–49.

28   Ibid., pp. 75–6, 81, 84.

29   Butcher, *St Hildegard of Bingen*, pp. 55, 61.

30   Ibid., p. 111.

31   Hildegard, *Divine Writings*, p. 261.

32   Hildegard, *Selected Writings*, p. 7.

33   Hildegard, *Selected Writings*, p. 78; from *Scivias*.

34   Ibid., p. 105; from *Causes and Cures*.

35   Florence Eliza Glaze, 'Medical Writer: "Behold the Human Creature"' in Newman, *Voice of the Living Light*, pp. 125–48 at p. 137.

36   Butcher, *St Hildegard of Bingen*, pp.23–4.

37   Ibid., pp.30–31.

38   Margot Fassler, 'Composer and Dramatist: "Melodious Singing and the Freshness of Remorse"' in Newman, pp. 149–75 at p. 149.

39   Ibid., p. 156.

40   Peter Dronke, *Women Writers of the Middle Ages*, Cambridge: Cambridge University Press, 1984, p.198.

41   Butcher, *St Hildegard of Bingen*, pp. 125–6.

42   Butcher, *St Hildegard of Bingen*, p. 74.

43   Hildegard, *Divine Works*, pp. 124, 128, 156.

44   Ibid., pp. 124, 128, 329.

45   Ibid., p. 156. n.74.

46   Ibid., p. 90. n.121.

47   Butcher, *St Hildegard of Bingen*, pp.137–38.

48   Ibid., pp. 136–43.

49   John, 'Hildegard of Bingen', p. 116.

CHAPTER THREE

Bonaventure:
The Journey to God

Life and work

Born the son of a physician *c.*1217 at Bagnoregio, near Orvieto in Italy, Bonaventure, as he came to be known (his birth name was Giovanni di Fidanza), became a student at the University of Paris at the age of eighteen. He spent twenty-one years there as a teacher, during which time (in 1243) he joined the newly emerging and rapidly flourishing religious order founded in the early years of the thirteenth century by Francis of Assisi. By 1250, this band of brothers, which had started out as a mere handful of followers and friends of Francis, had grown to more than 30,000 friars. While in Paris, Bonaventure became the fifth master of the friars' school there in 1252 and five years later he was elected the seventh Minister General of the order. In exercising this massive leadership role, he travelled extensively throughout Europe, including Italy, Spain, France, Germany and perhaps England, to meet with communities of friars. At one stage he was offered the post of Archbishop of York, but turned it down. In 1273, he was made a bishop and cardinal by Pope Gregory X, who asked him to help prepare for the Second Council of Lyons, which opened in 1274. Bonaventure died later that year, while the Council was still in progress. He was canonised in 1482 and declared a Doctor of the Church in 1588.

William Short has explored how Franciscans were perceived as a disruptive force in the university.[1] They threatened the livelihood of secular clergy, being popular and effective preachers. They heard confessions and buried the dead, and through their begging for alms reduced the revenue that would have gone to the already established clergy. They took jobs in the university that secular clergy thought were reserved for them. They were answerable to an authority (within their religious congregation) that was not under the jurisdiction of a bishop and thus it was difficult to supervise or control their activities. They also posed a threat because they represented a very different vision of the Church from that prevailing at the time, which was linked to tithes, benefices, property and working closely with secular powers. In contrast, Franciscans advocated poverty, simplicity, humility and fraternity. Championed and protected by the Pope, they seemed to represent a church that answered only loosely to national or regional authorities. In particular, in handing over chairs in theology from one friar to another, Franciscans threatened the access of secular clergy to such prestigious positions. This hostile environment was just one of the challenges faced by Bonaventure. Could Franciscans play a legitimate role in the university? Given their charism, could they operate as genuine academics?

Another challenge came from members of the order who were suspicious of any involvement with the university and the institutional affiliations that required, fearing that prioritising academic learning would jeopardise the very essence of the Franciscan mission. Would it distract from Francis' prioritising of poverty? Would engagement in academia pose a threat to humility and lead pride? Would it create divisions among the brothers, setting some apart from others? Should the Franciscan order be operating in the university at all?

Although sensitive to these diverse concerns, Bonaventure set out to demonstrate the essential harmony between the life of faith, as outlined by Francis, and intellectual engagement in university studies. He took seriously the injunction in Matthew 22:37: 'You shall love the Lord your God with all your heart, and with all your soul, and with all your mind.' He promoted a form of learning that embraced all three dimensions: affective, spiritual and intellectual. He turns the academic journey – the search for knowledge – into a spiritual journey – an encounter with God. Both involve rigour and desire. Academic work, for Bonaventure, can make a legitimate and valuable contribution to spiritual discipline.

One advantage of revisiting the medieval worldview – especially in the face of fragmenting academic disciplines, the loss of confidence in metanarratives that explain our place in the world, the disconnection between academic work and any particular moral tradition, and the erosion of trust in the possibility of attaining truth – is to learn from its strong sense of the coherence, integrity and harmony of creation. The medieval mindset was convinced that an objective order is to be found in the world and that there was a necessary connection between our moral character and spiritual state and the effectiveness and comprehensiveness of our cognitive reach. Bonaventure assimilates all academic disciplines into the life of discipleship. He steers between an unwarranted confidence in reason and our natural powers and a disabling distrust of these. For him, of course, we do need grace but should recognise that grace builds on and perfects nature; grace does not ignore or bypass our efforts. His task was to hold together Assisi and Paris, faith and reason, devotion and intellect, the divine and the human dimensions of life. Personal and intellectual integration requires an appreciation of the plurality and multi-dimensionality in creation and in humanity, but also of an ordering and unifying principle. Rigorous study conducted with the illumination of faith could give access to the richness and diversity of the world as well as provide the key to how it all fits together.

Bonaventure combined the roles of teaching, preaching, writing and administration, giving a high priority to reconciling conflicting groups within the order, to pastoral oversight, and to upholding Francis' vision for the Church. Bonaventure wrote sermons, biblical commentaries, a biography of Francis, spiritual treatises, doctrinal syntheses, a commentary on the major theological textbook of the time (Peter Lombard's *Sentences*) and a treatise on the organisation and unity of knowledge (*De Reductione*), which might be called his philosophy of education, plus an exploration of disputed questions in theology. He lectured on the Ten Commandments (1267), the gifts of the Holy Spirit (1268) and the six days of creation (1273). His style of writing strikes us today as unusual and can take some getting used to, as he often blended logic, metaphysics, symbolism and mysticism. His language and arguments are soaked with biblical references; they make great play with the significance of numbers; and are penetratingly analytic and highly systematic. He often makes connections that might seem unfamiliar or even far-fetched to us. The combination of intellectual rigour and devout faith is challenging for those who usually see these as either diametrically opposed to one another or, at least, uneasy bedfellows.

Despite these complexities, his aims are always clear and sharply focused. At the forefront of all his writings are questions about our origin, our purpose and our destiny. To find the answer to these questions we must come to know Christ as the key to understanding both the cosmos and our personal lives. The contemporary Franciscan theologian Ilia Delio summarises Bonaventure's goal as showing that 'Creation has a sacred purpose, and that is to awaken the human spirit to God – to love, praise, reverence and give thanks.'[2]

I end this opening section with two assessments of Bonaventure, the first by Ewert Cousins:

His life embodied many forms of the coincidence of opposites. He united the simplicity of Assisi with the sophistication of the University of Paris, the mystical contemplation of La Verna with the ecclesiastical politics of the Council of Lyons. He combined the humility of a friar with the dignity of a Cardinal, the speculation of the theologian with the practicality of an administrator, a high degree of sanctity with the most technical learning of his time. Within the Franciscan Order he emerged as the leader who through his own integration of sanctity and learning, of mysticism and practicality, was able to maintain unity within the Order and guide it in a direction that would preserve the primitive ideal while adapting it to the practical necessities of change and evolution.[3]

For anyone involved in Catholic education and seeking to hold together the tasks of teaching, leadership, and deepening and witnessing to one's discipleship, Bonaventure is a fine resource on which to draw. Jean Gerson (1363–1429), as Chancellor of the University of Paris, was already acknowledging this evaluation of Bonaventure, lamenting that Bonaventure had not received the recognition he deserved: 'if you look for enlightenment of the mind and ignition of the heart you are in the best hands with him.'[4]

For the purposes of this chapter I will limit my analysis of Bonaventure's writings to three of his works, each of which casts light on the purposes and essential features of Catholic education. First, *The Soul's Journey into God* (1259), his most frequently quoted piece of writing, because it locates our intellectual journey within a cosmological and spiritual context. Second, I examine an earlier and much shorter treatise, *On Reducing the Arts to Theology* (1254) – a rather unfortunate title, given that some modern readers may associate it with a form of reductionism in reverse or an exercise in theological imperialism. I hope to show that the treatise, far from being an assault on academic freedom, constitutes instead a valuable contribution to our understanding of how the diverse forms of knowledge cohere together, if properly contextualised. Third, I refer, selectively, to Bonaventure's last work, a series of lectures given in 1273, *Collations on the Six Days of Creation* or the *Hexaemeron*.[5] Although unfinished, this work highlights some essential qualities required for any serious study of creation. Drawing on these analyses, in the final part of the chapter I identify some of the implications of Bonaventure's writings for the work of Catholic educators, for those who teach in Catholic universities and Catholic schools.

Journey towards God

The best-known and most commented-on work of Bonaventure is *Itinerarium mentis in Deum* (*The Soul's Journey into God* or *The Mind's Journey to God*). Two recent commentators on this work demonstrate the breadth of meaning of the word translated as mind or soul in Bonaventure's writing. 'If we take into consideration Bonaventure's entire work, the best translation [of *mens/mentis*] may be "the entire human person with all one's capacities, powers and possibilities," or "the human person in one's physical, psychological and spiritual dimensions".[6] Thus Bonaventure is not speaking narrowly about either an intellectual search or a spiritual pilgrimage towards God, but the movement of the whole person, in all her or his multiple dimensions, in reaching out to the divine. *The Soul's Journey* is for 'the exercise of affection more than the erudition of the intellect'.[7] Its goal is not merely cognitive possession, but a relationship of loving communion – with God, through creation.

Bonaventure shows us how to read the world in such a way as to recognise, appreciate and respond appropriately to God's presence – in creation as a whole and in ourselves in particular. He aims to show readers that only when we recognise creation as an expression of the inner nature and purpose of the Creator do we have a key to reading the world rightly. *The Soul's Journey* is a reflection on the significance of Saint Francis' vision of a six-winged seraph and constitutes an attempt to connect the implications of this vision with how our understanding of the world as an arena filled with signs of God's presence and of God's invitation to a union with him that will be completely fulfilling of our nature, moving us towards wisdom and making us utterly at peace. The six wings of the seraph are compared to six types of illumination or six steps by which we can ascend – with divine assistance – to an intimate relationship with God. The person of Christ is pivotal for Bonaventure in manifesting God to us, in conveying his healing and loving power, in modelling a truly human response to God, and in enabling us to overcome sin, develop the virtues, elevate our natural capacities and enter more fully into God's embrace. As Cousins observes, 'There is a natural link between the Franciscan attitude toward material creation, as sacramentally manifesting God, and the Franciscan devotion to the incarnation as the fullness of this manifestation'.[8]

The six steps occur in three stages, each having a pair of aspects: one based on our natural powers, the other aided by grace or revelation. The first stage involves looking outwards at the natural world to find the vestiges (or footprints) of God. Step one does this by careful use of our senses, while step two enhances this by drawing upon our imagination, which, in Bonaventure's thinking, is illumined by God. The second stage looks inward, at the workings of the human person, in order to find the image of God; first, in step three, by examining the operation of the mind, then, in step four, by considering the working of the will. The third stage looks above, or upward, in order to find God: in step five, by focusing on God as Being; and, in step six, on God as Goodness. As Bonaventure proposed: 'by the eye of flesh man sees those things that are outside himself, by the eye of reason those things that are within himself, and by the eye of contemplation those things that are above himself'.[9]

There is a steady progression in how we detect God and gradually enter into relationship with him: first, without being aware of it, we come into God's presence as we encounter inanimate matter; then, step by step, we increase our awareness of his presence by detecting the shadow of God (as Creator and source of all being), moving from finding vestiges (or signs) of God's presence in creatures, until we reach the stage of recognising the image of God in ourselves and humanity as a whole. Once fully converted with the aid of grace that builds on a life of virtue and devotion, and enlightened by revelation, there is the possibility of similitude, that is, a real likeness between ourselves and God, although a yawning gap remains. Our relationship with God is one of filiation, not identification: as with the rest of creation, we come from the Creator who is the source, cause and sustainer of our being. However closely in tune with God we might speak as his 'words' among creatures, there remains a 'distinction between the Word and the small words that are creatures.'[10]

Bonaventure's work is full of symbolism: tree of life, journey, tabernacle, temple, mountain, mirror, circle, centre and lines, ladder, fire, desert, six-winged seraph. He favours three metaphors or images for depicting the world. The first is seeing the world as a ladder, by which we ascend to God. The second is seeing the world as a mirror, in which we can perceive God's reflection. The third is to envisage the world as a book in which we can read God's intentions and appreciate his artistry. God speaks to us via our senses, imagination, reason, understanding and conscience. If we apply these capacities properly when considering features of creation (and ourselves within it) – their origins, magnitude, multitude, beauty, fullness, activity and order – we can detect God's power, wisdom and goodness.[11]

Perhaps the most quoted extract from this work is in the Prologue: 'Do not think that reading is sufficient without sincerity, reflection without devotion, investigation without admiration, observation without exultation, industry without piety, knowledge without charity, intelligence without humility, study without divine grace.'[12] For Bonaventure, human effort and divine grace reach out for, and call forth, each other; they collaborate and are ultimately in harmony, not in competition. Therefore,

> Whoever wishes to ascend to God must first avoid sin, which deforms our nature, then exercise his natural powers: by praying, to receive restoring grace; by a good life, to receive purifying justice; by meditating, to receive illuminating knowledge; and by contemplating, to receive perfecting wisdom. ... We must first pray, then live holy lives and thirdly concentrate our attention upon the reflections of truth.[13]

None of the properties of creatures can be adequately understood without contemplating their relationship to God, from whence they came, whose presence shines forth in them, and to whom they are being led back (see *Hex.* 3.2). Such contemplation, if it is to be effective, must be accompanied by virtuous living and prayerful devotion but virtue and devotion also require serious intellectual effort as a necessary (though insufficient) element in growing into closer union with God. The key human powers of memory, intellect and will enable us to discern and to approach God. But without God's providential ordering of things, the world would not be intelligible to us and our cognitive potential and aspirations could have no reliable purchase on reality.

Bonaventure linked knowledge of the sciences to knowledge of the Trinity. When he used the word 'philosophy', he meant it in a way closer to our use of the word 'science' or the phrase 'form of knowledge' than to the specialist academic subject of philosophy. For him, philosophy could be divided into three categories: natural, rational and moral. 'The first deals with the cause of being and therefore leads to the Father; the second deals with the basis of understanding and therefore leads to the wisdom of the Word; the third deals with the order of living and therefore leads to the goodness of the Holy Spirit.'[14] Natural philosophy was divided at this time into metaphysics, mathematics and physics; rational philosophy into grammar, logic and rhetoric; and moral philosophy into individual, domestic and political. As Ian Wei points out, '*The Soul's Journey* sought to reconcile university learning with the spiritual traditions established by Francis.'[15] Wei comments on Bonaventure's intention for this book: 'It was not, however, a programme of study to be followed step by step'.[16] Rather it was a way of demonstrating the essential harmony between intellectual endeavour and spiritual development. For if every creature shows, to some degree or another, the signature and presence of the Creator, then every act of knowledge, wittingly or not, reaches out to God. Therefore, all study, in some way, has a spiritual dimension. Sin can distort our vision and prevent our seeing things in God's light. But the more Godlike we become, the more effective will be our search for truth. As noted by Junius Johnson,

> it is the relationship of creatures to the Creator that will be determinative for every subsequent understanding of the creature and that will ground any possible paths for the creaturely mind to ascend to knowledge of the Creator. ... While it [*The Soul's Journey*] remains first and foremost about the elevation of the intellect in contemplation, it is also now seen to be mapping the progress of the human creature in every aspect of its reality towards God.'[17]

For the believer, coming to understand some aspect of the world (when seen as God's work of art and part of God's self-expression) can be at the same time an act of communion with the divine. There is no separation here between the secular and the sacred in learning.

Knowledge

The second work by Bonaventure I wish to focus on is a very short treatise from 1254. *On the Reduction of the Arts to Theology* is its most common title, but it could equally be entitled *Retracing the Arts to Theology*.[18] By the arts, Bonaventure means all the disciplined ways we create a culture through practical and intellectual means. The Latin word *reductio*, as used by him, does not mean that the various academic disciplines can be 'reduced' in the sense of diminished or controlled by, or their workings fully explained according to the principles of theology. Rather it means led back to, raised up to, or sublated by being brought into the realm of theology. To sublate something is to take it up and include it, integrating it in a higher unity. The 'subject' continues to operate as before, but we see more dimensions of its potential and meaning. When something is sublated to a higher level of activity, as when physical and chemical elements and interaction provide building blocks for the emergence of life at the biological level, or when the playing of instruments is brought into harmony in a symphony, in each case the normal functioning of the respective item or activity or stage of development is not suppressed or interfered with, but is used in such a way that it serves a higher purpose than is possible at a prior level. When Bonaventure speaks of leading the arts back to theology, he really means something close to my description of sublation. Thus, the arts are not rendered empty or useless or lacking real knowledge. They do attain knowledge, but without knowledge of God, the real nature and meaning of what they know escapes them. When encapsulated within an awareness of their relation to God, what these arts can reveal is appreciated in greater depth, with more coherence and as having greater significance.

One might justifiably claim that what *The Soul's Journey* does in treating creation as a ladder by which we can ascend to God, *On the Reduction of the Arts to Theology* does with regard to the university curriculum. Each of the disciplines is best appreciated in the light of the economy of salvation. When this happens, each of them can play a part in leading us to God. As Bonaventure puts it, 'This is the fruit of all the sciences, that in all, faith may be strengthened, *God may be honoured*, character may be formed, and consolation may be derived from union of the Spouse with the beloved, a union which takes place through charity; a charity in which the whole purpose of Sacred Scripture, and thus of every illumination descending from above, comes to rest.'[19] Once again, we find in Bonaventure an essential harmony between intellectual endeavour and spiritual growth and a refusal to acknowledge any separation between sacred and secular knowledge – because God is the source, either directly or indirectly of all knowledge.

John Webster describes Bonaventure's *Reduction of the Arts to Theology* as 'an exquisite text, an elegantly patterned, economical, and spiritually charged articulation of a Christian metaphysics of created intelligence in which all the arts are moved by divine wisdom'.[20] The theme of light dominates the treatise which can be examined as a valuable contribution to the philosophy of education. Bonaventure is guided throughout by a text from James 1:17: 'Every good gift and every perfect gift is from above, coming down from the Father of lights.' As a way of structuring knowledge, four lights and six illuminations are described by Bonaventure. There is the external light of mechanical skill, the lower light of sense perception, the inner light of philosophical knowledge, and finally the higher light that come via grace and revelation. The six illuminations expand a little on this categorisation by referring to sacred scripture, sense perception, mechanical knowledge, rational philosophy, natural philosophy and moral philosophy.

In his sermon 'Christ Our One Teacher', Bonaventure warns his fellow Franciscans that 'the light of a created intellect does not suffice for a certain comprehension of anything without the light of the eternal Word.'[21] He goes on to quote Augustine's *Soliloquies I*: 'Just as the earth cannot be seen unless it is illuminated by light, so it must be believed that the subjects of the various fields of study … cannot be understood unless they are illuminated by him as if he were their sun'.[22] We should ask this teacher (i.e. Christ): 'Teach me goodness, discipline, and knowledge.'[23] For Bonaventure, knowledge consists in grasping what is true, discipline in wariness of what is bad, and goodness in the choice of what is good. The first concerns truth, the second sanctity, and the third charity.

And, of course, beyond our personal relationship with Christ and our openness to the working of the Holy Spirit, the greatest source of light for Bonaventure comes from scripture. As Webster notes, the illumination given by scripture 'pervades and interpenetrates the whole of creaturely knowing; it is its surrounding atmosphere, not simply another set of materials to go to work on.'[24] Bonaventure connects all the 'lights' from which we learn to the light from scripture: 'As all these lights have their origin in a single light, so too all these branches of knowledge are ordered to the knowledge of Sacred Scripture; they are contained in it; they are perfected by it; and they are ordered to the eternal illumination by means of it.'[25] Once we begin to interpret everything in creation as coming from God, and as being capable of leading us into union with God, then everything we find ourselves engaged in – whether home-building or politics, poetry or sport, educating children and young people or developing a business, scientific investigation or playing music – can reveal God's nature and purpose for us. Here theology is more of an environment, an ambience, rather than something focused on an entirely separate and distinctive subject – God – in isolation from everything else. This theological atmosphere never dispenses us from getting to grips with the specific knowledge made possible by each particular discipline; piety does not make technical competence in any subject area redundant.

Bonaventure was conscious, not only of the huge positive potential of learning, knowledge and study, but also of the potential dangers if this became unbalanced in any way. Given the hostility shown by some Franciscans to the presence of their members in the university, he had to be sensitive to the possible pitfalls of academic endeavour. Kevin Hughes comments on this point:

> Bonaventure's sense of the 'danger' of the sciences is not intrinsic to their nature; they are dangerous, as all created goods can be, insofar as they may be given pre-eminence beyond their scope. That is, they may be treated idolatrously. Treated, as they are in the *Reduction*, as illuminations within the created order of intelligibility, the sciences are good and rightly related to the higher lights of theology.[26]

Elsewhere he notes that 'The same knowledge that can prepare and dispose one for the knowledge of God can also beguile one and become an occasion of sin.'[27] If they do not lead us to charity, all forms of knowledge can send us in the wrong direction. Thus, in the spirit of Bonaventure, we might claim that our task as human beings is to learn how to love. This is our route to entering more deeply into our humanity (and also our divinity). Learning how to love depends on learning how to learn. These go together; otherwise, learning is likely to lead us astray and our loving will lack wisdom or the capacity to be effective.

Studying creation

Bonaventure's last work was the *Hexaemeron*, a series of collations or talks delivered to an audience of over 160 Franciscans between Easter and Pentecost in 1273. These talks, which read like a blend of sermon and conference paper, invite their audience to seek a union between Paris, the world of scholarly endeavour, and Assisi, the model of Gospel simplicity, humility and discipleship. Christian wisdom is the goal, a wisdom that acknowledges Christ as the pattern and the path, and a wisdom whose culmination is that we are made deiform, like God. The steps towards wisdom start with an earnest yearning for it, which must be shaped and guided by a life of justice, discipline, love and sanctity (*Hex.*, 2.2).

In these talks, Bonaventure sought to form the Franciscans as individuals and as a community. He intended to shape their collective consciousness, their habits, outlook, expectations and priorities. His goal was to set them on the path to wisdom, to guide their orientation to the world, and to direct how they read themselves in the light of scripture. He wanted their personal moral behaviour and their communal ethos as a peaceful brotherhood to lead to a life of obedience to God's law and of personal sanctity that issued in constant praise of God – for 'there can be no praise where there is no peace, nor divine peace where there is no observance of the law' (*Hex.*, 1.2). One authoritative commentator compares Bonaventure's most famous work, the *Itinerarium*, with the *Hexaemeron*:

> The *Itinerarium* employs the six days of creation as it symbolically relates to the soul's ascent and union with God. The *Hexaemeron* expands this vision by speculating how the six days of creation form the symbolic framework for all history and the journey of the church towards God within this eschatological framework. In this sense, the *Itinerarium* may be interpreted as a microcosm while the *Hexaemeron* refers to the macrocosm.[28]

In the first of these sermons about the six days of creation, Bonaventure draws on and brings into harmony diverse modes of knowing, i.e. disciplines or sciences, with Christ as centre of all things. 'It is in Christ, who holds the centre in all things, that everything has its beginning and it is through him that everything comes to its Creator. Our intent is to show that in Christ are hidden all the treasures of wisdom and knowledge, and that he himself is the central point of all understanding' (*Hex.*, 1.10–11). Each 'day' commented on by Bonaventure takes us ever closer to appreciating God: first from natural understanding, and then via faith, scripture, contemplation, prophecy, and rapture. For Bonaventure, 'the whole world is like a single mirror full of lights presenting the divine wisdom, and like a glowing coal emitting light' (*Hex.*, 2.27). The task he sets himself is to challenge, encourage, facilitate and support his fellow Franciscans in learning how to see and act rightly, and to feel appropriately, so that their lives are illuminated by these lights. Kevin Hughes offers the following overview: 'The *Collationes in*

Hexaemeron offer a theology of history, an anthropology, a masterful exegetical "summa" of the order of knowledge, but above all these, collectively they are an exhortation to a form of life, a Franciscan form of holy scholarship, attempting to keep Scholastic rationality intimately connected with the logic of Scripture.'[29]

Bonaventure contextualises knowledge within the economy and providence of God. Without an awareness of this broader context within which we know anything, it is too easy to be blind to the true significance of what we think we know. Therefore he taught that 'no one can have understanding unless he considers where things come from, how they are led back to their end, and how God shines forth in them' (*Hex.*, 3.5). To study any aspect of creation effectively requires that we do so conscious of that aspect being located within a network of relationships and as an expression, however dim to our eyes, of its source: 'Creatures ... are a road leading to the exemplar. ... The divine ray shines forth in each and every creature in different ways and in different properties (*Hex.*, 12.14; 2.23). As Hughes explains: 'To know things in abstraction from their source and exemplar in God is to be lost in the numerous cul-de-sacs of surface knowledge, without a map or a thread as a guide.'[30]

To turn such contextualisation into a regular and constitutive feature of our approach to learning does not come easily. It requires a constant willingness to allow oneself to become conformed to the nature and demands of God's reality. This depends on our attentiveness and receptivity, the operation of grace and the gifts of the Spirit (which are outside of our control), and the degree to which we develop in virtue and resist our inclination to sin. Bonaventure proposes four conditions for study: order, diligent effort, taste and measure (*Hex.*, 19.6). He assigns an expansive role for grace, claiming that its function is 'to re-create, to reform, to fill up with life, to illuminate, to assimilate, to unite, to lay the groundwork, to make acceptable and to raise up the human soul to God.'[31] The gifts of the Spirit 'expedite' our development in that they urge us on and remove obstacles, and they empower, liberate and fortify us. These gifts are 'wisdom and understanding, counsel and fortitude, knowledge and piety, and fear of the Lord'; they are drawn from Isaiah 11:2–3.[32] Seven sins are opposed to the seven gifts of the Holy Spirit: 'The first is pride; the second sin is envy; the third, anger; the fourth, sloth; the fifth, avarice; the sixth, gluttony; and the seventh, dissipation.'[33]

Diligent study should be joined to an ascetical life, which Bonaventure summarises as constituting four practices: recognition of one's own interior defects, mortification of the passions, ordering of the thoughts, and raising up of the desire (*Hex.* 19.24–7). He identified two vices as being particularly dangerous in their power to grip a person and make him swerve from the right path: *cupiditas* and *carnalitas*. Hughes describes *cupiditas* as 'selfish love that is the perversion of the *shared* good that follows from divine law' while *carnalitas* is 'the tainted love that "wallows in the mud" and that excludes the *spiritual* good of divine law'.[34] As a follower of St Augustine, Bonaventure is here drawing attention to what happens when human beings direct their love towards objects that are unworthy. Pride, malice and cruelty are also listed in the first talk on the six days of creation; these vices obstruct the pursuit of truth and wisdom. Pride always hovers close to anyone who seems to be making excellent progress, whether this be in their professional life, academic endeavours or spiritual development. Therefore, humility and the habit of opening oneself constantly to divine illumination and to ecclesial guidance, correction and fellowship, are needed to keep us on the right path.

> Just as a fountain of water will not last unless it has a continuous connection with its source, so it is with light. In a similar way, the grace of the Holy Spirit will not thrive in the soul unless it is referred back to its original source. ... The humble person remains in contact with his source, but the proud person cuts himself off.[35]

Catholic education

Bonaventure has something valuable to say to all Catholic teachers, but because he served so many years as the equivalent of today's university professor, I will begin by commenting on his relevance for the twenty-first-century Catholic university. The emphasis today on research, publications, income generation and reputation scores can contribute to marginalising religious faith – which can be relegated to the private sphere, as happens so often in the wider society. For those who want them, chaplaincy, liturgy, charitable service, Bible study and faith discussions can be available but do not necessarily influence the big decisions in the university. The central task of promoting higher learning is often untouched by faith perspectives.

What should distinguish a Christian university is not simply the *adoption* of aims not shared by other universities, but by the fact that *all* aims are understood and addressed in the light of a range of beliefs including the centrality of Christ, the goodness of creation, the reality of sin, and the need for, and offer of, salvation. The academic disciplines would be seen as avenues for revealing the potential within every field of human endeavour to 'read' and respond to God's creation, to recognise the pervasiveness of idolatry, to discern our place in salvation history, and to hear the call to witness the Gospel. Education would be nourished by prayer and worship. The challenge of scrutinising through the lens of faith the underlying assumptions that govern our work would be accepted as both necessary and worthwhile.

Bonaventure offers the university a vision of knowledge as interconnected and constituting part of our journey towards God. His vision supplies an alternative to one that treats the academic disciplines as fragmented and autonomous, as competing, rather than complementary, and as disconnected from our spiritual life and destiny. Seeing the world as God's work of art – where we can discern his signature and as the sphere where we can be divinised – makes all the difference. If, as Bonaventure frequently quotes from James 1:17, 'every good gift is from above, coming from the God of lights', then not knowing the source or purpose of the gifts may lead us to misread and misuse them.

We need to beware that our academic ethos and methods do not lead us to a false sense of mastery and the habits of manipulation rather than a true appreciation of mystery. The goal of mastery tempts us to treat our knowledge and the world as our possessions and under our control; in contrast, receptivity to mystery orients us to receive our learning as a gift and as a theophany, a manifestation of God. A mastery mentality encloses us in immanence while a mystery mentality opens us up to transcendence. Any danger lies in the pursuit of knowledge, if one reads the university in the light of Bonaventure, stemming not from the sciences themselves but from distorting by separating them from the true light, which in turn disrupts their right ordering and leads us to expect from them more than they can deliver. If the *Hexaemeron* sermons are aimed at prompting holiness and wisdom, Bonaventure's *On the Reduction of the Arts to Theology* clarifies how all forms of knowing relate to the knowledge of God. The various fields of study are led back to their source of life and of light; in doing so, they are raised to a higher level of integration and purpose.

A comment in a recent book on Christian faith and the university reflects a Bonaventurean theme: 'If we want to control and manipulate reality, we will organize knowledge into a map, but if we want to conform our souls to reality, we will understand knowledge as taking us on a pilgrimage.'[36] And the recent papal document *Veritatis Gaudium* also echoes Bonaventure in referring to 'the particular feature, in the formation of a Christian culture, of discovering in the whole of creation the Trinitarian imprint that makes the cosmos in which we live a "network of relations" ... situating and stimulating all disciplines against the backdrop of the Light and Life offered by the Wisdom streaming from God's Revelation'.[37]

Bonaventure links knowledge to holiness and love of God. Both conscience and desire must be activated and enlisted in the search for truth and in the ever-growing deepening of a sense of God's presence. He emphasises the interconnectedness of all truth as being ordered, harmonious and intelligible. He makes much of the notion of the light given to us by God in order to see reality. He believes that faith illuminates all aspects of our experience and knowledge. We tend to think of faith as believing in certain divine truths but give less attention to how faith alters how we see everything else.

A key theme for Bonaventure is that true knowledge requires the precondition of conforming ourselves to Christ. Today we resist the notion of conformity because it threatens our individuality and authenticity. But for Bonaventure, not to be conformed to Christ was to be out of sync with reality and to fail to have one's faculties operating at their full potential. It would be to regard oneself and other creatures in a false light: 'It is in Christ, who holds the centre in all things, that everything has its beginning and it is through him that everything comes to its Creator. ... Our intent is to show that in Christ are hidden all the treasures of wisdom and knowledge, and that he himself is the central point of all understanding' (*Hex.*, 1.10; 1.11). Conformity to Christ has both a spiritual or devotional dimension and the requirement of virtue that is counter-cultural the world of academia today.

In terms of virtue, Bonaventure refers to seven pillars or steps to wisdom: 'The first is chastity of the body; the second is innocence of the mind; third is moderation of speech; fourth is docility in affect; and the fifth is generosity in action; the sixth is maturity in judgment; and the seventh is simplicity in intention.'[38] Access to truth depends on the quality of one's character as well as the depth of one's devotion. 'The mirror presented by the external world is of little or no value unless the mirror of our soul has been cleaned and polished.'[39]

Conformity to Christ will align our thinking with God's purposes in creation. As one commentator on Bonaventure has pointed out, 'one who regards creatures simply in themselves without attending to the way in which they represent the deeper mystery of God fails to see their full intelligibility.'[40] Bonaventure puts great emphasis on discerning God's signature: first, God's signature as found in creation, then as found within oneself, and finally as found more directly in God. For Bonaventure, all things reflect the divine light in some way. Creation can be considered as a mirror, reflecting God's power, wisdom and goodness, and as a book in which we can discern the vestiges, images and likeness of God, each more closely reflecting God. Bonaventure sees the world as sacramental, signifying God's presence, even if under a veil. As Ilia Delio puts it, 'We are created to read the book of creation so that we may know the author of life.'[41]

In the *The Soul's Journey Into God,* Bonaventure shows us how to see God through the visible or material world, through the soul or interior life, and as we respond to God directly – thus modelling how to hold together the scientific, existential and the spiritual dimensions: 'The university of things is the stairway to ascend to God.'[42] Underlying this quotation is an application of the notion that the movement of our minds derives from God, in all their workings, not just in our obviously spiritual aspirations. Bonaventure can help us bring back together, in a healthy relationship, the intellectual and the spiritual – a task that should be at the heart of the work of a Catholic university.

What can Catholic teachers in schools learn from Bonaventure? Drawing from the analysis given above, I focus on some key, foundational principles for consideration. First, knowledge separated from relation to God is incomplete and precarious. Second, given that our best picture of God and of how human beings can relate to God comes through familiarity with the person of Jesus Christ, any school claiming to be Christian in inspiration must be Christ-centred. Ilia Delio reminds us that 'In Jesus Christ, the Word incarnate, the potency that lies in humanity to receive the very personal self-communication of God is realized. The Incarnation, therefore, is the perfect realization of what is potentially embedded in human nature, that is, union with the divine. ... The Incarnation *completes* creation.'[43] For Bonaventure, Christ is the fulfilment of the potential that lies at the heart of creation (union with God) and he is the goal to which creation is directed. Delio proposes that 'We might say that Christ becomes the fullness of the universe when each of us lives in the fullness of Christ.'[44] If Jesus of Nazareth stands at the centre of reality, then 'any attempt to understand man and his world without that centre is doomed to frustration.'[45] A third principle follows, namely that Catholic teachers should strive for an integration, in themselves and their students, of spirituality and scholarship.

From these foundations follow three implications for the curriculum. First, every effort (individually and collaboratively) should be made to promote interconnectedness in the curriculum. As Hayes points out, 'no science stands in isolation; all the arts and sciences of man – if they are true to the reality of the world – must finally be seen within the totality of things and in their relation to the unifying Word of God in which all reality finds its final intelligibility.'[46]

Second, a truly Catholic curriculum goes well beyond providing religious education (RE), the opportunity for occasional worship, and the supportive ambience of pastoral care in a hospitable community, important as all these are. It must embrace a holistic and coherent approach to the full range of knowledge, seen in the light of the Gospel. As Michael Merrick points out, 'The Catholic vision of education is all-encompassing, able to speak to all of what T.S. Eliot called the languages of human inquiry.'[47] Unfortunately, Merrick has good reason to complain that 'In practice we tacitly reject that vision, treating subjects as secular domains independent of the Catholic imperative. … In so doing, we present the faith in an emaciated form. By contrast, a Catholic philosophy of education cares about what happens in the history classroom, the art classroom, the English classroom, every bit as much as the RE classroom.'

Third is that the ethical implications of knowledge should be highlighted. Here I am referring to two ethical aspects, the second of which is often entirely ignored at all levels in education. There is nothing controversial in suggesting that students should be encouraged to question the uses to which people put the knowledge derived from science, technology and the diversity of human inventions. What is their impact of these forms of knowledge on humanity and the planet? Who is gaining and losing from their deployment? Can we find ways to use our knowledge to enhance human flourishing and the common good, instead of merely seeking personal advantage from our learning? Are teachers orienting students towards serving those in need? Are they fostering a concern for the environment? What is less likely to receive attention is the role played by the virtues in arriving at knowledge in the first place; here Bonaventure provides a jolt, welcome or not: 'Like a book written in a foreign language, Bonaventure states, creation became illegible because the human mind, clouded by sin, became enveloped in darkness.'[48] Therefore, moral education and formation in the virtues, together with training in prayer, are essential aids to recognising and embracing the truth. Humility and gratitude are not often included as necessary dispositions for learning.

There are also implications for pedagogy if one embraces Bonaventure's educational vision. The role of the emotions in learning is not to be neglected. There is a need to respect, encourage to speak and to listen carefully to every student (and colleague) because, as Delio observes:

> Just as the Word is the expressed 'image' of the Father, the human person is created to be an expressed 'image' of the Word. We might say that God utters each of us like a word containing a partial thought of himself. And when that word is spoken in and through our lives, God is made visible in the world.[49]

For the teacher, as well as for the student, knowledge as mastery is less important than knowledge as receptivity. In contrast to our materialistic society, our faith tells us that letting go is a necessary step for receiving – and learning. If, according to Bonaventure, 'the highest wisdom … is pure preparedness to receive the divine impress', then in the exercise of authority in the classroom the teacher should cultivate his or her capacity to listen carefully to students, both in order to learn from them and to more effectively meet their needs: one of the ways God speaks to the teacher is through the voices (and also via the unspoken communication) of students.[50]

Bonaventure sets the bar high for teachers when he comments on four essential features of the firm and stable faith they need to display: certain knowledge, outstanding reputation, harmony with each other, and strong conviction (*Hex.*, 9.9). They must know well what they are to teach. Their lifestyle and example must be such as to mirror the truth they represent and seek to share, thereby making it attractive to their students. There must be harmony and evident collaboration between teachers; disagreement, divisiveness, petty disputes and lack of cooperation undermine the effectiveness of their conjoined witness before students. The fourth quality, strength of conviction, Bonaventure points out, must be permeated by love, be prepared to endure suffering (for example, disappointment at lack of success, recalcitrant students, lack of recognition by others) for God's sake, and must exude an inner joy in serving God in this work (*Hex.*, 9.27).

As for the fourth implication for pedagogy, LaNave pinpoints an interesting and perhaps surprising feature in Bonaventure's thinking when explaining how, for Bonaventure, 'The magister [teacher] who would be a theologian must strike a balance between his proper subordination to and humility in the face of the authorities and the need for his theology to be his own.'[51] If we apply this to the role of RE teachers, it suggests that they should be more than mouthpieces for the Church, that they need to internalise the content of their teaching, making it their own, so that it comes across as genuinely theirs rather than someone else's preordained script. It is difficult to see how teachers can promote authenticity, agency and personal transformation in their students if they have not exercised such agency and creativity in their own appropriation of the faith.[52] These qualities are, of course, desirable in all teachers and are a goal for all students in all disciplines of the curriculum; they are not relevant only for RE teachers. The special feature that Bonaventure highlighted in his model, Francis of Assisi, should apply to teachers of any subject: 'Bonaventure is willing to regard Francis as a theologian because he manifests a legible expression of the truth that he perceived.'[53] The most effective teachers are those who live out and put into practice what they teach, demonstrating the powerful difference for good doing this has already made and continues to make in their own lives.

***

Bonaventure's vision enhances our regard for education because it sets it within the context of developing our capacity to reach out to, and rest in, God. The coherence of his thinking poses a challenge to common ways of approaching knowledge and learning. In contrast to our tendency to analyse, to break things down into their smallest parts and then to reduce everything to the rules operating at this lowest level, and that the viewpoint from which we can establish the best perspective is our own, Bonaventure's faith-infused outlook tells us that things don't make sense on their own; parts only make sense in the light of the whole to which they belong. Only a sense of the greater makes possible our judgements about the lesser. So, until we allow ourselves to come face to face with the bigger picture, our judgements are incomplete and shaky at best. And in contrast to our tendency to confuse information with knowledge and to separate learning from the rest of life, Bonaventure reminds us that learning is addressed to the whole person, with all our parts, and that it depends on all our parts being activated and interactive with one another, and brought together by attending to God, from whom they came. Finally, instead of relegating morality and spirituality to a private and purely optional realm, disconnected from intellectual pursuits, Bonaventure presents the view that we won't arrive at worthwhile knowledge without living justly; in this view, our access to knowledge and our ability to benefit from it are closely connected to the quality of our lives and our openness to God and to the bigger picture through prayer.

ENDNOTES

1   William Short, 'Shapers of the Tradition: Bonaventure and Scotus', in *Spirit and Life*, Vol. 2, New York: The Franciscan Institute, St Bonaventure University, 1992, pp. 45, 49, 52-3, 55– 6.

2   Ilia Delio, *Simply Bonaventure*, New York: New City Press, 2013, p.101.

3   Ewert H. Cousins, *Bonaventure and the Coincidence of Opposites*, Chicago, IL: Franciscan Herald Press, 1978, p. 42.

4   Gerson, cited by Marianne Schlosser, 'Bonaventure: Life and Works', in Jay Hammond, Wayne Hellmann and Jared Goff (eds), *A Companion to Bonaventure*, Leiden: Brill, 2013, pp. 9–59, at p. 57.

5   Bonaventure, *Collations on the Hexaemeron*, translation and introductions by Jay M. Hammond, New York: Franciscan Publications, 2018; hereafter *Hex*.

6   Josef Raischl and André Cirino, *The Journey into God. A Forty-Day Retreat with Bonaventure, Francis and Clare*, Cincinatti, OH: St Anthony Messenger Press, 2002, p. 125.

7   Bonaventure, *The Soul's Journey into God; The Tree of God; The Life of St Francis*, translation and introduction by Ewert Cousins, London: SPCK, 1978, Prologue, p. 56.

8   Ibid., p. 13.

9   Quoted by Ian P. Wei, *Intellectual Culture in Medieval Paris*, Cambridge: Cambridge University Press, 2012, p. 127.

10   Emmanuel Falque and Laure Solignac, 'Thinking in Franciscan', translated by Stephen E. Lewis, *Logos*, Volume 21: 4 (2018), pp. 31–59, at pp. 45, 48.

11   Bonaventure, *Soul's Journey*, p. 63.

12   Bonaventure, in Raischl and Cirino, *Journey into God*, p. 25.

13   Bonaventure, *Soul's Journey*, p. 63.

14   Ibid., p. 85.

15   Wei, *Intellectual Culture*, p. 142.

16   Ibid.

17   Junius Johnson, 'The One and the Many in Bonaventure: Exemplarity Explained', *Religions*, Vol. 7, No. 12, 144, (2016), pp.1, 15; doi:10.3390/rel7120144.

18   Wei prefers 'Retracing'.

19   Bonaventure, *On the Reduction of the Arts to Theology*, translation and introduction by Zachary Hayes, St Bonaventure, NY: Franciscan Institute, 1996, p. 61.

20   John Webster, '*Regina Artium*: Theology and the Humanities', in Christopher Craig Brittain and Francesca Aran Murphy (eds), *Theology, University, Humanities*, Eugene, OR: Cascade Books, 2011, pp. 39–63, at p. 42.

21   Bonaventure, 'Christ Our One Teacher' in Robert Pasnau (ed.), *The Cambridge Translations of Medieval Philosophical Texts*, Vol. 3, Cambridge University Press, 2002, pp. 79–92, at p. 84.

22   Bonaventure, 'Christ Our One Teacher', p. 84.

23   Ibid., p.90, quoting Ps 119:66.

24   Webster, '*Regina Artium*: Theology and the Humanities', p. 45.

25   Bonaventure, *Reduction*, p. 45.

26   Kevin L. Hughes, 'Reduction's Future: Theology, Technology, and the Order of Knowledge', *Franciscan Studies* 67 (2009), pp. 227–42, at p. 238.

27   Hughes, 'Remember Bonaventure? (Onto)Theology and Ecstasy', *Modern Theology*, Vol. 19, No. 4 (October 2003), pp. 529–45, at p. 539.

28   Jay Hammond, in J.A. Wayne Hellmann, *Divine and Created Order in Bonaventure's Theology*, translated by Jay Hammond, New York: Franciscan Institute, 2001, p. 217. n.87.

29   Hughes, 'Bonaventure *Contra Mundum?* The Catholic Theological Tradition Revisited', *Theological Studies* 74 (2013), pp. 372–98, at p. 387.

30   Hughes, 'Bonaventure *Contra Mundum?* The Catholic Theological Tradition Revisited', *Theological Studies* (74), 2013, pp. 372–98, at p. 388.

31   Bonaventure, cited by Charles Carpenter, *Theology as the Road to Holiness*, New York/Mahwah: Paulist Press, 1999, p. 36.

32   Bonaventure, *Collations on the Seven Gifts of the Holy Spirit*, translated by Zachary Hayes, St Bonaventure, NY: Franciscan Institute Publications, 2008, p. 43.

33   Ibid., p. 47.

34   Hughes, 'St Bonaventure's *Collationes in Hexaemeron*: Fractured Sermons and Protreptic Discourse', *Franciscan Studies* 63 (2005), pp. 107–29, at p. 118.

35   Bonaventure, *Collations on the Seven Gifts of the Holy Spirit*, p. 35.

36   Jeffrey Bilbro and Jack R, Baker, 'Putting Down Roots: Why Universities Need Gardens', in T. Laine Scales and Jennifer L. Howell (eds), *Christian Faith and University Life,* Palgrave Macmillan, 2018, p. 61.

37   Pope Francis, *Veritatis Gaudium – On Ecclesiastical Universities and Faculties,* Rome: Libreria Editrice Vaticana, 2018.

38   Bonaventure, *Collations on the Seven Gifts of the Holy Spirit,* p. 188-189.

39   Bonaventure, *Soul's Journey into God*, p. 56.

40   Gregory LaNave, 'Bonaventure's Theological Method', in Jay Hammond, Wayne Hellmann and Jared Goff (eds), *A Companion to Bonaventure,* Leiden: Brill, 2013, p. 116.

41   Ilia Delio, 'Theology, Spirituality and Christ the Centre', in Jay Hammond, Wayne Hellmann and Jared Goff (eds), *A Companion to Bonaventure,* Leiden: Brill, 2013, p. 373.

42   Bonaventure, *Soul's Journey into God*, p. 60.

43   Delio, *Simply Bonaventure*, pp. 90–1.

44   Ibid., p. 169.

45   Zachary Hayes, 'Toward a Philosophy of Education in the Spirit of St Bonaventure', *Spirit and Life* Vol. 2, New York: The Franciscan Institute, St Bonaventure University, 1992, p. 21.

46   Ibid., p. 31.

47   Michael Merrick, 'Our Catholic heritage is full of treasures. Let's bring them into the classroom', *The Catholic Herald*, 20 August 2018. Originally posted online 9 August https://catholicherald.co.uk/our-catholic-heritage-is-full-of-treasures-lets-bring-them-into-the-classroom/

48   Delio, *Simply Bonaventure*, p. 62.

49   Ibid., p. 72.

50   Gregory LaNave, *Through Holiness to Wisdom: The Nature of Theology according to St Bonaventure*, Roma: Istituto Storico dei Cappuccini, 2005, p. 184.

51   Gregory LaNave, 'Bonaventure's Theological Method', in Jay Hammond, Wayne Hellmann and Jared Goff (eds), *A Companion to Bonaventure*, Leiden: Brill, 2013, p. 106.

52   See John Sullivan, 'Living Tradition and Learning Agency: Interpreting the "Score" and Personal Rendition', in Ros Stuart-Buttle and John Shortt (eds), *Christian Faith, Formation and Education*, London: Palgrave Macmillan, 2018, pp. 93–114. And also John Sullivan, 'The Role of Religious Education Teachers: Between Pedagogy and Ecclesiology', in Sean Whittle (ed.), *Religious Education in Catholic Schools: Perspectives from Ireland and the UK*, Bern: Peter Lang Publishing, 2018, pp. 11–32.

53   LaNave, *Through Holiness to Wisdom*, p. 200.

PART TWO

INTERIORITY AND ENGAGEMENT

CHAPTER FOUR

Edith Stein:
Education for Personhood

Edith Stein (1891–1942) made a significant contribution to education as a schoolteacher and at university level, in her public engagements as a conference speaker for academics and for professionals, in her writings about education, and through her involvement in spiritual formation within a religious congregation. Few teachers in Catholic schools and universities are familiar with her work and many would benefit greatly from her insights into the intimate connections between an understanding of persons, of education and of spiritual development. Although, as is the case with every writer, her work is marked and shaped by the particular challenges of her time, she continues to have relevance for anyone exercising an educational role, in particular for those wishing to integrate professional work and Christian discipleship.

The chapter is in five parts. An outline of Edith Stein's life and work is followed by a presentation of the chief features of her examination of the human person, which, for her, is an essential foundation for any subsequent educational endeavour. Her anthropological analyses combines philosophy with a Christian understanding of personhood and here I give special attention to interiority and mystery and then to empathy and community. Third, as an extension of her broader treatment of personhood, I review Stein's comments about the nature and role of women, summarising her stance on gender differences and her nuanced feminism and how these should influence women's education. Fourth, I examine Stein's approach to spirituality. She explores interiority by reference to the soul and our relationship with God, indicates various factors that influence the soul's development, especially prayer, asceticism and living eucharistically, and engages fruitfully with the theology of her Carmelite model, St Teresa of Ávila. The final part of the chapter picks out key themes in Stein's educational writings: the agencies that provide education; the mediation of cultural goods by teachers (highlighting the importance of the materials put before students); the religious foundation of education; the qualities required by teachers in the face of the challenges they encounter. I end with a few examples of the impact Stein made on those she taught.

Life and work
Edith Stein was born into a Jewish family in Breslau. Her father died when she was two years old. A gifted linguist, she could read Latin, Greek, English, French and Dutch, as well her native German. Edith entered the University of Breslau in 1911, studying philosophy, psychology, history and German philology. Jews were strongly represented in German universities in the early years of the twentieth century, a situation that changed rapidly when the Nazis came to power in 1933 and almost immediately expelled Jews from university positions. Very soon she fell under the sway of a leading phenomenologist, Edmund Husserl, to whom for a time she became almost a disciple, following him to the University of Göttingen in 1913. She quickly embarked on her doctoral studies, and, in addition to the influence of the German philosopher Edmund Husserl and the philosopher and Catholic scholar Max Scheler (about whom Karol Wojtyła, later Pope John Paul II, wrote a dissertation), encountered several academics who combined their intellectual work with a deep spirituality that impressed her, even during this period when her own faith had fallen into abeyance.

These academics influenced her in a number of ways. They demonstrated for her the excitement and satisfaction, as well as the demands, of the intellectual life. She also experienced something that was still rare at the time (just before the First World War): women being accepted as valuable members of philosophical gatherings. One of these, Hedwig Conrad-Martius, was to remain a close friend and confidant for the rest of her life. Edith had been involved with feminist causes before going to Göttingen, while at university in Breslau and even while still at school, supporting groups advocating for women to have the right to vote and access to equal opportunities in the world of work.[1] Her experiences at Göttingen reinforced her commitment to this cause. Finally, most of the people in her academic circles were religious, some being recent converts to Christianity (for example, Dietrich von Hildebrand, later to become a famous Catholic philosopher).

She served for a time as a nurse on the Russian front during the First World War, caring for Austrian soldiers suffering from dysentery, cholera and typhoid fever. She returned to her doctoral studies in February 1916, combining these with secondary school teaching as she completed and submitted her thesis and underwent her examination. She was awarded the degree with the highest honours. After working for a time as an assistant to Husserl in Freiberg im Breisgau, she taught for almost a decade at the girls' school and teacher-training institute of St Magdalena in Speyer, run by Dominican nuns. It was not long before she was once again engaged in (part-time) academic studies and by 1927, five years after her conversion, she was recognised as a leader of the Catholic women's movement, regularly in demand as a speaker in Germany, Austria and Switzerland, where she gave lectures on education, personal responsibility, social justice, and woman's role in church and society.

She encountered obstacles to her career, both as a woman in a society that only slowly and reluctantly yielded equal rights to women, and later, in a society poisoned by the growing spectre of anti-Semitism. She failed in several attempts to obtain a professorship because of these prejudices. Although in teenage years she stopped praying and became indifferent to the practice of her family's Jewish faith, she always considered herself as committed to respecting and caring for her people. Even after converting to Christianity, Stein continued to speak up in defence of Jews, writing to the Pope when the Nazis came to power, urging him to condemn their disgraceful treatment of Jews and later dying with her people in Auschwitz. She had foreseen, as Hitler rose to power, the disaster coming because of Nazi hatred for Jews and other minority groups; once they had attained control of the state, their plans for brutal ethnic cleansing were evident to her.

From an early age, she had a vocation to academic research, writing and teaching, particularly in philosophy but also to teaching more generally, and later to religious life and mysticism. Perhaps her principal legacy is the intimate connections she demonstrated between anthropology, education and the spiritual life. If anthropology is neglected or only shallowly understood by teachers, they will not build properly on the nature, potential and limitations of their students, and thus approach education without sound foundations. If the spiritual life is not taken sufficiently into account (both as a goal and as a source of life), then education runs the risk of serving false gods and selling students short.

Many factors influenced her conversion to Catholicism in 1922, but she referred to three experiences as being particularly influential. First, she was deeply impressed by how the widow of the German philosopher Adolf Reinach, whom she knew from her student days, responded to the news of her husband's death. Stein observed faith profoundly operative during a crisis point in Frau Reinach's life, sustaining her despite her grief. This experience shattered Edith's unbelief. Second, she happened to visit a Catholic church during a weekday, when there was no service taking place. She was surprised and touched by the sight of a woman arriving with a shopping bag and kneeling for a time in quiet prayer before leaving to get on with her day. The familiarity and informality of the woman's awareness of the presence of the divine as an integral part of her life struck Stein as remarkable and aspirational. Third, when visiting a friend she chanced to pick up a book that she was then invited to borrow. By her own account she read it right through in one overnight sitting and was overwhelmed by the experience. This finally propelled her into the world of Christian faith. Here is the truth in the light of which everything in my life has to change, she thought. That book was the autobiography of Teresa of Ávila. Immediately afterwards she bought a missal and a catechism in order to inform herself properly about the nature of Catholicism and sought baptism as quickly as possible.

However, despite her new-found conviction, the decision to convert was neither straightforward nor easy; she was deeply sensitive to her mother's anguish and anger at what seemed to her to be a betrayal of their Jewish faith and of their family. Many years later, one of Edith's sisters followed her, both by getting baptised as a Catholic and by joining the Carmelite order. Edith's move to Christianity was ever afterwards a cause of great tension between Edith and her mother, so much so that, in recognition of the pain she had caused and the even worse pain she knew she would bring if she followed her heart's desire since 1922 to become a Carmelite sister, Edith delayed entry into the order for another eleven years. Another factor in that delay was her spiritual director, who urged her to continue working in the world, where her rare abilities and remarkable strength of character were badly needed. Eventually, when the Nazis came to power and her teaching and academic work were forced to end, she joined the Carmelites in Cologne and took the religious name Teresa Benedicta of the Cross.

For a brief period in 1932–3, Edith Stein served as a lecturer at the Institute for Scientific Pedagogy in Münster, preparing students who intended to become teachers. Her two essays, 'The Structure of the Human Person' and 'What is a Human Being?' contribute to laying the anthropological foundations for a theory of Catholic education: 'respect for nature as a given and for its laws of development; mutual trust and attention as a precondition for understanding; and responsibility towards, as well as trust in, God'.[2] Educators must take into account all the dimensions of the human being, 'as a material thing, an organism, an animal, a soul, and a social person'.[3] In contrast to secular scholars, who omitted reference to spirituality, Stein claimed that 'the human, finite being cannot be understood in isolation from the Infinite upon which it depends'.[4] In other words, a theological perspective is needed in order to fully understand the nature of human beings.

In her Introduction to *Selected Writings*, Marian Maskulak describes Stein as a 'scholar; philosopher; seeker of truth; victim of gender discrimination; educator; author; translator; public speaker; loving daughter and sister; faithful and trustworthy friend; person appreciative of history, culture, and the arts; Catholic convert ever proud of her Jewish roots; Carmelite nun; victim of anti-Semitic policies and hatred; and above all, a love of God'.[5] As a scholar, she fused traditional sources with currents of modern thought; thus Plato and Aristotle, Augustine and Aquinas, were brought into dialogue with twentieth-century phenomenology, existentialism and personalism, and quantum physics and evolutionary theory.

Lebech divides Stein's intellectual work into four periods. From 1917 to 1925, she worked on phenomenological studies, such as her doctoral thesis *On Empathy*, then *Philosophy of Psychology and the Humanities*, followed by her substantial essay *On the State*. From 1925 to 1930, she taught at Speyer and, at the request of the Jesuit Erich Pryzwara, translated some of the writings of John Henry Newman and Thomas Aquinas into German. From 1931 to 1935, she was engaged in full-time academic work, even after joining the Carmelites in 1932, now with a marked interest in philosophical anthropology (on the nature and powers of the human person). The final phase (which Lebech labels 'ontological'), from about 1935 until her arrest and execution in 1942, was spent in more explicitly spiritual studies as a Carmelite, although she wrote the major studies, *Finite and Eternal Being* and the not fully completed *Science of the Cross*, a work that was published after the war, during this final phase.

The unifying theme in these four periods was her focus on the human person, including inner experience, bodily expression, external forces and influences, and the community context in which personhood either flourishes or is distorted and diminished. She explores the causal relations between the body and consciousness, pointing out that this kind of necessity (how our physical bodies affect our thinking) is 'radically different from logical necessitation or spiritual motivation'.[6] Lebech notes Stein's claim that psychology depends on the distinction between causation and motivation. In causation, we are acted upon by biological necessity or by external forces; in motivation, we exercise agency in response to values that matter to us. While she did not seek martyrdom, she was ready for it when it came; her whole life had equipped her to stand alongside her persecuted Jewish brothers and sisters and to witness to her Christian faith.

Her manuscripts were buried underground by her Carmelite sisters and thus preserved for later publication. The scope of her work is breathtaking, especially given that none of it could be classed in any way as superficial or unscholarly; her writings engage with phenomenology, philosophy, anthropology, psychology, theology and spirituality, which she weaves together in a blend that always aims to do justice to the relationships and interconnections at the heart of life. Hers is very much a holistic vision of human persons and of their formation and development via education. She takes account of the multiple dimensions of life: physical, psychological, emotional, intellectual, spiritual, social and cultural. Although her most strongly developed intellectual gifts were deployed in philosophy, her studies in that field were 'related to psychology, ethics, the arts, religion, the social sciences and education'.[7]

She was a prolific letter-writer and her correspondence shows she was much in demand for guidance on personal, professional, intellectual and spiritual matters. In all cases, she did not hesitate, in responding to queries put to her, to be candid and direct in her advice, aware that such advice might sometimes seem critical or difficult to follow. A large selection of these letters have now been published.[8] They reveal the many questions, events and situations, the issue, dilemmas and concerns and the relationships (personal, professional and religious) of her life.

Because of her desire to protect her fellow Carmelite sisters in Cologne from the growing threat of Nazi anti-semitism, from which former Jews who converted to Christianity were not exempt, at the end of 1938 Edith moved to another convent in Echt, in Holland, hoping to be safe there. However, in reprisal against the Dutch Catholic bishops who spoke out against the deportation of Jews to concentration camps in Germany and Poland, there was a round-up of Catholics of Jewish descent. Along with her younger blood sister Rosa, Edith was arrested, sent to a camp and executed.

As Sister Teresa Benedicta, she was canonised by Pope John Paul II in 1998 and, in the following year, named co-patroness of Europe, along with saints Catherine of Siena and Birgitta of Sweden. The Pope picks her out as one among a handful of thinkers who successfully integrated faith and reason.[9] He admired her work and felt a special affinity for her inseparable commitment to truth and the human person; also because they had both come under the influence of the same teachers, and both pursued similar problems in their studies.[10] He observed at her canonisation that what we can learn from Edith/Teresa was 'Do not accept anything as truth if it lacks love. And do not accept anything as love which lacks truth! One without the other becomes a destructive life.'[11]

For those who knew her, through her teaching or otherwise, Edith was gentle, patient, modest and humble, as well as steeped in scholarship and acutely penetrating and perceptive in her judgements. She combined a sharp and capacious intellect with a warm and generous heart and a profound spiritual depth. A teacher who worked with Stein at Speyer recalled how Edith would put together and deliver packages for the poor at Christmas.[12] 'As a speaker, she appeared on the platform without fear but also without vanity to serve the cause of religious education with electrifying eloquence.'[13] Another commentator recalls that Edith was 'courageous, honest, direct, faithful, dedicated, realistic, spiritual, and, above all, prayerful'.[14] The intellectual, personal and spiritual qualities that she displayed throughout her life, together with the manner of her death, have contributed to the powerful impression she made on so many, and to the fact that today 'there are schools, institutes, libraries, community centres, student residences, streets, and public squares all bearing her name'.[15]

Personhood

Stein believed that each of us lives in search of our essential personhood and that education should serve this search. An understanding of anthropology is foundational for all teachers, and a Christian anthropology is vital for Christian educators. This entails appreciation of certain elements that might otherwise be neglected. Some of these elements are referred to in this section and others are examined in the later section on spirituality. Here the focus is on interiority linked to mystery and then on empathy linked to community.

Teachers cannot effectively carry out their work if they ignore the nature, predispositions, capacities and purposes of their students: 'Like any communicative practice, education projects an understanding of shared humanity, which it poses implicitly as a goal and standard for the communication.'[16] Philosophical anthropology, along with other social sciences such as psychology and sociology, is the study of human persons. For people of religious faith, these disciplines, however necessary, have to be supplemented by, and seen in the light of, theological anthropology, which, through the lens of divine revelation, reveals that people come from, depend on and are made for union with God. For Christians, education has to orient the whole person towards the goal for which he or she is destined; to do anything less is to fail to promote the full development of students and to act against the grain of reality. As a recent commentator on Stein observes, 'Any anthropology that lacks inquiry into divinity and into potential sources of divine revelation will fall short of interpreting human being accurately and adequately.'[17] For Stein, the definitive revelation of divinity and humanity was to be found in Christ, 'the archetype and head of humanity, the final form to which every human being is ordained and to whose life he gives his meaning'.[18]

Edith Stein's vision of education integrates three dimensions: a rich understanding of personhood, as expressed in feminine or masculine natures, in a unique individuality, and as a communal being; the comprehensive and harmonious development of the whole range of human capacities, intellectual, emotional, physical, aesthetic, social, moral and spiritual; and the religious foundation and goal of all formation. The religious foundation provides insight into who human persons *should* be and who they *can* be, with the help of God; without being properly aware of this, teachers cannot help students move in that direction – they will either mislead their students or at best leave them rudderless.

Stein explains the human person on several closely interlocked levels: the physical, the psychical, the spiritual, and the soul. Each level or dimension builds on and extends the scope of the previous one. A person is influenced, but not determined, by the body and its level of health and fitness. Stein includes energy (physical and mental) and moods in the psychical level. At the spiritual level, we are in the realm of conscious thinking and rationality; here we are self-conscious and capable of self-direction and self-transcendence. Stein particularly emphasises the concept of self-formation. The soul is the very core of our being from which our uniqueness flows; it is also the dimension of our being that enters into contact and union with God (or, alternatively, which refuses such union). Van den Berg notes that 'the levels of our psychic and spiritual being are shareable' while 'the things that happen on the purely physical level and that happen in our soul are in principle unshareable.'[19]

Without reference to the soul, Stein believes that humanity cannot be properly understood; it could be said that she anticipated the view expressed at the Second Vatican Council, that the essential clue to unlocking the mystery of humanity's nature and calling is Jesus Christ: 'in reality it is only in the mystery of the Word made flesh that the mystery of humanity truly becomes clear'.[20] Yet the Christian narrative reverses many of our usual assumptions about the world. In this narrative the greatest are least and least are greatest; the meek inherit the earth; seeds, children, and pearls are paragons of majesty; kings wash the feet of their subjects; wealth is handed over to poverty; ... women are on par with men; enemies are loved; sins are forgiven; ... freedom is accomplished through obedience and responsibility; infirmities are healed; life is found when lost; first are last and last are first; mercy triumphs over judgment; tables of counterfeit wealth are overturned; bread becomes body and wine becomes blood; the accused stands in the place of judgments; power is made perfect in weakness; the dead are raised to new life. In this order, the one who rules is the one who serves and the chief ruler is donned in robes of nakedness, wears a crown woven of thorns, holds a reed as his sceptre, and is fastened to his wooden throne with sharp nails.[21]

Stein sees self-giving as a major characteristic of God and the supreme act of freedom. She identifies a close connection between self-possession and self-surrender, and between self-actualisation and self-transcendence – both in relation to others and to God. Human dignity is based on interiority, and interiority is linked to the capacity for elevation or transformation. 'Human souls have the capacity to be regenerated and elevated by the divine Spirit.'[22] Education involves enlisting the motivational drives and interests of learners so that they cooperate in the task of elevation and transformation.

There is a certain incommunicable mystery about each individual that defies analysis and eludes the understanding even of that individual, let alone that of other people: In order to indicate the mystery contained in each person and the limits of our capacity to know them adequately, Stein points out that 'What I am as a spiritual individual is not fully accessible to rational knowledge.'[23] Furthermore, within the mystery of each person we should acknowledge the presence of an influence that transcends the merely human: 'There is in every human being a place which is free of earthly bonds, which does not come from other human beings and is not determined by other human beings.'[24]

On interiority being a vital element of human nature, Sarah Borden says:

> Stein believes that our senses, reason, heart, and body are all interconnected: Information is received through our senses; it is understood by our reason; its meaning is retained by our hearts; and its formation is expressed through our bodies. All work together and function best when each is fully developed. Our faculties, however, are ultimately united and rooted in the interior of the soul, in the centre of the person. This centre is the energy source, the heart of who we are. It is here that we hear the voice of conscience and have our most profound meetings with God.[25]

It is easy to lose touch with the core of our being, and when this happens our lives are likely to become fragmented, our faculties fail to operate harmoniously and, consequently, our freedom is impaired. Thus education should serve to protect the interiority that is vital to each person and to assist people to enter into it consciously, develop it deliberately, and deploy it wisely. Education helps us to open up our interior core to the world beyond ourselves. This is necessary because only in the engagement with others that follows such exposure can our unfinished nature, which is always capable of becoming more, come to fulfilment. From her talks on education and also according to the testimony of her students, it seems likely that Edith Stein would have embraced as her own the credo of one of Fergal Keane's teachers, as recalled by the BBC foreign correspondent: it is the duty of a teacher to keep faith with the possibility of a pupil as a person.[26] 'To teach is to accompany the awakening, structuring and growth of an interiority which only grace can open towards God.'[27]

The final theme to be mentioned in this section is Stein's treatment of empathy and how this is related to community. In her thesis on empathy she writes:

> Age, sex, occupation, station, nationality, generation are the kind of general experiential structures to which the individual is subordinate. ... I consider every subject whom I empathically comprehend as experiencing a value

as a person whose experiences interlock themselves into an intelligible, meaningful whole. How much of his experiential structure I can bring to my fulfilling intuition depends on my own structure. ... By empathy with differently composed personal structures we become clear on what we are not, what we are more or less than others. ... At the same time as new values are acquired by empathy, our own unfamiliar values become visible. ... Every comprehension of different persons can become the basis of an understanding of value. [28]

I think it likely that Stein might have exchanged the phrase 'finds herself deeply and inescapably influenced' for 'is subordinate', in light of her later emphasis on interiority and the essential mystery of each person; human beings are never totally determined by, and subordinate to, the conditions and constraints of their biology, upbringing and circumstances. In this passage she stresses that, in empathy, to some degree at least, we enter into another person's world and reach some understanding of how that world makes sense to that person. In so doing, we learn more about ourselves, by noting similarities and differences between that person's experiences, personality and character and our own; such an empathetic encounter prompts us to appreciate more fully the nature and purchase of the values we hold (either jointly or separately). Empathy is not only about my understanding of the other person, but also about 'the way our mutual understandings of one another are partly constitutive of our larger sense of ourselves in the world. The way *others* may sometimes have a better understanding of *me* than I have myself is a commonly experienced part of this process'.[29] Gestures and other bodily signs made by the other person give us some clues to that person's inner life, and this process is reciprocated. Empathy contributes to our respective 'world-building'. As one of the most important recent commentators on Stein points out, 'her emphasis on empathy allows us to comprehend how our experience influences that of others, how in turn it itself is influenced by their experience, and how intersubjectivity, as a consequence, is structured and "socially constructs" the world in which we live'.[30]

In seeking to understand how personhood develops, Stein is adept at showing how personally chosen decisions (which can be wise or unwise) and the influence of diverse external pressures (which can be positive or negative), contribute to human development in ways that serve both to assist and constrain it. Unlike her contemporary Martin Heidegger, she sees other people not only as a possible source of inauthenticity, for example, when we want to blend in with a crowd, but also as sources of advice, support and nourishment. As Royal observes, 'the authentic self is indebted to various communities for its very life and even for its subsequent ability to criticize such communities'.[31]

A vital aspect of human beings is their relationships with their communities. Every person receives from, and contributes, to communities, both positively and negatively, and this includes receiving and conveying spiritual gifts. Interdependence is basic, necessary and inescapable for human beings, materially and spiritually. Maskulak links Stein's emphasis on community to the conviction that, within God's plan, every life matters:

> The idea that the fulfilment of the human race is dependent on the fulfilment of each human being speaks strongly of the value of every human life. Each person is not in the world for himself/herself alone, but for the whole of humanity. This holds true not only for the strong and gifted, but also for the weak and disabled. For instance, in the case of the specially challenged human being or terminally ill patient, the love, service, and compassion which they elicit from others may be precisely what the others need for their own growth.[32]

Drawing on Stein, Regina van den Berg notes that 'Communities on this earth are always a school, and it is through life in community that human persons are able to develop and to become what they are meant to be as individuals.'[33] Given the power of communities to transmit many assumptions and values, it behoves churches and educational institutions to examine what messages, explicitly and implicitly, are being conveyed in their community life.

Nature and role of woman

Commentary on gender differences continues to be controversial. While, in the past, differences between men and women were used to justify attributing different social roles, generally to the detriment of women, modern analysts such as Judith Butler have argued that gender identity is independent of biological sex and almost totally underdetermined except where this results from an overbearing patriarchal ruling system.[34] According to such a view, people are socialised into specific gender roles, so much so that these can be said to have been imposed.

Stein did not live to see such arguments. She adopted a position that was radical by the standards of her time, especially in Catholic circles, but that appears more traditional in current perceptions. Antonio Calcagno points out that 'she was the first to introduce the question of sexual difference' and the specific nature and role of women in phenomenological studies.[35] She emphasised biological differences between the sexes but did not tie such differences to social roles that limited women's opportunities. Indeed, she resisted all unjust and unwarranted limitations on women, for example, she petitioned politicians to revoke regulations that prevented women from access to university posts as professor, and she argued that women were capable of joining all the major professions; further, she assumed that, generally, 'all women should learn a profession – a view that is amazing if not revolutionary for her time'.[36] She also campaigned for women's suffrage and got involved with vocational counselling for female students at university and in political parties.[37] In her lectures in 1931 she criticised the ruling that women teachers who got married should not be allowed to continue in their post.

She embraced the traditional emphasis on the role of motherhood while interpreting this in ways that did not restrict the motherly role to the biological. In her view, one could give birth or foster another person's quality of life through 'the spiritual power to enable another human being to live a real life'.[38] Similarly, in claiming that women are inclined by nature to act as companions towards others, she did not limit such a role to their life partner (if they had one), but linked it to the ability to 'be there' for others. In contrast to the idealisation of women's nature, as suggested by some men, perhaps in compensation for maintaining the subordinate role of women, Stein warns against any over-idealisation of the female character and even suggests that so-called feminine qualities can become unbalanced or excessive. She further nuances traditional understandings of women in two ways: by stressing the enormous individual differences in the characteristics to be found among women; and by arguing that, in the Christian life, all persons, male and female, are called to the same level of perfection, in accordance with the pattern laid down in Christ, and 'the higher one rises in the assimilation to Christ, the more similar men and women become. ... This annihilates the control of gender by means of the spiritual.'[39]

Stein believed that sexual difference transcends biology; it affects the whole structure of a person. Therefore, education could not be indifferent to matters related to masculinity and femininity and must be adjusted to take into account specific gender needs. Because she felt women's nature and needs had not been adequately taken into account in the educational literature and practices of her time, she set out to address this situation. She called for education to support the development of women's humanity, 'womanhood' and individuality.

The Association of Catholic Women Teachers and the Association of Catholic University Graduates frequently asked her to speak at their conferences in Ludwigshafen, Heidelberg, Zürich, Salzburg, and the industrial region of the Rhineland. One participant described one of these gatherings:

> There appeared a small, delicate, surprisingly unpretentious woman, simply and tastefully dressed, who clearly had no intention of impressing you by her demeanour and her dazzling wit. ... She spoke unrhetorically, with quiet charm, using clear, attractive, unpretentious words. Despite this, you immediately sensed a tremendous strength of intellect and an extremely rich, intensely disciplined interior life springing from absolute conviction.[40]

Stein thought that there *were* essential differences between the sexes (due to physical differences) and that these differences both limited and enabled their respective gifts and capacities in complementary ways. But she also acknowledged differences within each sex as well as between them and prioritised developing the individuality of each woman. And, for Stein, however central gender is to human experience, ultimately it is less important than the power of divine grace to transform lives. The following extract from Stein illustrates her views.

Many women have masculine characteristics just as many men share feminine ones. Consequently, every so-called 'masculine' occupation may be exercised by many women as well as many 'feminine' occupations by certain men. ... The same gifts occur in both [men and women], but in different proportions and relation. In the case of the man, gifts for struggle, conquest, and dominion are especially necessary: bodily force for taking possession of that exterior to him, intellect for a cognitive type of penetration of the world, the powers of will and action for works of creative nature. With the woman there are capabilities of caring, protecting, and promoting that which is becoming and growing. ... She is psychically directed to the concrete, the individual, and the personal: she has the ability to grasp the concrete in its individuality and to adapt herself to it, and she has the longing to help this peculiarity to its development. ... True feminine qualities are required wherever feeling, *intuition*, empathy, and adaptability come into play. Above all, this activity involves the *total person* in caring for, cultivating, helping, understanding, and in encouraging the gifts of the other.[41]

In commenting on the value of Stein's writing about women, Lebech points out that, while gender is central to a person's identity and should be factored into their education, it is not the most important aspect of that person. Lebech offers two insights that are pertinent for educators. First, in urging teachers to take proper account of gender, teachers should be aware that we cannot know *exactly* what it is to be a man, or to be a woman: both express the relational dimension of the human being, its standing in relation to something other than itself, but it is not a relation that ultimately can be completely understood in its specificity because it has no fixed content independent of cultural interpretation of its symbolic value.[42]

Second, if making sure gender differences are understood and appreciated is important, nevertheless,

It is the attempt to reduce the individual characteristics of the human being to its gender specificity, or let gender *expectations* determine how we allow individuality to develop that is unhelpful at least to some, and therefore not of benefit to all.[43]

Stein was radical in her feminism by the standards of her time. She argued that there was no profession that should be out of reach for women. She also felt that society would benefit from the participation of women across the full range of professions.[44] Vincent Aucante notes that she did not hesitate to ask herself if women might one day be called to the priesthood.[45] After all, just as individuals are called by God to undergo a continuous and endless process of development and transformation, so too is the Church. She rejected any attribution of passivity as appropriate for women. She advocated that women should exercise responsible roles, not only in the home and in religious life, but also in the professions and political and social life.[46]

She maintained that education should prepare women not only for homemaking but also for professional proficiency and for political and social responsibility. Both training of the intellect and schooling of the heart were necessary to equip women for these tasks. Stein believed that single-sex schools catered best for the particular developmental and learning needs of girls and also that the teaching body in girls' schools should be predominantly, but not entirely, female; in response to a questioner, she suggested that 'a mixed faculty might be preferable'.[47] Most education of girls at this time was in the hands of men, which prevented women from serving as role models for their female pupils. While schools should introduce girls to the same intellectual disciplines as those studied by boys, she emphasised the importance of fostering the capacities for spiritual companionship and spiritual motherliness. She picks out a paradoxical combination of qualities to be fostered in those growing into womanhood:

> The soul of woman must be *expansive* and open to all human beings; it must be *quiet* so that no small weak flame will be extinguished by stormy winds; *warm* so as not to benumb fragile buds; *clear*, so that no vermin will settle in dark corners and recesses; *self-contained*, so that no invasions from without can imperil the inner life; *empty of itself*, in order that extraneous life may have room in it; finally, *mistress of itself* and also of its body, so that the entire person is readily at the disposal of every call.[48]

It must be remembered that she was articulating these ideas about women as a corrective to the pernicious ideologies that reduced women to roles either of child-bearing (in the case of the Nazis) or of contributing to the labour force (in the case of the Communists). Her goal was to promote the uniqueness, dignity, giftedness and vocation of women and to set out the conditions required for their development.

Spirituality

Our life task, which should also constitute the goal of education, is to learn how to live from the core of our being, from the soul, so that our actions reflect who we really are, rather than emerge in response to unworthy motives or the external pressures of the moment. Authentic and effective self-donation – giving of one's time, talents and care in response to the needs of others – is a practice that is guided and empowered by a strong interior life, by the soul as the core of the person; it is here that God takes up his abode.

> It is our interior in the truest sense: that which is filled by suffering and joy, what rouses itself to indignation over an injustice and inspires to a noble deed,

what opens lovingly and trustingly to another soul or refuses it entrance; that which not only intellectually understands and highly esteems beauty and goodness, fidelity and holiness, but absorbs and 'lives' from it, and in that way becomes rich and wide and deep.[49]

According to Stein, the soul is

the 'space' in the centre of the body-soul-spirit totality. As sentient soul it abides in the body, in all its members and parts, receiving impulses from it and working upon it formatively and with a view to its preservation. As spiritual soul it rises above itself, gaining insight into a world that lies beyond its own self – a world of things, persons, and events – communicating with this world and receiving its influences. As *soul* in the strictest sense, however, it abides in its own self, since in the soul the personal 'I' is in its very home. In this abode there accumulates everything that enters from the world of sense and from the world of spirit. Here in this inwardness of the soul everything that enters from these worlds is weighed and judged, and here there takes place the appropriation of that which be*comes* the most personal property and a constituent part of the self.[50]

Only by putting oneself in God's hands can self-realisation occur: in the sense of understanding and appreciating one's true and unique self, and in the sense of allowing this self come to fruition. A signature theme that she reiterated was '*How to go about living at the Lord's hand*.'[51] Discerning one's vocation and living with trust in God's providence are vital elements in the synergy between nature and grace: 'When grace flows into a soul, it provides it with what perfectly suits that person and that person alone.'[52] Such grace is made to measure for each of us. It can lead to a radical transformation and a new birth that does not efface the essential nature of that individual soul, because that soul lives more deeply than one's dispositions and reactions would normally allow. [53] For grace to be fruitful, it must be freely received.[54] 'God leads each of us on an individual way; one reaches the goal more easily and quickly than another. ... But one may not set a deadline for the

Lord.'[55] Returning to one's inner centre in no way entails neglecting one's responsibilities in the world; in fact, being in close touch with the depths of ourselves is a pre-condition for effective work in the world. If at the core of our being we find the abode of God, being nourished from this core will enhance the quality and fertility of our actions and ensure that the fruits of our efforts exceed what was otherwise achievable unaided by grace.[56] For a while after her conversion to Christianity, Edith believed that 'to lead a religious life meant that one had to give up all that was secular and to live totally immersed in thoughts of the Divine' but gradually came to realise that 'even in the contemplative life, one may not sever the connection with the world' and that 'the deeper one is drawn into God, the more one must "go out of oneself," that is, one must go to the world in order to carry the divine life into it'.[57]

Well-versed in a variety of spiritual practices, including contemplation, immersion in scripture, spiritual reading, and participation in liturgy and a range of devotions, Stein advised those who came to her for guidance that 'it is important to find what is most appropriate for each particular person if they are to draw benefit from one's advice'.[58] However, nothing is more important for fostering the spiritual life than prayer. Prayer is the door that grants access to the inner self (and thus also to finding one's true vocation). For Stein, the mystics offered a better way into self-knowledge than the psychologists who failed to take into account the role of faith. Ever since she had been baptised, Edith had given herself over to a regular and substantive life of prayer. She never separated her personal prayer from the prayer of the Church, believing that, in prayer, one not only comes before God, but at the same time joins with all those others who are on the road towards God.[59] These fellow pilgrims support and strengthen one's growing in holiness, just as one's own prayers support and nourish their Godward journey. As a result of many years of engaging in these spiritual practices, even before she joined the Carmelites, an observer noted of Stein that 'you couldn't help feeling the spell of the great holiness that emanated from her tranquil personality'.[60]

The soul is the dimension of the self that has the capacity to receive God and to be open to all beings. Freedom and reaching out to others are key features of a spiritual nature. Although we are made for union with God, through self-transcendence and with the help of grace, this does not happen easily; it requires self-discipline and mastery of our bodily appetites and our psychic drives. This is why asceticism also has a part to play in the spiritual life. 'If a person finds herself too preoccupied by the demands of the flesh to be open to other dimensions of our life, then a degree of asceticism is required which makes it possible to access our interiority.'[61] Not only does it free the soul from being overruled or even enslaved by the body, it also breaks through the psychic structures that have built up through previous decisions and habits, undermines their conditioning power, and releases a person to direct their lives on the basis of deliberation rather than being driven by unconscious forces and needs.[62] Ascetic practices contribute to the health and flourishing of the body itself and, at the same time, through facilitating self-mastery, they contribute invaluably to the emergence of personal freedom. However, to guard against excessive asceticism, Stein warns: 'If one is intent on having all of one's life consist exclusively of sacrifices, the danger of pharisaism is around the corner.'[63]

If asceticism relates to the disciplining aspect of spiritual life and fosters a readiness to be open to grace, the nourishing aspect comes from reception of the Eucharist and participation in the liturgical cycle, both of which were vitally important for Stein; these feed the life of the spirit within us and open us up gradually to the meaning of the story of salvation being worked out in history. Asceticism is not about denigrating the body; indeed, Stein stressed the body's importance, reminding a correspondent that 'we are not pure spirits' and that the body influences the spiritual state of our life; the body manifests the inner state.[64] She links this to the potential influence of the liturgy for the development of the whole person – the body (through movement, gesture and discipline), the mind (through scripture, teaching and doctrine), and the spirit (in opening up to the story of salvation).

Éric De Rus explains the link between the liturgy of the Eucharist and education: 'If to educate is to participate in the work of grace, *it is in the Eucharist that Edith Stein locates the sacramental source which provides the ultimate meaning of the anthropology of education*, since it is in the loving offering of Christ to the Father through the Spirit that there resides the perfection of every elevation. But the essence of education consists precisely in this movement of elevation.'[65] Stein aims to bring love for the Eucharistic Saviour to the hearts of others by 'teaching eucharistically'. The prerequisite for teaching eucharistically is that 'we *live eucharistically*', which means '*allowing Eucharistic truths to become effective in practice*'. This is communicated 'by *example, instruction*, and *habituation*'. Teachers can give this example if their being fed by the Eucharist becomes evident, not only in how the Eucharist is clearly the centre and source of all that radiates from them, but also in their strength, peace, love, and readiness to help.[66] If this is the case, their teaching will be appealing. In addition to underlining the importance of the Eucharist, Stein felt that 'the significance of the Divine Office for religious education has not yet been sufficiently grasped. … Here one is always lifted out of the pettiness of earthly life and filled with the life of the church which one ought to bring to the children.'[67]

Stein reflected deeply on how Teresa of Ávila affected the people around her. She noted Teresa's qualities of humility, obedience, love of God and God's creatures, and detachment. Interior peace, joy and serenity lead to fruitful encounters with others.[68] In Teresa she felt she encountered a kindred spirit, one who went through experiences similar to her own: 'psychosomatic disorders, swings between self-reproach and self-applause, perfectionist zeal, depressions, tugs of deep family affection and attachment, as well as their similar prizing of female ambition, autonomy and intellect.'[69] Like Teresa, she hungered to find and hold onto truth. As did Teresa, she saw the vital importance of enlisting and training the will as a necessary prerequisite for recognising and living in that truth. Therefore, for Edith, education went beyond the imparting of new knowledge to the intelligence of learners; it addressed the will and it penetrated their souls; it assisted in a process of 'recreating' persons.[70] Several aspects of Teresa stand out in establishing her as a master teacher for Edith: her leadership ability to enlist others to collaborate in bringing projects to fruition; her competence in formation, as shown in her reform of the Carmelite order; and the effect of her charisma and sanctity on the people around her.[71]

Education

Edith Stein reflected deeply on education and her writings offer valuable insights for teachers, in all sectors, today. I focus here on the agencies that provide education, the cultural goods to be mediated in the curriculum, the religious foundation for education, the qualities required by teachers, and the challenges faced by them; I end with some evaluative comments made by former students about her as a teacher.

Stein considers that the main agencies for education are the family, the State and the Church, and that each has a legitimate part to play. Each faces limits on the scope of its actions, so that the assistance of the others is necessary. The State lacks a personal connection and assumes responsibility for education only after much human development and learning has already taken place. Furthermore, its interests tend to focus on ensuring that education produces people who will contribute to the economy and behave like good citizens, whereas those who know children as individuals are more concerned about their personal welfare, happiness and sense of fulfilment. The Church no longer touches all aspects of the lives of her people and, while having a keen interest in education, tends to focus more on spiritual formation than on passing on cultural goods or developing intellectual knowledge and skills. Although the family has primacy, it is limited by its inability to introduce young people to the broader culture and also because of the danger that the family 'could enchain the individual for life and possibly even impede the free development of her personality.'[72] Educational institutions, while well placed to supplement and extend what the family can offer, also have limitations. 'First of all there is a lack of the close personal tie, of the heart-warming natural love which envelops the child in her home. Individuality suffers neglect or even oppression through an institutional system.'[73] On their own, schools lack sufficient contact with outside groups that could enrich the educational experience. Ultimately, teachers should never forget that 'formal education is only *one* part of the integral educational process. ... The primary and most essential Educator is not the human being but God Himself.'[74]

Education for Stein occurs at the conjunction between the appropriation of culture, experience of community life, pedagogical initiatives, personal activity, and, underlying and permeating all these, the operation of divine grace. In addition to strongly emphasising the nature of persons and nourishing interiority, Stein stresses the importance of culture and cultural goods. All societies express their spirit through the culture they construct around their common life. This culture includes both external artefacts, such as buildings or artistic creations, and also less visibly, but no less potently, ideas, values and assumptions, which direct the attention of members of society towards some features of the world and blind them to others.

If education cannot bypass the nature of personhood, neither can it operate without offering cultural goods, objects and practices for students to engage with through processes of initiation, exercise, interrogation and evaluation. Activating students' faculties is inseparable from developing those faculties.[75] Thus, not only is respect for students necessary, so too is discernment as to the quality, moral significance and educational efficacy of the material mediated by teachers. Teachers should be aware of the formative role of culture and cultural objects such as great works that offer insight and meaning into life and which have enduring significance.[76] They also need to help students to develop the capacity for critical judgement that allows them to discriminate between benign and malign influences and social pressures.[77]

For Stein, cultural goods and cultural life are outcomes or fruits of the human spirit. She notes that 'The human spirit is aimed at creating, understanding, and enjoying culture. It cannot fully unfold if it does not come into contact with the variety of cultural fields, and the individual human being cannot attain to that for which he is called if he does not learn to know the field to which his natural aptitude points him.'[78] Thus, for her, there are two kinds of material that the teacher engages with and brings together: the material to be formed, i.e. the nature and dispositions of students, and what she mediates for her students as the substance of the curriculum. Although she favoured a subject-centred approach as more likely to do justice to the intellectual development of young people, Stein thought that the possible limitations of such a system, for example, fragmentation of the curriculum and less time spent with teachers, who would then exert less influence, could be tempered by ensuring that 'homeroom teachers' teach several subjects to their classes, such as German, history and English.[79] She also shrewdly noted that 'an over-loaded curriculum is the greatest danger to an effective educational process'.[80]

Although she put great weight on the necessity for teachers to mediate to students the cultural goods of society, she was also very conscious that education that is inspired and guided by Christian faith must adopt, after careful discernment, a counter-cultural stance in the face of assumptions, values and blind spots exhibited within that culture. For example, she claims that

> The eternal order demands a categorical rejection of the claims raised by another Weltanschauung. It demands rejection of a social order and of education which ... seek to consider all individuals as similar atoms in a mechanistically ordered structure. Such a society and educational system consider humanity and the relationship of the sexes merely on a biological basis, fail to realize the special significance and the higher level of the spiritual as compared to the physical, and, above all, are lacking completely in any supernatural orientation.[81]

Teachers today need to be on their guard against elements within our culture that undermine essential truths about human persons. What distinguishes a Christian notion of empowerment and humanisation through education from some secular notions are two considerations: the importance for Stein (along with other Christians) of the link between fulfilling personal potential and attaining one's ultimate end, that being communion with God and with God's creation; and an acknowledgement of the debilitating power of sin. Without making this connection, fulfilling potential can become reduced to expressing one's desires, dancing to tunes that fail to open one to transcendence, and having a limited appreciation of what is possible to human persons if they were to allow themselves to be transformed by grace. Without an acknowledgement of the power of sin, utopian expectations of education will fail to allow for weakness of will, vulnerability in the face of temptation and disappointment, deficient understanding because of failure to develop the habits and disciplines essential for recognising and responding to truth, and a tyrannical sensuality that subjects the spirit to the flesh, so that one's actions end up by imprisoning the self instead of leading to liberation. In her educational philosophy, Stein opposed all attempts to reduce the dignity and potential of human persons, believing that sanctity is the ultimate form of realism.

Resemblance to Christ is for Stein the ultimate goal of education, though each person has to achieve this in her or his own way. In the depths of the soul, persons can become fit hosts for the abode of God. She envisages education as a spiritual adventure that should ultimately be carried out with the aim of helping individuals to become the persons God intends them to be, capable and willing to share in the divine life. Teaching is a vocation, a significant way to respond to God's call to teachers to invite pupils to open themselves to the workings of grace and to develop the dormant powers of their souls in accordance with God's image. There should be synergy between nature and grace in the journey towards natural flourishing and supernatural destiny. The educator collaborates with God, whose grace assumes the primary role and the teacher a subordinate one. The resources of nature, on their own, are insufficient because human nature is wounded and weakened by sin. Without alignment to God's will and purpose, all attempts to achieve mastery over our lives are doomed to frustration and failure.

For Stein, prayer is the greatest activity the human spirit is capable of and education is a humanising activity of supreme excellence. These twin convictions pervade many of her writings. What brings them together are two features of each: first, that in both prayer and education, nature and grace interact, and, second, the interior of a person has to be fully engaged and brought into relation with the world exterior to her. With prayer, one willingly opens oneself up to God; in education, however compulsory, nothing worthwhile happens without the willing consent and effort of the learner; freedom of spirit is integral to prayer and to education. Again, for Stein, prayer and education have in common the feature of being activities that build, deepen and reinforce personhood, of being humanising. In opening oneself up to God in prayer and seeking to align one's will with God's purposes and to share God's life, a person does not lose her or his individuality, but becomes more truly the unique self they were made to be. Similarly, in the process of learning, when one opens oneself up to, engages with and actively responds to what is received from outside oneself, this enhances rather than narrows one's capacities, perspective on the world, self-knowledge, and readiness to act freely and responsibly.

One of the reasons that prayer and education are both possible and necessary is that we enter the world unfinished, incomplete, capable of change and in need of assistance to become a more perfected self – reflecting more closely the image of God and able to engage maturely and with informed initiative in the world. A teacher can find that her efforts to move souls in the right direction, which will lead to their ultimate fulfilment, seem powerless and ineffective. Stein advises teachers in that situation to continue to pray for their students, and thus to serve as vessels of grace, even as sacraments.[82] In her understanding of the essential link between prayer and education, she portrays education (in its broadest sense, which includes spiritual formation) as equipping people to pay loving attention to God in their lives, in such a manner that relating to God and engaging in the world are not two distinct activities but one: the fruit of integration. Indeed, as she expressed in a letter to a friend in 1932, education is 'a privileged way of participating in the great work of salvation'.[83]

If Christ is the model of humanity to be aspired to, then *how* teachers portray Christ makes a vital difference to what is conveyed to their students. The following remarks by Stein illustrate her insistence on the need for teachers to have internalised and appropriated for themselves Christ's words and deeds and to have developed a committed relationship with him, which continues to nourish them:

> It is a different matter whether someone simply reports the facts of Scripture like any other subject matter which he has made his own in terms of content, or whether someone tells of the Saviour who, through long, intimate contact, has wholly assimilated his image and, to a certain extent, is permeated by him.[84]

When this happens, 'what he carries within will spontaneously press to his lips on this or that occasion'. Furthermore,

> the teacher who so lives with the Saviour will not only speak of him during religious instruction. Wherever a practical decision is concerned, his way of acting in this or that situation will appear before and be a guideline for the decision. ... Whoever constantly attends the school of Scripture as a teachable student will take the Saviour with him into *his* school, and the children will sense that he is present with them and assists with the work.[85]

One can only teach along the lines advocated by Stein if one is filled with the spirit of faith to such a degree that one's life is fashioned by it, rather than by the norms of the world.

Stein refers to four types of knowledge required by teachers: (i) an understanding of the nature and development of persons, as individuals and as members of one or more communities and needing to belong to, benefit from and contribute to such communities; (ii) understanding the meaning and task of the social structure of the school where they work; (iii) the capacity to recognise the particularity of their students, along with their context and the ensuing challenges and opportunities; (iv) and familiarity with, and competence in, conveying the cultural tradition.[86] Teachers should also possess self-knowledge and awareness of how their personality and character influence their students. They must be clear about their purposes and goals, be familiar with their students, aware of the resources at their disposal, and well informed about the factors that enhance or inhibit learning.

Stein was aware of the difficulties facing those she advised about teaching: 'We must contend with our own fatigue, unforeseen interruptions, shortcomings of the children, diverse vexations, indignities, anxieties.' She continues, 'Or perhaps it is office work: give and take with disagreeable supervisors and colleagues, unfulfilled demands, unjust reproaches, human meanness, perhaps also distress of the most distinct kind.'[87] However, despite such obstacles, she remained clear about the potential to exert an influence for good that is at the heart of the teacher's vocation. 'The most effective educational method is not the word of instruction but the *living example* without which all the words remain useless. … The soul formed by God's word acts spontaneously to form the souls in the same sense.'[88] That is why she reiterated that 'it is of extraordinary significance that the child's education be placed in the hands of people who themselves have received proper emotional formation.'[89] In teachers who have enjoyed emotional and spiritual formation, their bearing and the very tone of their voice can exert a powerful influence. 'The inflection of the voice, the face – in short, everything that is conveyed by the term *expression* – permit pupils to gain access to the teacher's personal life and to a hitherto unknown spiritual world.'[90] Furthermore, she reminds teachers that 'Speech always has its repercussion on other souls. The word can enrich other souls, stimulate and guide them; it can injure them and cause them to retreat into themselves; it can make a deadly mark on them.'[91] Therefore, necessary tasks of correction and admonishment should be done with care and trepidation. 'Revealing another's shortcomings must be driven only by pure love, with consideration for what the other is able to bear, awareness of one's own blindness, and in reliance on God's guidance.'[92]

What did students make of Stein as a teacher? One of her students at Münster remembered that 'All her spare time was lovingly placed at her students' disposal' before continuing, 'All of us considered her a model, both of humanity at its purest and noblest and of a life lived out of Christian conviction.[93] She always concealed that great erudition of hers beneath the veil of an equally great modesty.' Another of her students reflected many years later on the impression Stein had made on herself and her friends: 'Though we were all very young at the time, none of us has yet been able to forget the spell that her personality exerted. ... Nobody ever saw her as anything but tranquil, dignified, and calm.'[94] As Herbstrith notes of Stein, 'Her firmness and personal rectitude rapidly gained her the respect of her students; her gentleness won their confidence.'[95]

Education must be in the service of personhood, not of the economy, or of the State, even though these have a legitimate call on human energies. Edith Stein espoused a view of persons that is neither utilitarian nor utopian, but rather one that is both reverent and realistic. She urges teachers to appreciate and respond sensitively to the precious interiority and mystery of the personhood of their students and to see this in the light of prayer and the graceful invitation of God to share divine life. Equally, she shows teachers the way to attend to their own personhood (as a necessary precondition for promoting that of their students) and to develop this according to the pattern of true personhood as modelled by Jesus Christ as the Way, the Truth and the Life.

ENDNOTES

1   Antonio Calcagno, *The Philosophy of Edith Stein*, Pittsburgh, PA: Duquesne University Press, 2007, p. 12.

2   Mette Lebech, 'Why Does John Paul II Refer to Edith Stein in *Fides et Ratio?*' in James McEvoy (ed.) *The Challenge of Truth*, Dublin: Veritas, 2002, pp. 154–80, at p. 173.

3   Ibid.

4   Ibid.

5   Edith Stein, *Selected Writings*, edited by Marian Maskulak, New York: Paulist Press, 2016, p. 2.

6   Lebech, 'Why Does John Paul II Refer to Edith Stein in *Fides et Ratio?*', p. 169.

7   Mary Catherine Baseheart, *Person in the World*, Dordrecht: Kluwer, 1997, p. 123.

8   Edith Stein, *Self-Portrait in Letters*, Lucy Gelber (ed.), translated by Freda Mary Oben, Washington, DC: ICS Publications, 1993.

9   John Paul II, *Faith and Reason*, London: Catholic Truth Society, 1998, #74.

10   Lebech, 'Why Does John Paul II Refer to Edith Stein in *Fides et Ratio?*', pp. 155–63.

11   Maria Ruiz Scaperlanda, *Edith Stein: The Life and Legacy of St Teresa Benedicta of the Cross*, Manchester, NH: Sophia Institute Press, 2017, p. 50.

12   Stein, *Selected Writings*, p. 243.

13   Editor's Introduction to Stein, *Self-Portrait in Letters*, p. 5.

14   Scaperlanda, *Edith Stein*, p. 196.

15   Waltraud Herbstrith, *Edith Stein*, San Francisco: Ignatius Press, 1985, p. 7.

16   Mette Lebech, 'Edith Stein's Philosophy of Education in *The Structure of the Human Person*', *Maynooth Philosophical Papers*, 2006, Vol. 3, pp. 163–77, at p. 164. Accessed 25 February 2021 from https://mural.maynoothuniversity.ie/3009/1/Stein%27s_Education_Theory_MPP.pdf.

17   Donald Wallenfang, *Human and Divine Being*, Eugene, OR: Cascade Books, 2017, p. xxviii.

18   Stein cited in Éric De Rus, 'Le geste educative selon sainte Thérèse de la Croix (Edith Stein): un art intégral' in Hervé Pasqua (ed.) Éducation et éducateurs chrétiens, Paris: L'Harmattan, 2013, pp. 143–84, at p. 144.

19   Regina Van den Berg, *Communion with Christ*, San Francisco: Ignatius Press, 2015, p. 118.

20   *Gaudium et spes*, 1:22, in Walter M. Abbott, (ed.) *The Documents of Vatican II*, London: Geoffrey Chapman, 1967, p. 220.

21   Wallengfang, *Human and Divine Being*, p. 27.

22   Wallengfang, *Human and Divine Being*, p. 88.

23   Vincent Aucante, *Le Discernement selon Edith Stein*, Paris: Parole et Silence, 2003, p. 20.

24   Stein, cited in Lebech, 'Edith Stein's Philosophy of Education', p. 177.

25   Éric De Rus, (2008) *L'art d'éduquer selon Edith Stein*, Paris: Cerf, 2008, p. 76. n.3.

26   Fergal Keane, 'The Teacher Who Inspired Me', *The Tablet*, 17 October 2020, p. 12.

27   De Rus, *L'art d'éduquer selon Edith Stein*, p. 180.

28   Edith Stein, *On the Problem of Empathy*, Washington, DC: ICS Publications, 1989, pp. 115–16.

29   Robert Royal, *A Deeper Vision*, San Francisco: Ignatius Press, 2015, p. 91.

30   Mette Lebech, 'Why Do We Need the Philosophy of Edith Stein?' *Communio*, 38.4 (2011), pp. 682–727, at p. 686.

31   Royal, *A Deeper Vision*, p. 98.

32   Marian Maskulak, *Edith Stein and the Body-Soul-Spirit at the Center of Holistic Formation*, New York and Bern: Peter Lang, 2007, p. 118.

33   Van den Berg, *Communion with Christ*, p. 119.

34   Judith Butler, *Gender Trouble: Feminism and the Subversion of Identity*, London: Routledge, 2006.

35   Calgano, *The Philosophy of Edith Stein*, p. 18.

36   Katharina Westerhorstmann, 'On the Nature and Vocation of Women: Edith Stein's Concept against the Background of a Radically Deconstructive Position'. Available from: http:www.laici.va/content/dam/laici/documenti/donna/filosofia/English/on-the-nature-and-vocation-of-woman-edith-steins.pdf; accessed 3 December 2020.

37   Ibid.

38   Ibid.

39   Stein, cited by Westerhorstmann, 'On the Nature and Vocation of Women', p. 10.

40   Herbstrith, *Edith Stein*, p. 96.

41   Edith Stein, *Essays on Woman*, second edition, revised, translated by Freda Mary Oben, Washington, DC: Institute of Carmelite Studies, 1996, pp. 81, 100, 82; emphasis in original

42   Lebech, 'What Can We Learn From Edith Stein's Philosophy of Woman?' in Cyril McDonnell (ed.), *Yearbook of the Irish Philosophical Society*, Dublin: Irish Philosophical Society, 2010, pp. 215–24, at p. 224; emphasis in original.

43   Ibid.

44   Stein, *Essays on Woman*, pp. 49–50.

45   Aucante, *Le Discernement selon Edith Stein*, p. 91.

46   Mary Catherine Baseheart, 'Edith Stein's Philosophy of Women and of Women's Education' in Linda Lopez McAlister (ed.), *Hypatia's Daughters*, Bloomington and Indianapolis: Indiana University Press, 1996, pp. 267–79, at p. 274.

47   Stein, *Self-Portrait in Letters*, p. 123.

48   Stein, *L'Art D'Éduquer*, Geneva: Editions Ad Solem, 1999, pp. 132–3; emphasis in original.

49   Stein in Maskulak, *Edith Stein and the Body-Soul-Spirit*, p. 8.

50   Ibid., pp.74–75.

51   Stein, *Self-Portrait in Letters*, p. 87.

52   Stein, *L'Art D'Éduquer*, p. 30.

53   My paraphrase and summary of Stein, *De la Personne*, Paris: Cerf, 1992, p. 37.

54   Stein, *De la Personne*, p. 42.

55   Stein, *Selected Writings*, p. 240.

56   De Rus, *L'art d'éduquer selon Edith Stein*, p. 86.

57   Stein, *Self-Portrait in Letters*, p. 54.

58   Stein, in Aucante, *Le Discernement selon Edith Stein*, p. 48.

59   Aucante, *Le Discernement selon Edith Stein*, p. 53.

60   Herbstrith, *Edith Stein*, p. 107.

61   Aucante, *Le Discernement selon Edith Stein*, p. 30.

62   Stein, *De la Personne*, p. 68.

63   Stein, *Self-Portrait in Letters*, p. 93.

64   Ibid., p. 72.

65   De Rus, *L'art d'éduquer selon Edith Stein*, pp. 141–42.

66   Stein, *Selected Writings*, pp. 160, 162.

67   Ibid., p. 209.

68   Stein, *L'Art d'Éduquer*, p. 70.

69   Joyce Avrech Berkman, 'The Blinking Eye/I: Edith Stein as Philosopher and Autobiographer' in Mette Lebech and John Haydyn Gurmin (eds), *Intersubjectivity, Humanity, Being*, Oxford and Bern: Peter Lang Publishing, 2015, pp. 21–55, at p. 23.

70   Stein, *L'Art D'Éduquer*, p. 48.

71   Ibid., pp. 35–36.

72   Stein, *Essays on Woman*, p. 224.

73   Ibid., p. 225.

74   Ibid., p. 107; emphasis in original.

75   De Rus, *L'art d'éduquer selon Edith Stein*, p. 2-4.

76   De Rus, '*Le geste educative selon sainte Thérèse de la Croix (Edith Stein): un art intégral*' in Hervé Pasqua (ed.) Éducation et éducateurs chrétiens, Paris: L'Harmattan, 2013, pp. 143–84, at pp. 158–60.

77   De Rus, *L'art d'éduquer selon Edith Stein*, p. 212.

78   Stein, *Selected Writings*, p. 70.

79   Stein, *Self-Portrait in Letters*, p. 123.

80   Stein, *Essays on Woman*, p. 234.

81   Ibid., p. 206.

82   Stein, *L'Art D'éduquer*, p. 88.

83   De Rus, *L'art d'éduquer selon Edith Stein*, p. 150.

84   Stein, *Selected Writings*, p. 201.

85   Ibid., pp.201-202.

86   Stein, *Selected Writings*, p. 122; *Essays on Woman*, p. 209.

87   *Essays on Woman*, p. 144.

88   Ibid., p. 6.

89   Ibid., p. 103.

90   Stein, in Maskulak, *Edith Stein and the Body-Soul-Spirit*, p. 101.

91   *Essays on Woman*, p. 232.

92   *Selected Writings*, p. 253.

93   Herbstrith, *Edith Stein*, p. 109.

94   Ibid, pp. 76–7.

95   Ibid., p. 77.

CHAPTER FIVE

Elizabeth Jennings:
The Poet's Gift

Language can serve a number of roles. It is constitutive of community. It is a medium for transcendence. It signifies identity. It is part of our search for meaning. It operates as a mode of stabilising for us the flux of experience and events. It is expressive of power. It reveals possibilities. It provides a gateway to perception and it shapes attention. All these uses of language apply in the realms of daily life, bodily activities, and human relationships; they also apply in the worlds of education and of the Church. Nobody was more aware of the potential and limits of language than the English Catholic poet Elizabeth Jennings (1926 – 2001).

I have always appreciated her straightforward writing style, her gentle use of imagery, her refusal to accept injustice. I have also enjoyed the way she combines Christian narrative with the curriculum of life at all its stages, and her blending of earth and spirit. Her work is Christian in content, purpose, background, assumptions, animating spirit and tone and points of reference. For Jennings, 'All making is a small participation in the divine and unceasing act of creation; and this is true whether the poet is aware of it or not.'[1]

A sacramental perspective permeates her writing, which is contemplative, calm (although it could be emotionally intense), restrained, clear, precise and unostentatious. Conversational, sensitive, gentle, simple, warm, quietly confident, infused with Christian faith and exuding close familiarity with Catholic ritual, practices, traditions and consciousness – these features are displayed throughout all her work. She sees the terrestrial and celestial as neighbours; the sacred and profane as interwoven. The mundane is a medium for the magnificent. What is, at first sight, merely earthy, has the capacity to be elegiac when suffused with the light of faith and saturated by the sustained downpour of attention. The very titles of some of her poetry collections give some indication of the nature of her work and offer hints of the state of her mind: *A Way of Looking*, *A Sense of the World*, *Recoveries*, *The Mind Has Mountains*, *Lucidities*, *Relationships*, *Growing-Points*, *Consequently I Rejoice*, *Moments of Grace*, *Extending the Territory*, and *Timely Issues*.

Influenced by George Herbert, Thomas Traherne, Gerard Manley Hopkins, David Jones and T.S. Eliot, among others, she found that words were given to her by grace and inspiration as well as through labour and craft. She detected intimations of transcendence within finite experiences and moved easily back and forth between the surface and depth of things, events and experience and a sense of intimacy and ultimacy. Admiration, gratitude, receptivity to presence and disclosure, joined to celebration of the intersection of the spiritual and aesthetic dimensions of life – these are hallmarks of her poetry and prose. They should also be among the qualities fostered in Catholic education.

This chapter has four parts. In the first, I provide a brief outline of Jennings' life. Part two examines her understanding of the nature and role of poetry and considers how the poet resembles the mystic in important respects. The third section explores some of the many themes that Jennings focused on in her writing: aspects of memory and identity, desire and love, loss and diminishment, religious faith and openness to the transcendent. Finally, I appraise some educational implications of her work that are of relevance to Catholic educators: the importance of poetic knowledge as a counter-force to a technocratic outlook; the value of her insights into the themes explored in part three; the necessity of self-knowledge for teachers and pupils; and her treatment of faith, spirituality and the sacramental perspective.

Life

Born in 1926 in Boston, Lincolnshire, Elizabeth Jennings moved to Oxford in 1932. Her family were fellow-parishioners and friends with the Tolkien family. As a child, 'In addition to being accident-prone, [her] maladies included insomnia, lung congestion, pneumonia, tonsillitis, and nightmares.'[2] She studied English literature at the University of Oxford at a time when the world of poetry was almost entirely male-dominated, and this contributed to her sense of being an anomaly, of being considered odd and at the margins of society. She worked first for a publisher and then as a librarian, before making a living by her pen. At the age of thirty, with the proceeds of a literary award for her poetry, she spent three months in Rome, where 'she rediscovered her faith, confirmed her vocation as a poet, and linked her religion to her craft'.[3] For periods of her life she enjoyed very close relationships with men from religious orders – for example, with the Dominican friars Fr Hildebrand James and Fr Sebastian Bullough – coming to depend on them emotionally in ways they could not possibly fulfil. 'She wrote constantly about her desire for non-possessive love, which would allow her to be both whole and free.'[4] She could also be 'gracious, thoughtful, loyal, caring, and good company'.[5]

Jennings often 'suffered from stomach ailments, anaemia, low blood pressure, and blackouts'.[6] In the mid-1960s she endured bouts of mental illness – and her poems explored sickness and hospitals, as well as other themes, such as family, faith, artists, places, friendship, love, nature, memory and the passing of time. She was physically and emotionally frail, managed only fleeting love affairs, and found herself in poverty by the age of forty, soon being hospitalised. She attempted suicide three times and endured periods of psychotherapy. Her loneliness and extreme bouts of anxiety and depression led her to turn often to alcohol as well as to hoarding and gambling. She lived alone, and destitute in her old age, often experienced isolation. Yet, in the midst of all these trials, 'the poet who in her personal life often reached the bottom of despair at the same time could preserve an unrelenting attitude of affirmation'.[7] Traumatic as they were, these experiences equipped and motivated her to engage sympathetically with others who were suffering: 'Using "imagined experience," she wrote touchingly and bravely in the first person about society's unwanted: the homeless, the ill, the mentally deranged, the criminal, the child, the unwed mother, and even the suffering Christ.'[8]

It is testimony to her commitment to her vocation as poet that, despite the many low points in her life, she remained a prolific writer, producing (as author or editor) forty-eight books of poetry, prose and anthology. The poet, novelist and critic, John Wain, who predeceased her by seven years, looked upon her poetry as 'growing out of tears but testifying to potent joy.'[9] Her range of topics was enormous and included relationships with family and friends, artists and musicians, the work of other poets, nature, illness, the various stages of life, time and transcendence, the power of the liturgy and of the sacraments, as well as many reflections on the nature and role of poetry. Described by Dana Gioia as 'England's best Catholic poet since Gerard Manley Hopkins'[10] she can be a rich resource for Catholic educators.

On poetry

In poetry we discover order in some aspect of the reality surrounding us and we find hope even when everything seems against us. Hope happens when we can locate our current experience within a larger context, which somehow allows us to feel pain while identifying reasons for joy. Poetry is a way of looking: 'It is a way to see, to learn, to celebrate.'[11] It can serve as 'a gateway to the numinous', revealing the world in a new light.[12] As Jennings wrote in 'Considerations,' 'But poetry must change and make/The world seem new in each design.'[13]

In this section, I explore four aspects of poetry, as Elizabeth Jennings viewed it: first, what it offers and its communicative impetus; second, how it is something received more than something achieved; third, the necessary tension and conflict that are integral to its power; and fourth, the similarities between the poet and the mystic.

Poetry offers an experience that steps outside time and is a foretaste of the eternal. Words can serve as windows that allow glimpses of the truth, beauty and harmony that exist around us, but which we often fail to notice. For Jennings, 'works of art, like sacraments in religion, show the given and the obvious, but simultaneously they illuminate the truth and take one "beyond," i.e., open the gates to transcendence'.[14] She envisages a resemblance between the poet and the minister of sacraments, in that both are 'tuned to the presence of the divine and predisposed to share it in communion with others'.[15] Poetry can provide 'an imaginative shortcut to truth'.[16] For readers who are unfamiliar with religious life and language, the poet needs to find 'images, symbols, and analogies from the material world to communicate the spiritual'[17] as the poet R. S. Thomas asks 'How shall we sing the Lord's song in the land of the electron, of the microchip?'[18]

To achieve such communication, poets must become intimate or form a relationship with whatever it is they are driven to write about. One cannot effectively convey to others an idea or experience that is foreign to oneself. This level of intimacy, when authentic, would display, according to Jennings, 'a sense of elation or enchantment, harmonious unity, anchorage in truth, personal humility and the closest possible intimacy with the contemplated object'.[19] Then, in Jennings' words, the poet's language 'flies higher than a kite' and 'dives more deep than submarines'.[20]

Jennings' enthusiasm for poetry began early. She remembers when she was thirteen being transfixed on hearing a poem by G.K. Chesterton being read in the classroom. She never forgot the thrill of that moment; nor the sense of how poetry can transport readers to a larger world. Among the artists whose work she admired and drew inspiration from was David Jones, like her a troubled and talented soul – and someone whose troubles and talents were also inextricably linked. Jennings recalled visiting him when he had spoken of art 'as gesture and as sacrament'.[21]

From start to finish, Jennings saw her the world in a sacramental perspective and her poetry as operating sacramentally, providing a meeting place that mediated between the material and spiritual dimensions of life. In her 1957 collection of reflections, *Pensées*, she argues that 'God's mercy, grace, charity and compassion must be reflected on and embodied, or incarnated, in poetry in order to help counter human sinfulness, especially the vices of pride, jealousy, selfishness and the desire to "possess" others.'[22]

One of the features of poetry she remarked upon was how the poet found herself a recipient of perceptions, rather than a discoverer of insights. Perception cannot be forced by sheer effort; it has to be surrendered to: 'as an invasion, not merely a speculation'.[23] The poet is not in control or in possession of an experience; rather she is possessed by it and her passivity is the channel that allows it to materialise without distortion. Gratitude is required, because 'words are offered/Like a Host upon the tongue'.[24] She was very conscious that in her poems she was receiving a gift that she attributed to God.

Another aspect of poetry is the conflict and tension inherent in how a poem is arrived at and then constructed. The tension at the heart of poetry is, for Jennings, a source of life. 'The poems which satisfy most are not those which simply give a sense of reconciliation and order, but those which show life and order as the fruits of conflict; and we need to *feel* this tension even in the most triumphant and reconciled poems.'[25] Furthermore, 'harmony and clarity are only reached after confusion and darkness and when they are reached, they are held only fleetingly'.[26] Discipline is an essential dimension of all art, which is in service of some vision of what is there to be seen or experienced, but that is not necessarily immediately obvious to the untrained eye or ear or to the unexercised imagination. 'Imagination is not to be exiled nor to be controlled. It is to be disciplined so that its deepest potentialities may be realized.'[27] Jennings wants to combine a surrendering and openness to mystery and inspiration as the receptive dimension of the poet's orientation to the world with a disciplined commitment to mastering the technical aspects of the poetic craft. If the subjective experience of the poet is to connect with objective reality and to communicate this authentically, the poet needs to hold her excitement in creative tension with prosaic discipline, her commitment to the vision and her capacity and willingness to detach herself from her own reactions to it. As she says in 'I Count the Moments', 'poetry is pain as well as passion'.[28] Or, in reference to the pianist, Arthur Rubinstein, a 'Player who keeps the passion in order/ To unleash larger fires'.[29]

In *Every Changing Shape*, her set of essays on different writers – mostly poets, but also dramatists and novelists – Jennings compares the poet to the mystic. Both the poet and the mystic introduce us to forms of knowledge that lie outside our usual ways of knowing. Here science cannot go; means-ends thinking is inappropriate; investigation in search of mastery is a non-starter. The training or formation of the poet and the mystic is similar in that it involves some form of asceticism. In referring to similarities between spiritual ascesis and poetic craftsmanship, Jennings notes that 'the poet's training corresponds in many ways with the training of the priest – the self-mastery, the ability to discard what is inessential, the patient waiting during the times when poems cannot be written, the terrible "dark night of the senses" in which everything seems plunged in meaninglessness and obscurity'.[30] Both professions offer a direct, suprarational union with the object of their attention – God in the case of the mystic, while in the case of the poet, this may be God, or an aspect of nature, or communion with some personal experience or something imagined. This intimate form of knowing is the fruit of love rather than scrutiny. For the poet, the sustained union is a passing one, because the poet steps back from it in order to convey it to others; whereas the mystic's priority is not to communicate but to immerse himself or herself in the experience in order to sustain and deepen it. For both the poet and mystic there needs to be a 'silencing of the self and dwelling lovingly upon the contemplated object in the intellectual poise of complete surrender so as to let oneself be possessed by the thing contemplated'.[31] 'Although it cannot be guaranteed, this devoted form of attention can lead to an intense experience of transcendence that needs to be shared, a sense of joyous rapture, the attitude of humility and an urge of love.'[32] Voluntary self-limitation rather than self-indulgence or self-promotion opens up inner space for both the poet and the person of prayer.

Key themes

Jennings touched upon a huge number of themes in her poetry. In order to give a flavour of these, within the limited space of this chapter, I restrict my attention to only a few examples: identity and memory as foundations for our way of looking at the world and life; desire and love; experiences of loss, suffering and diminishment; and faith in and openness to transcendence.

Identity, memory and a way of looking

Jennings often revisits her memories. Memories function as an essential source and foundation for our sense of identity. There is a thread, or, put more strongly, a bond, linking our past to our present. Memory holds the potential to be a source of learning to face life's challenges. She captures acutely the magical, unregulated, playful outlook of a child, comparing a child to a bird who is partly tamed and describing her childish self as 'instinct coupled with climbing imagination.'[33] And she depicts the mentality, especially the uncertainty, of teenagers in a similarly perceptive way, as they display 'So many ways to be unsure or bold.'[34]

On the home front – a term I use deliberately to recall the experience Jennings had of the Second World War – she notes how we can be burnt by past experience and become cold, frozen into defensive stances that prevent us from developing further. By holding on to past pains we block the way to future gains.

Our attention is too often limited, in scope and intensity, causing us to fail to see clearly. Our observations can be disoriented and driven by narrow and often selfish concerns that prevent us from seeing things as they truly are, leading us to live in a make-believe world. The year before she died, Jennings returned to the themes of memory and identity. In 'Song in November' she makes two points. First, our sense of identity depends heavily on our perception of how others recognise and 'read' us. We cannot help but see ourselves, at least partly, through the eyes of others (even if this mirror can sometimes be distorting). Second, even in our declining moments, memory can be a treasure and the seed of vitality.[35]

Desire and love

Many of Jennings' poems are about desire and love which take many forms, often related to family or friends, or to erotic, and even mystical love. In her hands, poems on this theme blend carnal, emotional, intellectual and spiritual dimensions. In 'A Child in the Night' she shows how the child's wonder at the world, where all is new and mysterious, and when being shines with fascination, gets lost or buried after childhood, until love rekindles it, albeit only too fleetingly.[36]

In 'More Than Spring' she intriguingly refers to a feature that seems innate to human beings, a yearning for something either forgotten, and to be retrieved, or for something not yet attained – our 'Eden-longings'.[37] In 'From Light to Dark', she asks if our happiness is rooted in our past, or is it ahead of us, inviting us to realms we have never entered?[38]

In 'Two Ways' she identifies two distinct types of love. One seeks to possess, the other to let be. One is restless and aching, the other looks out with friendship and ready acceptance. Having identified them, she expresses the desire to hold them together, both the receiving and giving aspects of love.[39]

Despite her various setbacks in life, Jennings never lost her aspirations and yearnings for something and someone ideal. In 'The Sonnets of Michelangelo XXXII' she hints at the persistent presence in us all of an irrepressible hope that, for many, remains a promise rather than a possession. The very existence in us of this dream of love keeps open the possibility of heaven.[40]

After separation from a much-loved friend, when love now belongs to the past, she shows appreciation and gratitude for a love than can progress no further rather than sorrow or regret.

You've cast your spell
And left a magic which I can live by.[41]

As a final illustration of her treatment of love, I choose one of her mature insights. In 'The Deepest Love', she acknowledges that, in the end, real love must be rooted in truth if it to be robust.[42]

Loss, suffering and diminishment

Many of Jennings' poems explore different facets of pain, both physical and mental. She shows great sensitivity to the feelings of those who are isolated, marginalised, neglected or misunderstood. Given her own experience of mental illness and of being institutionalised, it is little wonder that many of her poems are set in hospital. One recent commentator claims, with some justification, that 'Solitude in Jennings' personal experience is both a heavy burden that she carried throughout her life and a source of creative energy. … For Jennings, solitude in life, like silence in poetry, opens up new vistas of perception and thus empowers the poet to touch transcendence and share that experience with others.'[43]

In 'Night Sister' she marvels at the care constantly displayed by the nurse who has to cope with such suffering, day after day, caring for men and women in the most diminished state. She asks: 'How is it possible not to grow hard,/To build a shell around yourself when you/Have to watch so much pain, and hear it too?'[44]

While in a hospital ward herself, she observes – and shares – the contagious fear and anxiety of the very ill people around her. In 'Euthanasia' she draws attention to the fear that leads some to hide their frailties, such as by pretending to hear when they can't, or by disguising their pain, or by claiming to feel fine when they don't.[45]

In 'The Way They Live Now' she refers to a different kind of loss, implying that the stricter social etiquette that governed relationships between men and women in the past offered some pleasures that a more liberal society renders unavailable to young people today.[46]

Faith in – and openness to – transcendence

In this final selection from the many themes of Jennings' poetry, I focus, first on the sacramental perspective, then on the centrality of the Mass and her reflections on the seasons of the liturgical year, and finally on the notion that we are dust made for heaven.

One of the most obvious features of Jennings' outlook on life that we see time and again in her poetry is her constant commitment to a sacramental perspective: God is to be found through all kinds of media, circumstances and experiences. She exemplifies Gerard Manley Hopkins' observation that 'God's signature is written on all creation.'[47] Anna Walczuk has written a major study of Jennings that interprets her whole corpus in the light of a sacramental reading of the world. 'The religious cast of the poet's mind makes her see sacramental figures in things of Nature.'[48] In 'A Full Moon' Jennings reflects that: 'Tonight the full moon is the Host held up, For everybody's eyes/To see and understand the high and deep/ Salvation in the skies.'[49]

In 'Trees', she speaks of how 'The broad kind chestnut's hand/ Lay on us like a blessing.'[50] In fact, from her perspective, not to read the world sacramentally may lead to reading it antagonistically: 'All the world is praise or else is war.'[51] Either we receive creation as a gift, which deserves praise and gratitude, or, we are prone to receive it as something hostile, requiring mastery and taming, something to fight over. The world is suffused with God's presence, even if we are too blind and inattentive to pick up the signals. For her 'God is "hidden", but He has not absconded; He has not withdrawn from the world or abandoned humankind.'[52] Furthermore, sacraments use material signs to mediate different aspects of the loving presence of the Creator, and 'To marry spirit with flesh, matter with form, the visible with the invisible, is the property of sacrament; and it is to this unifying power that Jennings' poetry constantly draws attention.'[53]

The source that sustains the sacramental outlook for Jennings, as for all Catholics, is the Mass. In 'A Reproach', Jennings laments the times when she falls short of proper attention as she recalls how easily her thoughts stray from the mystery being unfolded before her in the sacred liturgy.[54] Then she recalls feeling upbraided when a friend who does not share her faith said to her that if she believed what Elizabeth does about the nature and purpose of Mass, she would go every day.

By way of contrast, in another poem, 'At Mass (II)', she is very much attuned to, and affirming of, what she gains through participation in the Eucharist: 'Our hearts are made/Bethlehems for God the Father's son. ... /And we return to find all usual things/Are shining with right purpose.'[55]

Jennings often links the liturgy of life with the Church's seasons, showing her readers how to sense the sacramental in ordinary aches, yearning, hopes and striving. For example, she comments on Epiphany, Good Friday, Easter, and Pentecost.

In 'Words for the Magi' she sees the gifts of the Magi visiting the newborn Jesus as foreshadowing the temptations he later faced in the desert. If each of us has to face our own temptations, so too, must we all face, at some point in our lives, a personal Calvary.[56] This is the focus of her poem 'Many Easters.' For Jennings, acknowledging the Cross of Christ as the culmination of the life and work of Christ, and as the path we must follow, should make us mindful of the multiple sufferings of so many others in our world, sufferings in which, if we are honest, we have perhaps played a part. This leads her to warn that our veneration of the Cross of Christ should galvanise us to show compassion for others who carry their own crosses.[57]

There is a wonderful reconstruction of Pentecost in 'Gift of Tongues' – a strange blending of fear followed by ecstasy, then an explosion of unimaginable communicative giftedness, and a sharing of mystery and of glory, before returning to a more reticent and quiet amazement.[58] In another reflection on Pentecost, a feast often celebrated as the occasion for confirmation, Jennings perceptively exposes how a ritual to mark maturity in faith so often takes place at a difficult and uncertain time for the adolescent, and when the vibrations of frighteningly turbulent hormonal upheaval are felt.[59]

Jennings is conscious of the paradox that the formula that expresses unity in belief and binds the congregation together, the Creed, is interpreted differently by those who recite it:

> Each re-makes
> The article he needs ...
> Christ turns to each of us
> A different face, the one we beg and need.'[60]

Although Christians share the belief that Jesus is our Saviour and Lord, who offers each of us salvation, what this means for each of us at the various stages of our lives differs, because our fears and hopes differ, our sins and strengths differ, and our experience and circumstances differ.

An openness to the transcendent permeates Jennings' poetry. One could justifiably claim that such openness is a signature theme in her work. This orientation begins with attention. Poetry prompts us to look again, and more carefully, at our surroundings. Too often we fail to notice what is around us. Being open to transcendence also depends on being conscious of an inner emptiness, a yearning for something missing, as illustrated in a line from 'For Albert Camus': 'The ache for the certainty that never ends.'[61] Yet, despite a sense of incompleteness and of the need for something not currently available to us, she expresses hope in an eponymously named but unpublished poem: 'It looks into a storm and sees the end/Even when thunder's clapping still.'[62]

Despite her constant awareness of human fragility, limitation and weakness, Jennings never took a jaundiced view of the human condition. For her, if human beings constitute dust, it is dust that is made for heaven. In 'The Contradictions' she confidently asserts of God's working within us: 'He took our dust/And taught it how to bless.'[63] And, again, in 'Frail Bone', using the image of humanity as sand falling through 'the hour-glass of the planet' she claims that the dust that we are 'delivers/Defiant speech to the last,/Anomalous oratory.'[64] Lowly dust we may be, but nevertheless it is dust with the power to speak and dust with divine potential.

Educational implications

Elizabeth Jennings was a powerful advocate for poetry as a humanising influence as well as being an outstanding exemplar of the poetic art. I hope that the potential use of her poetry in education has already become apparent in this chapter. In this final section, I briefly explore four implications for teachers and students. Without doubt, other educational implications of her work for teachers and students, although other educational implications could doubtless be identified. First, there is the importance of including poetic knowledge and an appreciation of the aesthetic dimension within the curriculum. Second, is the potential of her poems to serve as a resource in the curriculum, prompting reflection on the themes explored earlier in this chapter. Third, her work can offer a gentle and non-intimidating stimulus to growing in self-knowledge, a quality that is vital for all teachers and essential for learners on their way to maturity. Finally, she provides many entry points for reflecting on the spiritual dimension of life.

Art invites us to participate in what it portrays. It helps to keep a Christian imagination fresh when bombarded daily by temptations to respond to the world in utilitarian ways. Poetic knowledge and the aesthetic sense are as valid and authentic modes of knowing as other forms of knowing that are awarded privileged status in our society. Poetry is particularly helpful for fostering receptivity and appreciative learning, in contrast with calculative and technocratic knowledge, which is concerned with manipulation and control. Poetry has the power to counteract the influence of the prevailing technocratic outlook. The Dominican Timothy Radcliffe notes that 'we live under the spell of what Pope Francis calls "the technocratic imagination" which sees everything as matter to be used for our own ends'.[65] When the technocratic imagination, which views nature as being at our disposal, is combined with insistent individualism, which views life as a zero-sum game, we risk being enslaved by the very tools we employ to master the world and thereby risk slipping into a superficial, empty and anxious existence, needing constant affirmation from virtual 'friends'. In fact, Radcliffe notes that

Many aspects of our contemporary imagination can enslave us. The seduction of violence, the cult of celebrity, the fear of the stranger, the Kingdom of Mammon. ... Every novel, poem, film or painting that opens us to our invisible brothers and sisters is an ally of the sacramental imagination. ... The traditional way in which Christians have resisted the gravitational pull of the banal has been to set aside moments each day to recite or sing poetry.[66]

In Jennings' poetic hands, the patient, receptive and appreciative attention given to phenomena and experience blends the tenderness of love with the discipline of intellect, thereby minimising the pull of the technocratic outlook and replacing it with a Christian imagination.

Each of the first three themes explored earlier in this chapter can be explored at any level of education, according to the students' maturity and vocabulary. All children, adolescents and older people have a sense of identity and can draw upon memories, happy and sad. Desire and love, too, affect every age group, although the nature of our wants and our loves alter significantly over time, even as we also note continuities. Loss, diminishment and suffering are also experiences that anyone can identify with, in themselves and in others. All three themes constitute essential elements in the repertoire of the human life and, if education is to connect with real-life issues, each of these themes deserves to receive attention at various points in the opportunities for learning made available. Furthermore, it should be possible to address them via different subjects in the curriculum, most obviously through English, the arts, science (especially the examination of nature) and personal, social and health education. Jennings' poems provide an accessible route to pondering who we are, what matters to us, how we are affected by our experiences, and how we see the world around us, as well as how we cope with our wants and needs, the challenges posed by life's set-backs, and the complex mixture of the joys and pains of love. She has the gift of drawing larger significance from specific and what at first seem minor details in her observations. Many of her poems are devoted to artists, for example, Mantegna, Rembrandt, Goya,

Giotto, Vermeer, Caravaggio, and Cézanne. As just one example, in 'Rembrandt's Late Self-Portraits', she leads us smoothly from consideration of the artist's craft to his character: 'Your brush's care/ Runs with self-knowledge. Here/Is a humility at one with craft'. She also attributes honesty and courage to this painter as his work shows that 'all the darknesses are dared'.[67]

This brings us to the third area where Jennings' poems can contribute to learning: self-knowledge. Both students and teachers need to grow in self-knowledge; the work of each depends upon a sound foundation of authentic, and gradually maturing, self-knowledge. Motivation to learn and to teach, appropriate interaction between learner and teacher, the capacity to cope when the going is tough, the wisdom to discern the difference between short-term wants and longer-term interests, the awareness of potential and also of limitations – all these are nourished by self-knowledge. And self-knowledge is supported by the cultivation of empathy and imagination, qualities that are nurtured and stretched in Jennings' poems.

The final aspect of her work that is of crucial relevance for Catholic educators is her treatment of faith, sacraments and the liturgical seasons, her depiction of explicitly religious practice, symbols and life, and her evocation of the spiritual dimension. Gratitude, wonder, affirmation, finding God in everything – these surface in her poems in response to people, events, nature and works of art. The body and the material world hold for her promises of the spiritual and echoes of transcendence. Jennings exemplifies a point made by Timothy Radcliffe: 'All the senses of the body open us to each other and to God. Our physical existence – hearing, seeing, touching, walking, smelling even - open us to transcendence.'[68] A huge admirer of Gerard Manley Hopkins, Jennings follows in his footsteps in expressing a sacramental perspective, as he did in 'God's Grandeur': 'The world is charged with the grandeur of God. ... [but] "All is seared with trade; bleared, smeared with toil;/And wears man's smudge and shares man's smell; the soil/Is bare now, nor can foot feel, being shod.'[69] She detects the eternal in what might superficially appear to be merely ephemeral. In the midst of a fragile and quickly passing experience she picks up signs of an underlying and enduring force beyond our reckoning. For her, there is no matter so small that it lacks the capacity to open us up to some aspect of the divine. Not only can Jennings' poems supply great support for the teacher of religious education in school or theology in university; they demonstrate that consideration of the spiritual is deeply relevant to many areas of the curriculum.

ENDNOTES

1   Elizabeth Jennings, *Christianity and Poetry,* London: Burns & Oates, 1965, p. 18; and Jennings, *Every Changing Shape,* Manchester: Carcanet, 1996, p. 30.

2   Dana Greene, *Elizabeth Jennings,* Oxford: Oxford University Press, 2018, p. 11.

3   Ibid., p. 53.

4   Dana Gioa, 'Clarify me, Please, God of the Galaxies', *First Things*, 1 May 2018, p. xvii.

5   Greene, *Elizabeth Jennings*, p. xv.

6   Ibid., p. 130.

7   Anna Walczuk, *Elizabeth Jennings and the Sacramental Nature of Poetry,* Krakow: Jagiellonian University Press, 2017, p. 13.

8   Greene, *Elizabeth Jennings*, p. xviii.

9   Walczuk, *Elizabeth Jennings and the Sacramental Nature of Poetry*, p. 23.

10   Gioa, 'Clarify me, Please, God of the Galaxies', p. 2.

11   Elizabeth Jennings, *The Collected Poems,* edited by Emma Mason, Manchester: Carcanet, 2012, p. 673. Unless otherwise indicated, all page references from her poems are taken from this volume.

12   Greene, *Elizabeth Jennings*, p. 189.

13   Jennings, *Collected Poems*, p. 262.

14   Walczuk, *Elizabeth Jennings and the Sacramental Nature of Poetry*, p. 241.

15   Ibid., p. 204.

16   Ibid., p. 45.

17   Barry Sloan, 'Poetry and Faith: The Example of Elizabeth Jennings', *Christianity and Literature*, Vol. 55, No. 3. (Spring 2006), pp. 393 – 414, at p. 395.

18   Jean Ward, *Christian Poetry in the Post-Christian Day: Geoffrey Hill, R. S. Thomas, Elizabeth Jennings,* Frankfurt am Main: Peter Lang Publishing, 2009, p. 46.

19   Walczuk, *Elizabeth Jennings and the Sacramental Nature of Poetry*, p. 112.

20   Jennings, *Collected Poems*, 'Movement and Meaning,' p. 681.

21   Ibid., 'Visit to an Artist,' p. 101.

22   Ibid., p. 974.

23   Jennings, *Every Changing Shape*, p. 211.

24   Jennings, *Collected Poems*, 'Questions to Other Artists', p. 397.

25   Jennings, *Every Changing Shape*, p. 108; emphasis in original.

26   Ibid., p. 215.

27   Ibid., p. 33.

28   Jennings, *Collected Poems*, p. 435.

29   Ibid., 'Artur Rubinstein Playing in Old Age', p. 874.

30   Jennings, *Every Changing Shape*, p. 197.

31   Anna Walczuk, 'Elizabeth Jennings and Poetry Reaching Out Towards Transcendence', *Anglica*, Vol. 24, No. 1 (2015), pp. 59–72, at p. 68.

32   Ibid., p. 65.

33   Jennings, *Collected Poems*, 'Partly Tamed', p. 519.

34   Ibid., 'The Young Ones', p. 180.

35   Ibid., p. 817.

36   Ibid., p. 380.

37   Ibid., p. 460.

38   Ibid., p. 461.

39   Ibid., p. 849.

40   Ibid., p. 132.

41   Ibid., 'Resolve', p. 616.

42   Ibid., p. 454.

43   Walczuk, *Elizabeth Jennings and the Sacramental Nature of Poetry*, p. 95.

44   Jennings, *Collected Poems*, 'Night Sister', p. 199.

45   Ibid., 'Euthanasia', p. 442.

46   Ibid., 'The Way They Live Now', pp. 669–70.

47   Jennings, *Every Changing Shape*, p. 97.

48   Walczuk, *Elizabeth Jennings and the Sacramental Nature of Poetry*, p. 194.

49   Jennings, *Collected Poems*, 'A Full Moon', p. 760.

50   Ibid., 'Trees', p. 678.

51   Ibid., 'Praises', p. 769.

52   Jean Ward, 'Elizabeth Jennings: An Exile in Her Own Country', *Literature & Theology*, Vol. 21. No. 2 (June 2007), pp.198 - 213, at p.207.

53   Ward, *Christian Poetry in the Post-Christian Day*, p. 71.

54   Jennings, *Collected Poems*, 'A Reproach', p. 602.

55   Ibid., 'At Mass (II)', pp. 743–4.

56   Ibid., 'Words of the Magi', p. 384.

57   Ibid., 'Many Easters', pp. 494–5; also 'The Eternal Cross', p. 647.

58   Ibid., pp. 82–3.

59   Ibid., 'Whitsun Sacrament', p. 320.

60   Ibid., 'One Creed or Many', p. 391.

61   Ibid., 'For Albert Camus', p. 188.

62   Ibid., 'Hope', p. 922.

63   Ibid., 'The Contradiction', p. 638.

64   Ibid., 'Frail Bone', p. 541.

65   Timothy Radcliffe, *Alive in God*, London: Bloomsbury, 2019, pp. 301–2.

66   Ibid., pp. 346, 324, 355.

67   Jennings, *Collected Poems*, p. 324.

68   Radcliffe, *Alive in God*, p. 301.

69   'God's Grandeur' in Gerard Manley Hopkins, *Poems and Prose*, edited by W.H. Gardner, London: Penguin, 1976, p. 27.

CHAPTER SIX

Paulo Freire:
Dialogical Pedagogy

Too often, those on the receiving end of education suffer from a degree of direction that seems too heavy an imposition and that pays too little attention to their own experience, context, questions and hopes. When this happens, no matter how well-intentioned the teachers' efforts, the possibility of developing a mature and responsible agency in students is impaired, or even stifled. Furthermore, a one-sided exercise of authority by teachers can inhibit a healthy relationship between teacher and student, one in which each brings their authentic self to the classroom. The Brazilian philosopher and educator Paulo Freire (1921–97) displayed a rare sensitivity to the tensions at work in educational encounters, such as those between authority and freedom, direction and dialogue, and between professional responsibility and the fostering of personal relationships. He also challenged teachers to question the assumption that the classroom can or should constitute a space that is protected from political concerns. The chapter is in four parts. The first provides an overview of Freire's life and work, while the second examines his treatment of the political dimension of education. Part three provides an analysis of what Freire meant by dialogical pedagogy and in the final part I explain the role played by those virtues and qualities that Freire believed were essential for the work of teachers.

Life and work

Paulo Freire was one of the twentieth century's most important educational thinkers and practitioners, probably second only to John Dewey in the extent of his influence. His ideas and practices were picked up and applied in many countries and across many different academic disciplines and spheres of activity – in education, politics and social welfare programmes, in Churches and in workers' organisations. He contributed to education in multiple ways, as teacher, adult educator, expert on promoting literacy, and educational philosopher, but also as a social critic, model practitioner of the theology of liberation, and as a prophet. He served as tutor and mentor, school teacher and university professor, adult educator, literacy coordinator, international advisor, political activist and educational administrator. He was, perhaps, the most influential educational thinker from the global south, a person whose life was marked not only by recognition and acclaim but also by imprisonment, exile, censorship, misunderstanding and criticism.

He worked at local, regional, national and international levels. For a period, he was employed by the World Council of Churches as its educational secretary, which led to him being asked to provide consultancy for educational and literacy projects in many different countries. He also served as a consultant to UNESCO (the United Nations Educational, Scientific and Cultural Organization). His experience of imprisonment as well as exile, far from dissuading him, only radicalised his convictions and reinforced his determination to persevere.

Freire was hostile to all forms of dehumanisation and oppression – authoritarianism, economic inequality, racism and patriarchy. He constantly fought to overcome the passivity brought about by poverty, to expose damaging patterns of behaviour and to replace them with more life-giving ways. His life was devoted to promoting democracy, justice, engagement and participation in society, and to advancing hope, liberation and a more abundant life. As Peter Roberts notes, 'The people with whom he worked endured high rates of malnutrition, infant mortality, and disease, with squalid housing conditions, low levels of literacy, and limited access to health care and educational opportunities.'[1] This experience of direct contact with circumstances that undermined the humanity and severely limited the opportunities of the poor depressed Freire, but also stimulated him to devote himself to addressing them with all the skill at his command. His was a faith that rejected fatalism. For him, there was an obvious link between spirituality and social justice: how could one be friends with Christ but not with the needy? The Jesuit educator Cristóbal Madero, in demonstrating Freire's continuing relevance for Catholic educators, emphasises his deployment of a theology of communion and his application of the theological virtues for his concept of dialogue.[2]

The theological underpinning and inspiration of Freire's life and work has been largely neglected, even marginalised, leading to a distorted and misleading reputation as a Marxist and secular thinker. Marx *was* a major influence, but never one that was accepted fully; Freire rejected the role of violence as a tool of revolution, and infused his humanism with the vastly different ethos of the Gospel. Other influences on Freire included Jean-Paul Sartre, Martin Buber, Frantz Fanon, Herbert Marcuse and Pierre Teilhard de Chardin. His mentor for several years was Archbishop of Olinda and Recife Hélder Câmara, a church leader diminutive in physical stature but immense in moral authority. From such diverse writers, but above all through his own experience as a social activist and teacher, Freire forged his own distinctive and original blend of religious radicalism, drawing on philosophy, history, social and political theory, theology, anthropology, linguistics, psychoanalysis and communications to fertilise his thinking.

The Brazilian Catholic left movement, within which one can locate Freire, had its own trajectory and contributory elements but was also influenced by a steady stream of European Catholic thinkers, and clergy who had been trained in Rome and who brought liberating ideas and a more holistic anthropology to Brazil. Among these were the Young Christian Workers who advocated throughout the 1950s for the process of See-Judge-Act. This was an approach to engaging the laity in social affairs in the light of the Gospel. Pope John XXIII incorporated this approach in his 1961 encyclical *Mater et Magistra* (paragraph 236):

> There are three stages which should normally be followed in the reduction of social principles into practice. First, one reviews the concrete situation; secondly, one forms a judgment on it in the light of these same principles; thirdly, one decides what in the circumstances can and should be done to implement these principles. These are the three stages that are usually expressed in the three terms: look, judge, act.

To this must be added the enduring effect on Latin America of the Second Vatican Council (1962–5), which in turn helped to change the mindset of many Church leaders, a process that came to a head at the landmark Medellin Conference in 1968.

Three French Catholic thinkers especially influenced Freire: Jacques Maritain, Emmanuel Mounier and Pierre Teilhard de Chardin. Each of these contributed in their own way to Freire's understanding of the nature and calling of the human person. Like them, Freire 'rejected privatized morality, reflexive submission to authority, and political quietism'.[3] He concurred with their view that the human person is made in the image of God, endowed with an inalienable dignity, and that people should be treated as subjects (not objects), who are called to contribute to, and participate in, the common good (thus avoiding the perils of either individualism or collectivism). Education should facilitate in each person a growth in freedom and creativity, their relationships with others and openness to the transcendent, and a willingness to share in God's life and work.

Liberation theology and Freirean pedagogy influenced each other.[4] Each stressed the need to nurture and encourage agency rather than passivity in learners regardless of their age. Freire became increasingly alarmed about the (mostly malign) rise of neoliberalism, which damagingly infected many societies with its crudely reductionist understanding of persons and society and its deluded advocacy of market forces. Freire saw clearly how politicians led by neoliberal ideology undermined educational values, diminished the dignity of human beings, and threatened the common good. Unfortunately, even today, some Catholic politicians fail to see how deeply at odds neoliberal thinking and reliance on market forces are with regard to Catholic faith, theology and social thought. But for Freire, Catholic thought 'constituted the well-spring of his worldview, moral vision, and social concern', impelling him to 'confront poverty, authoritarianism, and injustice'.[5]

Especially since the Second Vatican Council, progressive elements within the Latin American Catholic Church had been raising critical questions about the Church's traditional alliance with social and political leaders and elites and they had pressed the Church to adopt a preferential option for the poor. This phrase refers to a pervasive theme in the prophetic books of the Old Testament as well as in the Gospels: the call from God to give a high level of importance to the well-being and needs of the poor and the marginalised in society. Freire was part of this new emphasis. As Kirylo and Boyd point out, 'The base community movement drew much of its approach from Freire's literacy work and its emphasis on "reading the world" and conscientization.'[6] It is unsurprising that among his closest supporters were leading pioneers and representatives of liberation theology such as Gustavo Gutiérrez, Leonardo Boff, Frei Betto and Hélder Câmara.

Freire could be described as a prophetic personalist. Personalism emphasises the uniqueness and dignity of each person, the centrality of justice as a virtue, and our mutual interdependence.[7] As a prophet, Freire not only criticised prevailing political and social authorities for facilitating dehumanising policies and practices, he also took a critical stance on Church leaders failing to defend the poor against the status quo. Too often, he felt, Church leaders were motivated by their desire to protect the rights of the Church, collaborating with the wealthy while advocating charity and helping to keep in place the very structures that ensured human suffering would continue. At best, they supported measures to equip people to fit into the world as it is, rather than seek to promote a different, better world. For Freire, the Church should be prophetic, avoid otherworldliness and strive wholeheartedly for the complete liberation (economic, social and political, as well as spiritual) of oppressed people by becoming an instrument of transformative action.

Political dimension

More than any of the other figures in this book, Freire illustrates the unavoidably political dimension of education. He considered that educators are necessarily politicians and that they inevitably engage in politics when they educate.[8] If education cannot help being political, however, engaging in politics cannot avoid also being a source of learning. In both education and politics there is always a tension between what should be maintained and what should be changed. Without continuity and stability, there would be confusion and chaos; without transformation leading to individual and social change, there would be sterility and the stifling of creativity. Acutely aware that he was working in a context marked by elitism, authoritarianism, discrimination, paternalism and exploitation, Freire wanted to help people move away from silence, oppression and colonialism and towards a more self-confident, active and self-determining role in the world.

The first step in coming to appreciate the political dimension of education is to realise that there is no such thing as a neutral educational activity. As Richard Shaull comments in his Foreword to Freire's most famous work, *Pedagogy of the Oppressed*:

> Education either functions as an instrument which is used to facilitate the integration of the younger generation into the logic of the present system and bring about conformity to it, *or* it becomes 'the practice of freedom', the

means by which men and women deal critically and creatively with reality and discover how to participate in the transformation of the world.[9]

Freire believed that the reason a political understanding of education was not in order to exert power over others, but to serve them by assisting in liberating them from all that threatens to dehumanise them. In contrast, an oppressive pedagogy is 'necrophilic', a term Freire borrowed from Erich Fromm to suggest that the desire to control, in the context of teaching people to adjust to the world as it is, has the effect of killing the spirit and inhibiting the creative capacities of students.[10] And if, as he saw clearly, 'humanization … is thwarted by injustice, exploitation, oppression, and the violence of oppressors' then, in the struggle against dehumanisation, and in helping the oppressed to regain their humanity, such assistance does not encourage the oppressed to become in turn oppressors themselves. Liberation should restore the humanity of all.[11]

The pedagogy of liberation that Freire advocated had several key features. First, it would focus on the situations in which the oppressed found themselves and examine the causes and modes of oppression. Second, it would aim to change the situation by committing to the struggle for liberation because, to be transformational, such education must transcend a merely theoretical understanding and embrace action. Third, it should be conducted in partnership with, and not just on behalf of, the oppressed. Thus, it must involve their agency and active participation; they must not experience themselves merely as potential beneficiaries of someone else's goodwill or benign paternalism. 'Attempting to liberate the oppressed without their reflective participation in the act of liberation is to treat them as objects which must be saved from a burning building; it is to lead them into a populist pitfall and transform them into masses which can be manipulated.'[12] Fourth, it must alert people to the degree to which they have unconsciously internalised their oppressors' perspectives –'Only as they discover themselves to be "hosts" of the oppressor can they contribute to the midwifery of their liberating pedagogy.'[13] Fifth, a liberating pedagogy can only be carried out in communion with others; it is not a matter of providing isolated individuals with the means of escaping their lot and achieving personal success at the expense of others.[14]

Before showing the link between Freire's political understanding of education as the practice of liberation and two central planks of his thought – his banking concept of education and the process of 'conscientisation' – it should be noted that he also saw teachers as requiring liberation. Oppressed and unfree teachers cannot function effectively in the liberation of their students. He argued that 'the struggle of teachers' defence of their dignity and rights should be understood as an integral part of their teaching practice. ... The struggle to bring dignity to the practice of teaching is as much a part of the activity of teaching as is the respect the teacher should have for the identity of the student.'[15] Sometimes teachers can experience within themselves a tension between their duty to address the immediate needs of particular students and their need to maintain the healthy flourishing of the teaching profession. An example of this might be when a teaching union calls a strike, for example, to seek better remuneration or improved working conditions, but the cost of joining such action might be that students preparing for examinations receive less tuition than they or their teachers believe they need. Freire is clear that students' well-being is affected by the presence or absence of healthy and flourishing teachers. Burnt-out, poorly paid teachers, who have to work in conditions that diminish their effectiveness, are unlikely to promote education that is liberating and humanising for their students.

Freire is usually known for his critique of the banking concept of education. The banking approach to teaching envisages students as receptacles to be filled by the teacher rather than as reciprocals who can contribute to the educational encounter as well as receive; who can modify the teacher's views as well as being open to influence themselves. The more meekly the receptacles permit themselves to be filled, the better students they are. 'Education thus becomes an act of depositing, in which the students are the depositories and the teacher is the depositor.' This severely reduces any scope for initiative or agency. Students find themselves expected to receive, store and reproduce (for example, in examinations) whatever deposits their teachers have been made in their minds. This process sets apart teachers and students, assuming that the latter are lacking, and that the former already possess, the necessary treasures of knowledge. Students are limited to a passive role of acceptance and assimilation while their teachers decide both the content and methodology of what is being taught, without reference to the needs or interests of students.

From a Freirean perspective, three defects of a banking approach to education stand out. First, it assumes that learning occurs as a result of transferring information and fails to allow for the active involvement by students so that they come to own, rather than merely to borrow, their knowledge. Learning, like faith, may begin as something second-hand, but eventually it must become first-hand, personally owned. Without real ownership there can be no real responsibility for how that knowledge is valued or deployed in life. A precondition of ownership is a sufficient degree of autonomy in learners, whereas the banking approach reinforces a fatalistic submission to domination. Second, banking education is, by its very nature, anti-dialogical, whereas 'problem-posing education regards dialogue as indispensable to the act of cognition which unveils reality.'[16] (The vital role played by dialogue is examined further in section three below.) Third, as Schugurensky observed, banking education 'has a predesigned, fixed, and static curriculum; in problem-posing education, the content emerges from the reality and dreams of the learners'.[17]

Freire's opposition to the banking approach to education goes beyond merely pedagogical considerations. He was also opposed to any objectification of human persons in the world. The banking concept turns people into assets for use by others and asphyxiates their creative powers. Teachers often feel their agency is excessively constrained by the controls exerted either by the authority of their institution or from beyond that, for example, legislation, government inspection, the pressures of league tables, a mandatory curriculum, and the examination system. For students and teachers, the banking approach to education threatens to turn them into objects and to ignore, even to suppress, their essential capacity for transcendence, to become more than they are at this moment. For Freire, this 'being-more' is not simply to be equated with self-actualisation, or a natural unfolding of what is within. As Catholic philosopher of education Samuel Rocha points out, 'Freire's call to "be more" remains radically open to an ontology and even a theology of transcendence.'[18] Rocha shows how Freire acknowledged the influence on his thinking of the personalist philosophers from earlier in the twentieth century, especially Martin Buber, Erich Fromm, Karl Jaspers, Max Scheler, Gabriel Marcel and Emmanuel Mounier.[19] He shared with them 'a sense of the sacredness and dignity of the person and the need to protect it from being depersonalized through objectification'.[20] It is important to note here that Freire saw no dichotomy between his desire to nurture learners' capacity for transcendence and his determination to address their current mundane realities.

Instead of the banking approach, teachers should engage in raising critical questions about students' life situations. Freire observed that, 'For the naïve thinker, the important thing is accommodation to this normalized "today". For the critic, the important thing is the continuing transformation of reality, for the sake of the continuing humanization of men.'[21] To counteract the pernicious effects of a banking approach to education, he proposed the alternative of 'conscientisation' (a term borrowed from Archbishop Hélder Câmara). This is the process in which actively engaged and critically questioning people develop a deepening awareness of the factors and forces that influence and shape their socio-cultural reality and their daily lives. 'As women and men, we are not simply determined by facts and events. At the same time, we are subject to genetic, cultural, social, class, sexual, and historical conditionings that mark us profoundly and that constitute for us a centre of reference.'[22] If we become conscious of our conditioning, we realise that we can avoid becoming trapped in this condition. Thus, although we cannot avoid being conditioned, we do not have to allow ourselves to be determined. A critical awareness of why we are where we are and what is pressurising us to remain there gives us an opportunity to exercise our free will to go beyond our current situation. Freire insisted that 'The educator with a democratic vision or posture cannot avoid in his teaching praxis insisting on the critical capacity, curiosity, and autonomy of the learner.'[23]

Three further points about conscientisation should be noted. First, it is not merely cerebral, a matter of questioning and reflection; it must include action. Such action may be social, cultural or political and must be followed by reflection and evaluation of both the nature and effects of such action. This combination of critical questioning, followed by action that leads to further reflection is what is meant by 'praxis'. Conscientisation can be distinguished from consciousness-raising by its emphasis on learning through action.

Second, Freire went out of his way to stress how important it is for the effectiveness of conscientisation that teachers know the real circumstances of their students' lives. Otherwise teachers may not appreciate the degree to which their students have developed 'certain habits, likes, beliefs, fears, desires'.[24] Too often there can be an unbridgeable gap between what is considered normal practice and desirable behaviour in the world as lived by teachers and students. Teachers need to be familiar with the everyday language used by their students, their dreams and aspirations, and the types of knowledge and values they encounter outside of school. Freire wisely observes: 'It is through hearing the learners, a task unacceptable to authoritarian educators, that democratic teachers increasingly prepare themselves to be heard by learners. But by listening to and so learning to talk with learners, democratic teachers teach the learners to listen to them as well.'[25]

Finally, he points out that the praxis at the heart of conscientisation should be carried out in, and as, a community; it is not performed by isolated individuals seeking personal advantage.[26] The kind of democracy advocated by Freire does not foster competitive individualism, but cooperation and collaboration on behalf of the common good.

Dialogical pedagogy

If the prophetic aspect of Freire's personalism is highlighted by his argument that education is always a political activity, as illustrated by his critique of the banking concept of teaching and learning and by advocacy of conscientisation, the personalist aspect is evident by his emphasis on the centrality of dialogue. Dialogue can be contrasted with monologue: 'Monologue has no concern for ascertaining a response. Dialogue, however, ... assumes that within the exchange of the word there is another side, another story, another point of view that, respectively, needs to be considered. In short, key to a dialogical relationship is authentic listening.'[27] 'Through dialogue [teachers and students] become jointly responsible for a process in which all grow. ... If it is in speaking their word that we transform the world by naming it, dialogue imposes itself as the way in which we achieve significance as human beings.'[28] Naming (in the accepting presence of others) the world as we experience it is vital for the emergence of authentic humanity. Furthermore, 'Dialogue with the people is neither a concession nor a gift, much less a tactic to be used for domination. ... Dialogue does not impose, does not manipulate, does not domesticate.'[29]

The conditions for eliciting commitment are quite different from the conditions for ensuring compliance and, for Freire, dialogue is an essential condition for encouraging commitment. Among the requirements for dialogue he included humility (which prompts teachers to open themselves to the questions and concerns of students, to invite students to contribute, and to foster a classroom environment that is affirming and inclusive), love for the world and for people, faith that people have the capacity to make a positive difference, and mutual trust and hope.[30] Trust does not necessarily precede dialogue but can be established by dialogue. And, as for hope, 'If the participants expect nothing can come of their efforts, their encounter will be empty and sterile, bureaucratic and tedious.'[31]

Dialogical pedagogy, in stark contrast to the banking approach to teaching, treats learners with respect, takes their interests, needs and perspectives into account and shows itself ready to learn from them.

For, as Freire shrewdly notes, 'Some of the paths and streams that students' at times almost virgin curiosity runs through are pregnant with suggestions and questions never before noticed by teachers.'[32] One recent commentator on Freire explains how dialogical pedagogy contributes to the humanisation of all involved:

> Growing into one's full humanity requires participation in an I-Thou relationship between two Subjects. ... All participants in dialogic pedagogy are Subjects who possess their own dignity, stature, integrity, and unique expertise. Because it is grounded upon radical openness, interdependence, and mutual vulnerability, dialogic pedagogy offers a life-giving venue for interlocutors. In contrast, banking pedagogy is an 'I-It' relationship, one that is based on hierarchy and subordination.[33]

The promotion of dialogue, the resistance to the assumptions of the banking approach, and the fostering of conscientisation may lead readers to assume that Freire's ideas are corrosive of any notion of teacher authority, and that they deny the asymmetrical nature of the relationship between students and teachers. This is compounded at a time when students, teachers, parents and the public more generally all inhale, wittingly or not, a prevailing cultural atmosphere of relativism, whereby institutions and individuals that claim authority are subject to constant scrutiny and questioning, and are often targets of ridicule and hostility. Traditional moral norms seem to have lost their influence over consciences. Religious subcultures seem to be dissolving. In the age of the 'selfie', one notes the celebration of an exalted sense of a self-made identity that can be made, set aside and reconstructed at will – and conveyed on social media. These phenomena cumulatively make it much more difficult than was once the case for the passing on of a Catholic faith and form of education, and to do so in a confident, coherent and consistent manner. Does Freire's advocacy of conscientisation and of dialogical pedagogy reinforce the cultural undermining of an approach to Catholic education that relies so much on a belief in authority and the importance of a living tradition? Given that changing cultural conditions pose major challenges for the passing on of religious faith, and that fears of being indoctrinatory bedevil attempts by teachers (and parents and adults more generally) to offer authoritative and directive teaching, I will devote attention in what follows to exploring my understanding of how Freire viewed the relationship between authority and freedom and between dialogical and directive pedagogy. I will do so with special reference to the teaching of religion in a school context. Here I go beyond Freire's writings (since he wrote very little explicitly about the teaching of religion), but remain firmly within the spirit of the whole corpus of his works.

He was not hostile to teachers being directive, so long as their relationship with students was life-giving; he believed they should share their convictions with learners, as neutrality is impossible, but by invitation rather than imposition. From his earliest writings, he reiterated the need for balance: 'The dialogical theory of action opposes both authoritarianism and licence, and thereby affirms authority and freedom.'[34] This theme continued in his later work: 'The need for dialogue does not in any way diminish the need for explanation and exposition whereby the teacher sets forth his/her understanding and knowledge of the object [being studied].'[35] He was confident that a balance between directiveness and democracy can be maintained if teachers can 'accept the directive nature of education without manipulating students and, at the same time, accept the democratic nature of education without leaving students to themselves.'[36] For Freire, this directiveness is both in service of, and subordinate to, the task of fostering critical consciousness and supporting humanisation in teachers and students.

Much hangs on the word 'directively' in the context of religious teaching. Does this mean teaching as if the teacher subscribes to the content without being willing to face questions about it, or as if everybody holds the content to be true, teaching accompanied by manipulation, or teaching without reference to its supporting rationality? These possible meanings of directive teaching undermine dialogue but dialogical pedagogy does not require teachers to hide what they believe to be true (through some spurious notion of neutrality); however, it does forbid any manipulation of pupils. For Freire, dialogical pedagogy requires rather than prevents personal witness by teachers, even as it fosters critical engagement and avoids indoctrination: the students' level of maturity and cognitive capacity must be taken into account and teachers must be aware of the weight they attribute to their own views, lest they do so too 'heavily'.

Non-directive teaching that introduces pupils to a debate or range of answers to a controversial topic still requires inducting pupils into criteria relating to accuracy, precision, supporting evidence, and the relationship and origin of an idea or practice to other ideas and practices. All teaching, if it is to avoid being superficial and insubstantial, and if it is to have meaning for pupils, needs to take into account personal relevance and practical implications as well as its potential significance for reading and responding to the world. The line between directive and non-directive is blurred. Religious education can be conducted with commitment to the criteria for teaching advocated by Freire and doing justice to the claims of a religious tradition on its own terms. It can be both liberating and faithful.

Is directive teaching hostile to a dialogical ethos? A teacher can express her beliefs, explain them, witness to their significance for herself and others, and seek to make them credible, while still making room for those who do not accept them. Her classroom can be a safe space for the expression of religious faith as well as for expressions of dissent and alternative positions. She cannot impose her faith as being true but neither can she pretend to be neutral. She should deliberately and explicitly make space and time for the airing of different views and help pupils probe the reasons and practices that sustain these positions. It is not anti-educational to convey as a teacher what one believes to be true, although great sensitivity, prudence and restraint must be exercised in *how* one does this. This stance is entirely compatible with the notion that pupils should be equipped to make decisions for themselves about the kind of life they wish to live and to reflect and act upon those decisions in a well-informed manner.

Religious beliefs are, of course, contested and controversial, including within a faith community, let alone between that community and people with different affiliations and commitments). To aim for a critical appreciation and creative appropriation of a religious tradition is a legitimate aspiration for a religious education teacher; although he or she should allow for the possibility that some students will decide in favour of modifying the tradition or even to reject it entirely. In aiming to engage seriously with the tradition, it is necessary to guard against limiting children's imaginative horizons by over-emphasising one particular worldview, and to offer them the opportunity to encounter and consider others.

Can a teacher's directions threaten pupils' personal autonomy? If they direct in an insensitive, non-inclusive manner, such a danger exists. However, this outcome can be avoided. Direction can present a template or a pattern for pupils to consider; it cannot impose this as the only possible template or pattern, nor can it compel pupils to adopt it. French philosopher Louis Lavelle pertinently observed that the greatest good we can do for others is not to communicate to them our riches, but to reveal to them their own.[37] Sometimes this means that teachers need to step aside. It often means that they must be demanding without being impatient, vigilant without being overbearing, and ready to love without expecting anything in return. It also means that, if they wish to be heard, they must be ready to listen before deserving to be heard themselves.

As we have seen, the word 'direct' is open to different interpretations. In the context of teaching, it can mean impose, compel, insist upon, give no choice about, offer no alternative; such direction can be freighted heavily with emotion, buttressed by over-bearing authority and punitive sanctions. Such directive teaching corrodes authentic dialogical and Christian teaching, regardless of the orthodoxy of the content. In contrast, when by 'direct' one means such actions as point to, witness to, model, explain, invite into, demonstrate the coherence and implications of, some body of content, this is entirely compatible with a dialogical and Christian approach. Along with Freire, one can claim that, although there is an inescapable creative tension between directive and dialogical teaching, they are not only compatible but also require each other in order to be fully operational.[38]

In a recent article, Drew Chambers notes the various down-to-earth ways that Freire recognised how teachers direct their classes: 'stimulating learners, pointing to objectives, and aiming to convince learners of some knowledge or belief. ... Directiveness, in Freire's intended sense, is less about making normative claims on "epistemologically controversial issues" and more about directing, on a day-to-day basis, the educational experience of a class.'[39] Teachers are charged with setting the agenda for their classes, although this can be done in collaboration with students, depending on their level of maturity, experience and willingness. Teachers are expected to discipline unruly behaviour that threatens the learning of others and they are required by the society that sponsors them to set before pupils certain readings, to foster specific skills that aid learning, and to make decisions (sometimes checked by external agents such as inspectors or via public examinations) about standards of work achieved.

Chambers selects statements by Freire that affirm the unavoidability of directive teaching: 'Educational practice, whether it is authoritarian or democratic, is always directive.'[40] Similarly, 'There is no education that is not directive.'[41] The challenge for Freire is how to exercise directiveness in a non-authoritarian manner. As Chambers comments, 'the goal is for teachers to connect course content to the world outside the classroom (and thereby to students' lives in their uniqueness and particularities), defend the teachers' own understandings, and provide a space for dialogue about other understandings and beliefs.'[42]

Qualities of teachers

Freire outlines a range of qualities needed by teachers who seek to promote liberation and humanisation. Perhaps his most succinct statement on the issue is as follows: 'without certain qualities or virtues, such as a generous loving heart, respect for others, tolerance, humility, a joyful disposition, love of life, openness to what is new, a disposition to welcome change, perseverance in the struggle, a refusal of determinism, a spirit of hope, and openness to justice, progressive pedagogical practice is not possible.'[43] These ideas appear time and again throughout his writings, with minor variations in their ordering and emphasis. I will focus on eight teacher qualities that he highlights in a different essay.[44] As he got older, Freire's writings became increasingly accessible and clear, and used a minimum of technical language; thus I will use his own words for the most part as they require little or no additional commentary.

Humility appears first. This quality:

> by no means carries the connotation of a lack of self-respect, of resignation, or of cowardice. On the contrary, humility requires courage, self-confidence, self-respect, and respect for others. Humility helps us to understand this obvious truth: No one knows it all; no one is ignorant of everything. We all know something; we are all ignorant of something. ... Humility helps me to avoid being entrenched in the circuit of my own truth.[45]

In contrast, an authoritarian teacher lacks humility, is too confident of fully possessing this truth and is convinced that it must be conveyed without regard for the concerns or resistance of others to it. Such a stance is likely 'to cause children and students to adopt *rebellious* positions, defiant of any limit, discipline, or authority. But it will also lead to apathy, excessive obedience, uncritical conformity, lack of resistance against authoritarian discourse, self-abnegation, and fear of freedom.'[46] Humility tends to reduce the temptation to believe that the teacher is already in full possession of the truth, respects the dignity and gifts of others, and is willing to be vulnerable enough to learn from them.

Freire lists love as a prerequisite for teachers. 'It is not possible to be a teacher without loving one's students, even realizing that love alone is not enough.'[47] Cognition and emotion should not be treated as if they are incompatible or to be separated. 'We must dare ... to speak of love without the fear of being called ridiculous.

mawkish, or unscientific, if not anti-scientific.'[48] As contributing to humanisation, teaching must be an expression of loving care and the climate of the classroom needs to be nurturing, with an atmosphere of positive regard for all students. However, Freire is quick to point out that 'one should never reduce teaching to merely a feel-good process, particularly a paternalistic nurturing that takes the form of parental coddling'.[49] Thus there is a strength that should underpin a teacher's love for students. Conscious of the huge and often conflicting demands made on the psyche, patience and energy of teachers, Freire insightfully observes, 'I do not believe educators can survive the negativities of their trade without some sort of "armed love."'[50] The arming of love comes partly from the other qualities, referred to below, as well as from teachers' disciplined commitment, professional knowledge, skill and experience, lifestyle, and the degree of support they receive from fellow professionals and in their personal relationships.

Freire describes two qualities as being indispensable for teachers but without giving further explanation: courage and joy, the third and eighth teacher qualities, respectively. This does not mean that they lack importance. A teacher may not necessarily always be called upon to display physical courage but moral courage and emotional resilience are integral to the role; without these qualities teachers will fail to strive for truth or defend individuals from injustice. They will be tempted to compromise their integrity in the face of malpractices that might be endemic in their institution. If sacrifice gives love the steel to take the strain in times of difficulty, then lack of courage will sap the willingness to pay the price of commitment or to persevere in the face of obstacles. As for joy, it is counterintuitive to believe that teachers who exude misery or a lacklustre attitude towards their pupils and the subjects they teach are likely to elicit enthusiasm or active engagement in their classrooms. In the context of religious teaching, attempts to convey the Good News in the tone of voice and the bearing of presenting a bad weather forecast are destined tarnish its inherent attractiveness. However burdened a teacher or lecturer might be by concerns outside of school or university, it remains important to demonstrate their subject's continuing positive impact on the teacher's own life, in order to maintain its credibility.

With regard to the fourth quality, tolerance, Freire simply says: 'Being tolerant does not mean acquiescing to the intolerable; it does not mean covering up disrespect; it does not mean coddling the aggressor or disguising aggression. Tolerance is the virtue that teaches us to live with the different. It teaches us to learn from and respect the different.'[51] One can detect a link here with humility.

The fifth quality, decisiveness, does not usually receive much attention in teacher education courses. Decisiveness means acting in response to discernment of what the situation calls for from us. That implies a period, however brief, of reflection before action. Wisely, Freire notes that '*indecision* is perceived by learners as either moral weakness or professional incompetence'.[52] The line between decisions taken too quickly and a state of indecision is perilously narrow.

To support teachers in getting the balance right, between rashness and indecision, the sixth and seventh qualities listed by Freire come to their aid. These are, on the one hand, a sense of security and confidence and, on the other, a capacity to maintain a balance between patience and impatience. A teacher's confidence, Freire claims, should benefit from his or her 'scientific competence, political clarity, and ethical integrity'.[53] While scientific and professional competence certainly receive a great deal of attention in the formation and training of educators, neither political clarity nor ethical integrity is developed to anything like the same degree. This is partly due to the shocking neglect of philosophy of education in professional formation and partly due to the influence of the insistent individualism and radical relativism that are rampant in western society.

Also relevant to being appropriately decisive is the ability to maintain a balance between patience and impatience. Freire proposes that:

Neither *patience* nor *impatience* alone is what is called for. Patience alone may bring the educator to a position of resignation, of permissiveness, that denies the educator's democratic dream. Unaccompanied patience may lead to immobility, to inactivity. Conversely, impatience alone may lead the educator to blind activism, to action for its own sake, to a practice that does not respect the necessary relationship between tactics and strategy.[54]

Freire advocates avoiding isolated patience and untampered impatience. 'The benevolent classroom discourse and practice of those who are only patient suggest to learners that anything, or almost anything, goes.'[55] Just as he argued that, alongside dialogue, the teacher should also be directive, so too he insisted that discipline has a crucial role in promoting learning. 'Without discipline, one does not create intellectual work, read texts seriously, write carefully, observe and analyse facts, or establish relationships among them.'[56] He opposed both 'the absence of discipline by the denial of liberty and the absence of discipline by the absence of authority'.[57] And, in *Pedagogy of Freedom* he asserted that 'true discipline does not exist in the muteness of those who have been silenced but in the stirrings of those who have been challenged, in the doubt of those who have been prodded, and in the hopes of those who have been awakened.'[58]

One final point on Freire's view of teacher qualities is called for. A theme Freire often revisited was the necessity for teachers and students to be aware of our unfinished nature. 'Women and men are capable of being educated only to the extent that they are capable of recognizing themselves as unfinished. It is our awareness of being unfinished that makes us educable.'[59] But even more so than for students, teachers need to bear in mind their essential unfinishedness – and thus their own capacity to change and the necessity for such change in order to become what they are called to be. Failure on the part of teachers to take proper account of their unfinished nature is likely to lead them to a defective deployment of their authority. 'Both the authoritarian teacher who suffocates the natural curiosity and freedom of the student as well as the teacher who imposes no standards at all are equally disrespectful of an essential characteristic of our humanness, namely, our radical (and assumed) unfinishedness, out of which emerges the possibility of true dialogue.'[60]

Teachers who are conscious of their unfinishedness will realise the need to adopt a patient and long-term view of human development and to accept that there will be many setbacks, mistakes and false moves made by learners along the way. It is possible to push too hard and adopt a punitive approach to pedagogy that discourages learners. However, in acknowledging that at no stage have we actually become the finished article, and that there is always scope for further development, teachers will resolve never to settle for whatever current attainment their students appear to have reached. In doing so, they run the risk of selling students short and failing to encourage their full potential. There is a similar need for teachers to have patience with their own shortcomings while refusing any temptation to be complacent or to resist continuing development of one's knowledge and pedagogical skills. Freire believed that it is part of teachers' personal witness before students that they be willing to make visible their efforts to live up their ideals: 'It's important that the students perceive the teacher's struggle to be coherent.'[61]

***

Education activates many gifts. These include how to read intelligently, think clearly and analyse ideas, how to weigh up the soundness and significance of claims and how to interpret evidence. An educated person is able to listen sensitively, take into account different points of view and judge carefully. She has self-knowledge and the capacity to express herself convincingly; at the same time she has learned to relate compassionately and cooperatively, to appreciate the gifts of others and to give herself to commitments and to other people. The fruits of education are recognisable in students who have developed a disciplined desire to find truth, beauty and goodness, who display confidence and competence in ongoing learning, and who have learned to love wisely. These capacities contribute to an education that is humanising. And, from belief in the Incarnation, it follows that if education fails in being humanising, it can never become divinising. Humanists and Christians surely have in common the desire for education to promote flourishing lives, although they might differ in their understanding of what a flourishing life looks like and what its constitutive features might be. Freire's educational ideas have been adopted by many people who do not share his Catholic faith and vision for humanity.

Freire poses penetrating questions that should challenge all teachers: Why do we teach? Whose interests are we promoting? What kind of personhood are we cultivating? What kind of society are we helping to build? We have seen in the preceding analysis that the teacher's virtues are described by Freire as including 'a generous loving heart, respect for others, tolerance, humility joyful disposition, ... a disposition to welcome change, perseverance in the struggle, a refusal of determinism, a spirit of hope'.[62] Freire places hope at the heart of education, at any level. All teaching should be an expression of hope and carried out in aid of hope. It should not impose on, but empower, learners. As Leopando comments: 'Dialogic interactions with students must be conducted with respectful presence, generosity of spirit, sincere attention, and a recognition of their own intellectual limits. ... Teaching is first and foremost an act of love, compassion, and care. Its overriding concern is nurturing the student's dignity, growth, and "being."'[63]

A key feature of Freire's pedagogy is its prophetic nature. It 'calls out' situations of injustice and oppression and the ideologies that promote inhumanity; it should provide hopeful and positive visions of human possibility; and it should demonstrate to students their capacity for agency in the world and challenge them to exercise responsibility for promoting a more just, peaceful and loving society. In their encounter with students, teachers should 'walk the talk' by modelling and embodying these humanistic values. This liberating education requires far more than any set of technical competencies to be instilled in the would-be teacher.

Freire's anti-authoritarian and humanitarian pedagogy was aimed at awakening people to the conditions of their lives, the factors at work in those conditions, and how these could be ameliorated through their individual and communal agency. He is famous for attacking the banking notion of education whereby students are considered to be receptacles to be filled with preconstructed knowledge transmitted by their teachers. A particularly interesting Freirean theme is the necessarily creative tension between the denunciation and annunciation tasks of a prophetic Church. Denunciation focuses on naming, critiquing and confronting assumptions and structures that promote injustice, oppression and dehumanisation. Annunciation emphasises the counterweight of hope and an alternative vision, and equipping people to enact this vision. The former equips people for making critical judgements of current reality; the latter offers affirmation and encouragement to change that reality. 'Denunciation alone degenerates into paralysis, cynicism, and despair; annunciation alone is rudderless, credulous, and ineffectual.'[64] On its own, denunciation leads to 'demoralization, burnout, and even nihilism'; similarly, annunciation, on its own, displays naive optimism but yields few practical results.

One has to look beyond Freire, for example to Edith Stein, in order to plumb the depths of the spiritual dimension of liberation, and to Hildegard of Bingen if one wishes to explore the relationship between the material and spiritual aspects of life. It might be regretted that the Catholic Church has still not fully accepted Freire's application of liberation theology to the realm of education, nor implemented his ideas in the context of the life, learning and communication that takes place in the Church. However, his prophetic personalism offers a striking alternative to 'the neo-liberal focus on self-interest, consumption, choice, competition, and the commodification of knowledge' that mar the educational landscape, and we can be inspired by his emphasis 'on love, dialogue, tolerance, honesty, curiosity, open-mindedness, rigor, and political commitment.'[65] In Freire's hands, education becomes humanising, hopeful, dialogical and life-enhancing.

ENDNOTES

1   Peter Roberts, *Happiness, Hope, and Despair*, New York & Bern: Peter Lang Publishing, 2016, p. 53.

2   Cristóbal Madero, 'Theological dynamics of Paulo Freire's educational theory', *International Studies in Catholic Education*, Vol. 7, No. 2 (2015), pp. 122–33.

3   Irwin Leopando, *A Pedagogy of Faith: The Theological Vision of Paulo Freire*, London: Bloomsbury, 2017, p. 128.

4   For an example of the application of Freirean pedagogical principles to the development of a curriculum for liberation theology, see Pastoral Team of Bambamarca, *Vamos Caminando. A Peruvian Catechism*, London: SCM, 1985.

5   Leopando, *Pedagogy of Faith*, pp. 3–4.

6   James D. Kirylo and Drick Boyd, *Paulo Freire: His Faith, Spirituality and Theology*, Rotterdam: Sense Publishers, 2017, p. 6.

7   For a careful and thorough introduction to personalism, see Juan Manuel Burgos, *An Introduction to Personalism*, Washington DC: Catholic University of America Press, 2018.

8   Paulo Freire, *Teachers as Cultural Workers*, Cambridge, MA: Westview Books, 2005, pp. 121, 129.

9   Paulo Freire, *Pedagogy of the Oppressed*, translated by Myra Bergman Ramos, Harmondsworth, UK and New York: Penguin Books, 1972, pp. 13–14.

10   Ibid., p. 51.

11   Ibid., pp. 20–1.

12   Ibid., p. 41.

13   Ibid., p. 25.

14   Ibid., p. 58.

15   Paulo Freire, *Pedagogy of Freedom*, translated by Patrick Clarke, Lanham, MD & Oxford: Rowman & Littlefield, 1998, p. 64.

16   Ibid., p. 56.

17   Daniel Schugurensky, *Paulo Freire*, London: Continuum, 2011, p. 73.

18   Samuel D. Rocha, '"Ser Mais": The Personalism of Paulo Freire', *Philosophy of Education*, Volume 2018, No.1, pp. 371–84, at p. 375. See also Rocha and Adi Burton, Adi 'The eros of the meal: Passover, Eucharist, education' Encounters in *Theory and History of Education*, Vol. 18 (2017), pp. 119–32.

19   Rocha,'Personalism of Freire', p. 377.

20   Ibid., p. 375.

21   Freire, *Pedagogy of the Oppressed*, p. 65.

22   Freire, *Pedaagogy of Freedom*, p. 91.

23   Ibid., p. 33.

24   Freire, *Teachers as Cultural Workers*, Cambridge, MA: Westview Books, 2005, p. 129.

25   Ibid., p. 155.

26   Ibid., p. 82.

27   Kirylo and Boyd, *Paulo Freire*, p. 66. n.15.

28   Freire, *Pedagogy of the Oppressed*, pp. 53, 61, slightly modified.

29   Ibid., pp. 107, 136.

30   Ibid., pp. 61– 4.

31   Ibid., p. 64.

32   Freire, *Teachers as Cultural Workers*, p. 32.

33   Leopando, *Pedagogy of Faith,* p. 131.

34   Freire, *Pedagogy of the Oppressed*, p. 145.

35   Freire, *Pedagogy of Freedom*, pp. 80–1.

36   Shugurensky, *Paulo Freire* p. 102.

37   Louis Lavelle, *The Dilemma of Narcissus*, translated by William Gairdner, New York: Larson Publications, 1993, p. 167.

38   See John Sullivan, 'Dialogical Pedagogy and Humanising Education' in Christiana Idike and Marcus Luber (eds), *Catholic Education and Humanism in a Global Context*, Regensburg: Verlag Friedrich Pustet, 2021, pp. 107–23.

39   Drew Chambers, 'Is Freire Incoherent? Reconciling Directiveness and Dialogue in Freirean Pedagogy', *Journal of Philosophy of Education*, Vol. 53, No. 1 (2019), pp. 2–47, at p. 23.

40   Ibid., p. 26; Freire, *Pedagogy of Hope*, London: Bloomsbury Academic, 2014, p. 79.

41   Freire, *Pedagogy of Solidarity*, London: Routledge, 2014, p. 20.

42   Chambers, 'Is Freire Incoherent?', p. 27.

43   Freire, *Pedagogy of Freedom*, pp. 108.

44   Freire, *Teachers as Cultural Workers*, pp. 71–84. Unless indicated otherwise, all quotations that follow are drawn from that essay.

45   Ibid., pp. 71-2.

46   Ibid., p. 73.

47   Ibid., p. 28.

48   Ibid., p. 5.

49   Ibid., p. 6.

50   Ibid., p. 74.

51   Ibid., p. 76.

52   Ibid., p. 78, emphasis in original.

53   Ibid., p. 78.

54   Ibid., p. 80, emphasis in original.

55   Ibid., p. 80.

56   Ibid., p. 155.

57   Ibid., p. 159.

58   Freire, *Pedagogy of Freedom*, p. 86.

59   Ibid., p. 58.

60   Ibid., p. 59.

61   Ibid., p. 95.

62   Leopando, *Pedagogy of Faith*, 204.

63   Ibid., p. 205.

64   Ibid., p. 177.

65   Peter Roberts, *Happiness, Hope, and Despair,* New York & Bern: Peter Lang Publishing, 2016, p. 66.

CHAPTER SEVEN

Marshall McLuhan and Walter Ong: Media and Communication

Theologians commonly concern themselves with truths, principles and beliefs, and they examine their interconnections and implications. Rarely do they take into account the physical senses through which we engage the world or the bodily dimensions of teaching and learning the faith. They often seem to take for granted the media and technology through which we receive and transmit religious faith, failing to attend to the effects of technological change on how a tradition is experienced. In this chapter I introduce key insights from two Catholic professors of English literature who made remarkable and prophetic contributions to our understanding of how deeply we are influenced by the communication media we use. These are the devout Canadian layman Marshall McLuhan (1911–80) and the American Jesuit priest Walter Ong (1912–2003). Both have continuing relevance for we how read and respond to the world and thus also for the work of Catholic educators. This chapter opens by considering important examples of technological change and its effects on culture, before detailing biographical information about McLuhan and Ong. In the third section of the chapter I analyse key themes from their work, and in the fourth part bring out some major implications for Catholic Christians of the thought of each of these thinkers. More direct implications for Catholic educators are suggested in part five.

Technological change

More than a generation ago the cultural theorist and religious thinker Walter Ong pointed out how changes in the media of communication used in a society alter the balance within what he called the 'sensorium', the relative attention given to seeing, hearing, touching, tasting and speaking in our engagement with the world around us. Changes in the communication media employed by people in general, and by teachers and learners in particular, affect not only our language but our perceptions and our thinking, our modes of reasoning and valuing. It seems timely at this point in our cultural development, when waves of digital innovation in communication technologies wash over us with increasing rapidity, for Christian educators to reflect on how our interaction with communication media might affect our understanding of the task of communicating Christian faith.

Wise educators should remain alert to the influence of culture and its communication media on the outlooks and mind-sets, the dispositions and expectations, the capacities and blind-spots of teachers and students. The messages that are conveyed, the language that is used, the relationships that are fostered, the modes of presence that are established and the kinds of learning that are facilitated in education cannot help but be deeply implicated in and pervasively influenced by the broader communication context.

The rapid development of new and increasingly more sophisticated communication technologies has an impact on our understanding of knowledge (its sources, nature, structure, reliability and interconnectedness or coherence), of text and of learning. It also modifies how we think about personal identity, self-expression, social conventions, community, authority and our perception of moral norms. As Sara van den Berg notes: 'Distance, time, memory, privacy, and truth are only a few of the assumptions that have been challenged or transformed by the immediacy and scope of electronic technology.'[1] As a result, the ways we read and respond to the world are shifting. Changes occur in our experience of time and space, our sense of presence – who is present to us and how; changes are also experienced in our views of what is possible, what is plausible and what is permitted. Our awareness and appreciation of stability, of continuity, of achieving depth through long-term engagement with and commitment to others, with texts and the world around us may become interrupted and inhibited.

Religious faith is inevitably influenced by the cumulative effect of all these unforeseen consequences of technological change, along with alterations in our thinking, our habits, our imagination, desires, our priorities and the people we are in touch with. Affecting us in tandem, new technologies 'modify our reflexes and expectations'.[2] Technology changes the storyline of society in several ways: it significantly adds to the sheer number of stories to which we have access; it loosens our connection to traditional reference points for the stories we inherit; it modifies how we encounter stories, for example, beyond face-to-face encounters and listening to elders, to sources and agencies with which we do not enjoy a direct and ongoing relationship or holistic reinforcement experiences. Nearly twenty years ago an observer of cultural trends could comment: 'Children used to grow up in a home where parents told most of the stories. Today television tells most of the stories to most of the people most of the time.'[3] Despite the continuing cultural dominance of television, it is likely that this judgement has been rendered outdated, given the proliferation of new communications media now being deployed by children and young adults who live in a hypermedia environment where there is a blend of 'text, still image, moving image and sound, all arranged through a series of controlling icons'.[4]

The specialist in the philosophy and ethics of information, Luciano Floridi, refers to four revolutions brought about by Copernicus, Darwin, Freud and Turing. Each of the first three of these revolutions displaces some aspect of our understanding of our place in the world and our own nature. As he says, with respect to the first three of these revolutions, 'we are not immobile, at the centre of [a] universe' that revolves around us, 'we are not unnaturally separate and diverse from the rest of the animal kingdom, and we are far from being Cartesian minds entirely transparent to ourselves'.[5] The fourth revolution, as described by Floridi, one inaugurated by Alan Turing in the 1940s, 'displaced us from our privileged and unique position in the realm of logical reasoning, information processing, and smart behaviour'.[6] Our own creations, computers and related information and communications technologies, alerted us to our situation as 'mutually connected and embedded in an informational environment (the infosphere), which we share with other informational agents, both natural and artificial, that also process information logically and autonomously'.[7]

Key elements in this infosphere include (among others) 'cloud computing, … smartphone apps, tablets and touch screens, GPS', as well as 'identity theft, online courses, [and] social media' … all of which have become 'environmental, anthropological, social and interpretative forces', forces which cumulatively work together in such a way as to modify, pervasively, profoundly, and relentlessly, 'how we relate to each other … and how we interpret the world'.[8] The infosphere evidently includes, for Floridi, not only the technological tools and their properties, but also the agents who use them and the interactions and relations they make possible. Our whole environment now has to be understood as one that is inescapably interactional, governed by informational processes. In a striking comment, Floridi observes that 'we grew up with cars, buildings, furniture, clothes and all sorts of gadgets and technologies that were non-interactive, irresponsive and incapable of communicating, learning, or memorising',[9] but this is no longer the case. Increasingly and inexorably everything around us seems to be interactive and mutually responsive, so that, in terms of information, even if not in terms of emotional bonding, we are totally connected. According to Floridi, information and communication technologies (ICTs) have affected our understanding of what it is to be real; where once it was thought that to be real was to be unchangeable (therefore only God has true being); then that to be real was to be capable of being perceived by the senses; through the impact of ICTs, to be real is to be something with which one can interact, even if that is transient and virtual, rather than real in the concrete sense intended when being perceivable was the yardstick.[10]

Christians are not immune from changes in the information and communication environment. They are inescapably influenced by what surrounds them – both in what they think is plausible and in how they express what is dear to them. They must face the challenge of evaluating and working out the implications for their mission of the various new features of our communication environment – whichever term one finds most helpful, whether this be hypermedia, the infosphere, the hive, connectivity or informational matrix. They need to be alert to how communication media is shaping our environment in its multiple dimensions – cognitive, economic, political, social, cultural, moral and even physical.

Major changes in modes of communication have impacted in hugely significant ways on cultural change: from oral to chirographic (writing), and from typographic (printing) to electronic media, which has expanded exponentially since the first days of telegraph, telephone and radio. If it took several hundred years after Gutenberg's printing press before a mass market for books became a reality; the rise of computers, from invention to mass availability and use, has been a few decades.

Johannes Hoff, in an unpublished lecture given to the Catholic Theological Association at their annual conference in Durham, September 2017, suggested that 'almost every alphabetised Western person who had forgotten her mobile phone felt like a nineteenth century man who had forgotten his trousers. ... A smart phone has the character of a symbolically charged reality that motivates and inspires responsive actions, and controls our everyday habits, for better or worse.' Hoff's comments alert us to the powerful links between our artefacts and our outlook, our possessions and the degree to which we are possessed by them.

Other commenters have pointed out the ambiguous potential of new communications technology. Trevin Wax, for example, suggests that:

> It's not *what* you're looking at on your phone but *that* you're always looking at your phone. It's not what you might access on your phone that is most influential; it's what your *phone* accesses in *you.* It's not enough to ask, 'What am I doing on my phone?' Instead, we've got to ask, 'What is my phone doing to me?' The primary myth the smartphone tells you every day is that you are the centre of the universe. If your phone is your world, and if the settings and apps are tailored to you and your interests, then with you at all times is a world that revolves around you.[11]

Sophisticated technology can be addictive to such an extent that users feel bereft without it; it is almost as if, without being connected online, they feel they no longer exist or that life lacks a purpose. When our outlook is so deeply dependent on such media, our attitude to faith and to the Church inevitably suffers. Wax shrewdly observes:

> When your entire world is tailored to meet your needs and fulfil your desires, you cannot help but start to see the Church the same way. You see your pastors as the people you pay to keep you happy. You see the programmes as a way of serving your own needs. In other words, you import your consumer mindset into the Church, and suddenly church is all about you and what you need, not about Jesus and what he has done, or about the Spirit of God and how he can empower you to serve others. Instead of the Kingdom Dream changing you, you let your American Dream change your church.[12]

Connectedness turns out to be rather different from real communion and being in touch with others virtually does not always translate into self-giving compassion and service.

The two thinkers who are the subject of this chapter did not live to see the effects of the digital revolution, but they saw enough to alert us to take seriously the ambivalent powers of our own inventions.

Others have followed in their footsteps, some deliberately taking forward their insights, while others do so unawares of our two pioneers in this field. James Bridle focuses our attention on the insidious and often scarcely visible influence of computation, the cloud and emerging new scenarios that would have seemed far-fetched even in science fiction less than half a century ago.[13] Psychologist Aric Sigman[14] warns parents that the attention of their children is being claimed for many more hours, days and even years by electronic media than it is given to their mother and father, to such an extent that parents feel disempowered about attempting to pass on their values and faith. In his encyclical *Laudato si'* Pope Francis indicates how abreast he is of these concerns: 'We have to accept that technological products are not neutral, for they create a framework which ends up conditioning lifestyles and shaping social possibilities along the lines dictated by the interests of certain powerful groups.' [15] And his fellow Jesuit Antonio Spadaro notes that: 'The internet is not an instrument: it is an *ambience* which surrounds us. ... If the internet is changing our ways of living and thinking, does it not also change (and thus is already changing) our way of thinking about and living the faith?'[16] Both McLuhan and Ong would have recognised the questions that new technologies for communication pose in the twenty-first century and they anticipated many of the questions now being asked.

Biographies

Marshall McLuhan was a fertile and provocative thinker. A university professor in the USA and Canada, he spent most of his academic career based at St Michael's College – a Catholic institution that was part of the secular University of Toronto – before that teaching at Assumption College in Windsor, Ontario. He became a Catholic in 1937 and from then attended Mass on a regular basis, often daily. He was usually up between 4.00 and 5.00am reading Scripture in different languages (which he said was like having different cameras on the same action). I am not sure what his wife, whom he married in 1939 and with whom he had six children, made of his discipline of early rising. In later years he suffered a brain tumour, surgery, heart attack and a major stroke, from which he never recovered. It so happened that he taught at St Louis University from 1937 to 1944, where Walter Ong was a student of his for a while.

McLuhan's range of reference was huge. He made connections with anthropology, history, literature, philosophy and psychology, as well dipping into other disciplines. Also wide was the circle of his interlocutors, which included people from a wide range of disciplines, roles and cultural contexts. He was interdisciplinary in his refusal to compartmentalise knowledge before this became an acceptable academic stance. In this respect he reflected the medieval and Renaissance scholars in whose work he was steeped. McLuhan had an increasingly eclectic and idiosyncratic writing style. Like G.K. Chesterton, he deploys language that is pithy, provocative and playful, using broad generalisations that sometimes slip into stereotypes that can be contested but which contain profound, if awkward and uncomfortable, truth.

His thought is suggestive rather than definitive; it remains unfinished and requires completion; it needs to be filled out and related to other insights; its assessment of the gains and losses brought about by technological developments needs to be updated (though these do not invalidate many of his major insights and observations). He was strong on unsubstantiated assertion but weak in argument; constantly jumping from one topic to another, not always careful about coherence. His use of terminology could be confusing, for example, about hot and cool media. He conveys the sense that he was more concerned with making an impression and to stir people up than to be convincing. There is a tendency in his work to offer over-simplifications, for example, claiming that printing was the direct and apparently single cause of the rise of nationalism, the desire for privacy, individualism, etc.

McLuhan's most famous saying is 'the medium is the message'. By this potentially misleading phrase he meant that the form in which a communication is conveyed exerts a more important influence on us than the particular surface message to which we attend. The form of the communication (its medium) remains largely unnoticed or is taken for granted, so much so that we are unaware of its effect on us. Furthermore, the media we use affect our collective consciousness as well as our individual awareness and these media modify a culture in ways that it is difficult to discern. Rather controversially, McLuhan claimed that the message is the effect of the medium in those who use it and the message can be seen in the changes the medium brings about in users. Thus, for example, the meaning of the Eucharist is the transformation it brings about in those who participate in it as they become part of the body of Christ.

Since McLuhan's death, the range of new communications media used by millions of people has significantly increased at a rapid pace. He did not live to see personal computers, Facebook, texting, YouTube, Skype, Twitter, Netflix, Google, Yahoo, iPhones and iPads, or the technology that allows us to save our thoughts in cloud storage. Often mistakenly interpreted as a techno-utopian, in fact he lamented many of the developments he wrote about. He is a writer (and speaker) who provokes one into thought, even if this is via disagreement. I wish he had engaged theology more directly and more frequently, rather than seeming to assume, after conversion, that his theological ideas were now sorted and settled, and could simply be assumed. For a person who made such an issue of the message that is being conveyed by the media we use, he seems to have given little thought to deepening and developing his religious thought in order to reach up to the needs of the times. However, the French Catholic philosopher Étienne Gilson, a specialist in medieval thought, but an erudite commentator on the whole range of Western philosophy – classical, medieval, modern and contemporary – told a group of students that in his view, McLuhan was a genuine genius.[17] A generation after that assessment, there continue to be positive evaluations of his enduring significance. For example, Anthony Wachs observes that 'McLuhan's thought at its best is rhetorically complex, historically deep, philosophically profound and far more extensive than the aphorisms that helped to make him famous. ... He was the single most influential scholar to bring attention to communication as a field of study during the twentieth century', though he does admit the conflicting nature of his reputation, 'as a prophet for some, and as a charlatan for others.'[18]

Although they wrote with greater scholarly depth and cogency than McLuhan, it is reasonable to claim that many academics who followed his lead on media studies, such as Walter Ong, Neil Postman[19] and a whole generation after them, would not have achieved what they did were it not for McLuhan's provocation, stimulus, excitement and example. McLuhan's significant impact on thinking about communication media was recognised when he was appointed in 1973 by the Vatican to the Pontifical Commission for Social Communications.[20]

Walter Ong also made connections between consciousness, communications and culture. As I have said, Ong was taught briefly by McLuhan at St Louis and viewed him very positively as a teacher. In a letter, Ong said of McLuhan: 'A superb teacher can make the thinking an overpowering activity, delightful even when it is disturbing and exhausting. By these criteria, MM was always a superb teacher. He could stir people's minds. Even those who found themselves baffled or exasperated generally find themselves changed'.[21] McLuhan supervised Ong's English literature MA thesis on sprung rhythm in the poetry of Gerard Manley Hopkins. Many years later, Ong dedicated the 1958 published version of his Harvard PhD thesis on Peter Ramus to McLuhan – and McLuhan in turn was influenced by and built on that thesis in his own book, *The Gutenberg Galaxy* in 1962.

Ong studied in France and the UK as well as in Harvard for his PhD. In Paris from 1950–53, his room was very near that of his fellow-Jesuit, Teilhard de Chardin. Later, Ong was one of the first Americans to write about Teilhard. After his doctorate, he went back to St Louis University to teach 1954–89. He made significant contributions to various areas of scholarship, including literary studies and linguistics, rhetoric, contemporary culture and communications, intellectual history, psychology, as well as to religion and the Jesuit ethos. For a short period (1966–67) he served as adviser on Education to President Johnson. Thomas Farrell claims that Ong is unique in building a link between personal interiority, consciousness, mediated communication and community.[22] Thomas D. Zlatic claims that Ong was 'on the front of intellectual currents, whether they be neo-Thomism, New Criticism, rhetoric, phenomenology, psychiatry, orality, media studies, cosmology, sociobiology, anthropology, structuralism, reader-response theory, deconstruction, or hermeneutics'.[23]

Key themes

McLuhan, like Ong, was interested in the interactions between our senses, the media we use and our assumptions and outlook. As mentioned, his most famous theme was 'the medium is the message'.

I have picked out five further key themes from his work. First, he pointed out how media can be understood as extensions of ourselves and secondly the powerful effects of the communication environment on how we think. Thus, while, through the use of various media, we impose ourselves on the world, at the same time, through the media with which we engage, much is imposed on us in ways we are only inadequately aware of. Third, he drew attention to how the figure/ground distinction (which I will explain) enhances our appreciation of what we take for granted and thus fail to see properly. Fourth, he raised important questions that should be put when assessing the effects of artefacts, ideas and communication media.

First, then, in a letter in 1969 to Jacques Maritain, McLuhan noted that 'Every technology is an extension of our own bodies. ... Each extension of ourselves creates a new human environment and an entirely new set of interpersonal relationships. ... Every new technology thus alters the human sensory bias creating new areas of perception and new areas of blindness'.[24] 'An extension appears to be an amplification of an organ, a sense or a function. ... Psychically the printed book, an expression of the visual faculty, intensified perspective and the fixed point of view. ... Socially, the typographic extension of man brought in nationalism, industrialism, mass markets, and universal literacy and education.'[25] In a different letter in the same year to Maritain, he claimed that 'Each new extension of ourselves creates a new human environment and an entirely new set of interpersonal relationships. ... Each new technology thus alters the human sensory bias creating new areas of perception and new areas of blandness.'[26] Yes, he wrote blandness, not blindness, a typical playful jolt to those who read or heard him. In a signature style of mosaic writing, *The Gutenberg Galaxy*, which piles up ideas in impressionistic daubs rather than connected analysis, McLuhan links the use of technology in extending our senses to changes in culture: 'if a new technology extends one or more of our senses outside us into the social world, then new ratios among all our senses will occur in that particular culture. ... And when the sense ratios alter in any culture then what had appeared lucid before may suddenly be opaque, and what had been vague or opaque will become translucent'.[27]

Second, McLuhan saw his role as alerting people to the unnoticed ways that our use of media altered our sense of self, of others and of the world around us. The regular use of new communications media did not simply add to the furniture of the world around us; rather it re-ordered *all* of the things we think about and give ourselves to, by changing how we relate to all these. We tend to focus on the content being conveyed through some medium of communication, but fail to discern its character, its underlying assumptions and its shaping power over us. Thus, without our realising it, 'Subliminal and docile acceptance of media impact has made them prisons without walls for their human users'.[28] Changes in the forms and channels of communication tend to have radical political consequences and alter our patterns of attention, both of which affect culture.[29] In a 1969 letter to Robert J. Leuver, editor of the Chicago paper *U.S. Catholic*, he noted that 'the environment is invincibly persuasive when ignored'.[30] Because of this, as early as the beginning of the 1950s, as he prepared his first book *The Mechanical Bride*, he wrote 'the problem which every educator must face today is that of immunising the student against his environment'.[31] An alternative rendering of this was his succinct assertion, 'Education is ideally civil defence against media fall-out'.[32] Neil Postman, who developed McLuhan's ideas, echoed his observations:

Technologies and techniques of communication control the form, quantity, speed, distribution, and direction of information; such information configurations or biases affect people's perceptions, values, and attitudes. ...[33]

... Every technology has a philosophy, which is given expression in how the technology makes people use their minds, in what it makes us do with our bodies, in how it codifies the world, in which of our senses it amplifies, in which of our emotional and intellectual tendencies it disregards.[34]

Third, one of the insightful ways McLuhan drew attention to how the media environment covertly shapes us was his use of the distinction (borrowed from gestalt psychology) between figure and ground. By 'the figure', he means what we explicitly attend to, the topic of our investigation or discussion, the idea or fact we are asking about, the notion we are considering, the target of our mental activity. By 'ground' he refers to the foundation from which we take a stance, the background assumptions we take for granted, where we are looking *from*, rather than what we are looking *at*. There are close similarities here (though I believe neither thinker is aware of it) with Michael Polanyi's distinction between proximal and distal awareness. In *The Tacit Dimension*, Polanyi observes, 'Thinking has a *from-to* structure. We attend from the proximal to the distal, from the subsidiary to the focal, thus achieving an integration of particulars to a coherent entity to which we are attending'.[35]

Wachs explains McLuhan's distinction thus:

... ground is the contextual aspect of reality that is not directly in the focus of attention, whereas figure is the object that is the direct centre of the focus of attention. Every situation contains a figure, or object of attention, and a ground, or the area of inattention from which all potential figures emerge and into which they recede. ... Figure and ground interplay with one another, and this interplay constitutes our consciousness and perception of reality.[36]

Fourth, McLuhan became increasingly intrigued by the literature on the two hemispheres of the brain, the left and the right, which appear to have different but complementary functions; the left being more analytical, the right being more holistic. He claimed in a letter to Jacqueline Tyrwhitt, written in 1968, that he had been using a two-hemisphere approach when he referred to the written and the oral, the visual and the acoustic, the medium and the message, as examples of the figure/ground distinction.[37] He continues, 'During the past century … there has been a new electronic milieu or environment which automatically pushes the right hemisphere into a more dominant position than it has held in the Western world since the invention of the phonetic alphabet. … My work has been a dialogue between the two hemispheres in which the characteristics of the right hemisphere are given so much recognition that I have been unintelligible to the left-hemisphere people.'[38] Elsewhere he explained the distinction between right and left hemispheres thus: 'The right covers the *field* of perception in its entirety, whereas the left concentrates on one aspect at a time. Gutenberg attaches itself to the left hemisphere; the oral, the acoustic and consequently the electric, to the right hemisphere. … Our school system, like our Catholic hierarchy, is completely dominated by the left side of the brain.'[39]

There are major implications for educators and for the Church if the role of the two hemispheres is properly appreciated, implications which we are only beginning to wake up to. The best work known to me on the different contributions of the two hemispheres is *The Master and His Emissary* by Iain McGilchrist (Yale University Press, 2009), a book I would put on a par with Charles Taylor's *A Secular Age* (Harvard University Press, 2007) for its contribution to understanding our culture. Even though McLuhan's thoughts on the topic were much less detailed, rigorous, coherent or strongly founded than those of McGilchrist, he deserves credit for his prescient and prophetic recognition of the need for us to appreciate how the two hemispheres operate in opening up for us different facets of the world.

The fifth contribution from McLuhan can be said to be the enduring investigative power and relevance of the four questions he constantly raised when considering different media of communication and their role in cultural change. Four questions can be applied to any artefact or idea, he claimed: What does it enhance or intensify? What does it render obsolete or displace? What does it retrieve that was previously obsolesced? What does it produce or become when pressed to an extreme?[40] He frequently commented with great insight on many different features of contemporary life (for example, cars and television) by probing their effects through deploying these four questions. Neil Postman posed similar questions about communication media:

> To what extent does a medium contribute to the uses and development of rational thought? To what extent does a medium contribute to the development of democratic processes? To what extent do new media give greater access to meaningful information? To what extent do new media enhance or diminish our moral sense, our capacity for goodness?[41]

Both sets of questions are important. If McLuhan's questions reveal features of our cultural landscape more generally, Postman's draw attention to their ethical implications.

Walter Ong has argued that Socrates' complaints at the end of the *Phaedrus* about writing – that it diminishes memory, lacks interaction, disseminates at random and disembodies speakers and hearers – are similar to late-twentieth-century worries about computers as well as fifteenth-century concerns about printing.[42] Not only, as Ong observes, might we apply this to computers; it has been lamented also with regard to many other technological innovations in communication. However, despite the need to be alert for how our technology can come to colonise our thinking, he offers a balanced assessment: 'Technology can dehumanise us and at times has dehumanised us. But it can also humanise us. Indeed, technology is absolutely indispensable for many of our absolutely central humanising achievements'.[43] Indeed, 'the use of a technology can enrich the human psyche, enlarge human spirit, set it free, intensify its interior life'.[44] Ong's primary concern is less the material nature of the 'hardware' used than the habits of mind and the human relationships brought about by modes of communication.

He was particularly insightful about how the modes of communication currently in use at any particular moment in history, together with the information-handling capacity of a culture at that time, influence the articulation of its theological understanding. How knowledge is discovered, stored, passed on to others and how it is accessed when required – all these inescapably have a bearing on what is taken to be theological knowledge, who decides what counts as such, what the scope of that theology is assumed to be, as well as how it is to be preserved and conveyed to inquirers and to the next generation. As one scholar of communication has observed, when discussing Ong's work, 'A textual discipline today, theology includes older oral, homiletic, liturgical, musical, architectural, chirographic, print and visual traditions that require different rules of interpretation'.[45] It is all too easy to forget that theology transcends what is transmitted via texts.

Two major insights from Ong deserve mention here: first, his account of the 'sensorium'; second, his analysis of key characteristics of media. In *The Presence of the Word* he describes the sensorium as the complete set of our bodily senses working together as an operational complex,[46] explaining that the way we use our senses and the relative weight we attribute to each of them has a different configuration according to the culture in which we find ourselves. 'Cultures vary greatly in their exploitation of the various senses and in the way they relate their conceptual apparatus to the various senses. ... a given culture ... brings [a person] to organise his sensorium by attending to some types of perception more than others, by making an issue of certain ones while relatively neglecting other ones.'[47] This is not to deny the fact that our senses provide both opportunities for, as well as constraints on, cultural developments; the influence between culture and senses is reciprocal. Our world is simultaneously personal, as constructed by us, and objective, given to us. 'The sensorial organisation specific to any given time and culture may bring us to overspecialise in certain features of actuality and to neglect others.'[48]

Following on from this, Ong draws attention to three characteristics of media. He shows how any particular medium used in communication addresses and activates one or more of the different physical senses of sight, sound, hearing, touch and taste, affecting social perception as well as bodily engagement. Then, he links different media with particular associated ways of managing information, including its storage, retrieval and dissemination, with attendant effects on how cultures develop and deploy systems of meaning. Finally, he shows how the use of different media frames the pattern of relationships and authority in a culture.

Similarly to McLuhan, Ong notes changes brought about by shifts from oral to writing cultures; then from a print-based culture to an electronic one. 'In one way or another, codes modify what they encode,' he says.[49] Print culture seemed to downgrade the role of oral communication and lead to a forgetting of the huge importance of sound, and to ignore the extent to which 'words are ultimately given their meaning by a nonverbal context'.[50] Though all the senses play a necessary part in our lives, sound was especially significant for Ong. It offered a 'special sensory key to interiority'.[51] For him, sight presents surfaces; distances the looker from what is looked upon; and privileges clarity and distinctiveness. In contrast, sound is a unifying sense, it brings together the emitter and the receiver; its ideal is harmony rather than distinctiveness or separation.[52] 'The word as sound signals interiority and mystery (a certain inaccessibility even in intimacy)'.[53]

Furthermore, just as was the case with McLuhan, Ong did not view communication as a matter of the transmission of a message; nor did he consider language to be a neutral vehicle for the transfer of information that had already been arrived at. Rather, language 'is a negotiation of meanings between human persons that is open-ended and without terminus'.[54] Furthermore, given that all interpretation is interdependent with the communication medium through which the negotiation is conducted, then 'different communications media engage the senses in different proportions with different effects on noetic processes, psychic drives, and personality structures'.[55] What matters for Ong is 'not a sharing of information but a sharing of selves' because what matters in human communication is not the exchange of messages, but 'a sharing of interiors'.[56] Here honesty is not seen as separate from one's personhood, character or actions, in the way that sometimes truth can seem to be something 'out there and distinguishable from us.

Ong's claims about sound and for the nature of orality in culture have come in for criticism in some quarters. Jonathan Sterne suggests that Ong's theory of orality is 'rhetorically powerful, but not very accurate. ... [I]n recent years, anthropologists, historians and countless others have chronicled organisations of sonic culture that call into question [Ong's] assumptions about sound, culture, and consciousness'.[57] However, even if one accepts that, with regard to orality, Ong is flawed in several respects, this need not prevent one from being enriched by his insights into the mysterious, yet real, connections between the history of communication media and human receptivity to God's revelation.

Implications for faith

This brings us to consider the implications for Catholic Christians of the major insights left to us by McLuhan and Ong. A very recent assessment of both these thinkers made clear that 'Their Catholicism was not incidental to their theories and their art; it was their structure, their spirit and their sustenance'.[58] As early as 1935, two years before becoming a Catholic, McLuhan had written to his mother 'I finally perceived that the character of every society, its food, clothing, arts and amusements are ultimately determined by its religion'.[59] This was a view being argued at that time by Christopher Dawson in his work on cultural history.

If religion was, for McLuhan a source of inspiration and integration in life, he was adamant that Christians must be open to learning from secular disciplines. For example, he wrote in 1944 to both Ong and to another Jesuit, Clement McNaspy, to convey his opinion that 'Increasingly, I feel that Catholics must master C.G. Jung. Modern anthropology and psychology are more important for the Church than St Thomas today'.[60] In the same letter, he also recommends management theorist Peter Drucker's books. So willing was McLuhan to take on board new thinking across a wide range of disciplines that he might be accused of being insufficiently critical of what he was assimilating and of lacking a parallel deepening of his understanding of the theological sources, development and coherence of his own faith tradition.

Despite this possible weakness, he was not slow to assert in a letter in 1946: 'It seems obvious to me that we must confront the secular in its most confident manifestations, and, with its own terms and postulates, to shock it into awareness of its confusion, its illiteracy, and the terrifying drift of its logic. There is no need to mention Christianity. It is enough to be known that the operator is a Christian. This job must be conducted on every front – every phase of the press, book-rackets, music, cinema, education, economics'.[61] C.S. Lewis made very similar comments around the same time.

Because of his insights into the effect of communication media on consciousness and culture, McLuhan was able to offer some striking, if sometimes acerbic, comments about developments in Christian history. Here are some examples. 'The early church began with a liaison with the Greco-Roman and the alphabetic. Ever since, the Church has made inseparable the propagation of the faith and of Greco-Roman culture, thus ensuring that only a tiny segment of mankind would ever be Christian'.[62] 'There was nobody at the Council of Trent who had any interest in the shaping power of the Gutenberg technology in creating private judgement on the one hand, and of massive centralist bureaucracy on the other hand. There was nobody at Vatican I or II who showed any understanding of the electro-technical thing in reshaping the psyche and culture of mankind. ... Since Vatican I and II the Catholic bureaucracy has moved resolutely into the nineteenth century, supported by plain-clothed priests and nuns.'[63] This was in a letter to Frank Sheed, the Catholic apologist and publisher. In the same letter, he said, of the Councils of Trent and Vatican I: 'The policies adopted at these Councils manifested the spirit of Don Quixote who donned the latest print technology as his armour and motive, and rode off valiantly into the Middle Ages.' He was calling for a much deeper understanding of how communication media modify cultural understanding. He lamented in an interview about liturgy with Pierre Babin, in 1977, 'I do not think that the powerful forces imposed on us by electricity have been considered at all by theologians and liturgists'.[64] In another interview with Babin he claimed 'Latin wasn't the victim of Vatican II; it was done in by introducing the microphone'.[65] As a factor influencing change in the Church, technology is often ignored.

As for Ong, I would select four important contributions which have implications for Christians today: his treatment of the need to engage with modernity; his analysis of the effect of the communications system in which we find ourselves immersed; the centrality of presence; and finally his creative use of the metaphor of yeast as leaven.

First, Thomas Farrell, one of the foremost scholars of Ong's work, noted that 'Ong stopped contending with modernity before the Second Vatican Council officially changed certain Church teachings'.[66] Farrell attributes this shift, from the usual Catholic counter-cultural position to a more open one, to 'his new understanding of Western cultural history, inspired primarily by Lavelle's work with the aural-visual opposition.' Ong found this key to his later thinking in the writing of the French philosopher, Louis Lavelle.[67] Four years before Vatican II opened, one can see Ong's cautious move towards advocating a positive approach to the modern world. 'As man's ideas of what the world is undergo radical revision and enlargement, the Christian mind must make some fundamental adjustments in thinking about his religion itself. But he must make them sensitively and within the economy of faith. ... not the adapting of revelation to the facts, but the integration of the new facts with revelation; not a new understanding of faith and of

God in the light of new discoveries, but a new understanding of the new discoveries in the light of faith and in relationship to God.'[68]

Surely, this interaction is reciprocal, working both ways, rather than unilaterally; for God is the source of knowledge, whether from 'above' or 'below'. Ong does acknowledge that 'the Church has elaborated her understanding of her mission, and indeed come to some new understanding of this mission, insofar as the relationship of man to the universe has been clarified through the scientific work of the modern world'.[69] He continues this line when he expresses the view that 'Thinkers in the Church must relate secular knowledges to theology and to her teaching, and thus not merely to "reinterpret" her teaching for the age but also to possess it themselves in its fullness. … The Church needs to be present to secular learning and to have it present to her in order to realise her mission as the Mystical Body of Christ, extending the effects of the Incarnation to all her members and, so far as she can, to all men – which certainly means to all the reaches of their intellectual activity. In fulfilling her mission to bring the entire world to Christ, the Church must reflect not only on divine revelation but also upon creation itself'.[70] In an article written mid-way through the Council he acknowledged that: 'Our present advances in theology, in the explication of divine revelation itself, have depended in great part upon advances in secular thought – advances, for example, in anthropology, in sociology, in cultural history, and in literary history.'[71]

Second, I have already mentioned Ong's treatment of the sensorium, his emphasis on sound, his commenting on the significance of moves from one type of communications medium to another. Like McLuhan, he was keen to point out the over-reliance of the Church on modes of thought facilitated by print culture and the need to attend to a broader range of media in order to receive and share the diverse ways God reaches out to us. Two years after Vatican II ended, in a series of lectures he gave at Yale University, he observed that 'post-Tridentine Catholic theologians, who were also post-Gutenberg men, conceived of tradition … by analogy with a written text', but 'The word of God comes to man and is present among men within an evolving communications system'.[72] Ong teaches us that the Church must become more aware of the ways that our modes and media of communication shape our perceptions, assumptions, priorities and practices – and thus modify the effectiveness and influence the reception of our mission in the world.

Third, Ong reflected deeply on the notion of presence; the ways that God is present to us, the ways we are present to one another and the central importance of sound and the voice in all of this. He notes that 'God is thought of always as "speaking" to human beings, not as writing to them'.[73] Sound resonates within and touches us in deeper ways than sight; sound provides a vital access to the presence of others. According to Ong's way of thinking, knowledge is about presence rather than possession. Just as God is always present to us, though we may not advert to that presence, we are called to learn how to reciprocate that presence, not only to God, but to each other (where God is also present). I would take the liberty of extending Ong's profound analysis of the aural, in contrast to the visual, and claim that two aspects of our faith-life might be revitalised by attending to how sound and voice are central to presence.

At some point in the Middle Ages a shift occurred in references to the Body of Christ – emphasising less the notion that God is present in the body of believers (though of course that was never lost) and stressing more God's presence in the bread and wine of the Eucharist that became the body and blood of Christ. Thus, the real presence moves from here, among us, nourishing us as a community to there, in front of us, to be gazed at and consumed by individuals. A communal attendance, among the faithful, to the presence of Christ and the working of the Holy Spirit in their midst should prompt us to engage more frequently in listening, sharing and discerning with one another, not only what the words of Scripture might be saying to us, but our experience of faith-life more generally, including what helps and what hinders us in our paths of discipleship. This calls for us to be really present to one another as well as really available and actively receptive to God's reaching out to us.

Similarly, the privileging of sight, reinforced later by printing, and the strong association between faith and fixed doctrine tended, in many people's minds, to reduce faith to assent to beliefs and to reduce obedience to compliance. Ong's restoration of sound and voice as central to presence should prompt us to revisit the roots of the meaning of obedience, which means deep listening to the other (including the Other) and acting upon what is learned in that listening. This type of obedience requires responsive agency on the part of the hearer, not mere passivity.

The fourth contribution from Ong is his use of the gospel imagery of yeast acting as leaven in dough to suggest how faith should work in a given culture (developed from the metaphor of yeast in Mt 13:33 and Lk 13:21). Ong likens yeast to Christian faith and the Church as the vehicle of its living tradition, while the dough into which yeast is inserted represents the world as a whole and, in the application of the metaphor made in an article in 1990, the dough represents the Christian university in particular and the academic disciplines taught there. Ong points out that: 'Yeast acts on dough, but it does not convert all the dough into yeast, nor is it able to do so or meant to do so. Its primary effect is to interact, and this interaction results in ferment and growth for both yeast and dough.'[74] Both Church and world benefit from and are enriched by such interaction. Ong makes it clear that the Church's encounter – with the world and with the university – is not intended as confrontation but as interpenetration with a view to mutual enhancement, an engagement that is not carried out only on the Church's own terms, an encounter that is meant to be an act of service and of mutual learning, not of unilateral imposition or of domination. The Church aims to function as a leaven, raising what it meets to a higher level, bringing out latent potential in those with whom it enters into dialogue, while at the same time coming to a fresh realisation of the implications and scope of the Gospel it proclaims as this is related to specific cultures and contexts, for example, in the university.

Educational implications

I hope it will be obvious how relevant to the work of Catholic educators are the three implications for Christians that I have drawn from McLuhan – the need to be open to secular learning, the duty to challenge prevailing cultural assumptions, and the necessity of understanding how the Church's engagement with communication media has shaped, for better or worse, how effectively the Gospel is conveyed. The four contributions that I have highlighted from the work of Ong should also be kept in mind by Catholic educators in schools and universities. A few additional comments on the bearing of developments in communication media on education seem pertinent here.

First, it must be acknowledged that 'no communication arrangement can guarantee to make accessible the truths of Christian faith'.[75] Such access is subject to and requires both the gift of grace and the free response of the one who receives it.

Second, technology can do much but still remains in service to the underlying and enduring inner capacities or gifts of humanity, including imagination. This point is illustrated in the following brief anecdote. 'When I grew up, I could not imagine a world without Kodak. Neither could the managers of Kodak. As a result of this assumption, Kodak has become history.'[76] Even as humanity becomes increasingly dependent on technology, the technology still depends on our inner capacities and qualities, such as sensitivity, listening, intelligence, conscience, empathy and judgement. Without these, connectivity will never lead to community or become mutual attunement.

Third, in order to move beyond mere connectivity, there is the need to nurture the willingness to engage in deeper listening. Many years ago Postman claimed that one of the benefits that education should give us is a built-in crap detector; the ability to tell when some person or group was trying to deceive or manipulate us.[77] Can we now hope that one of the benefits that education will give us is a better hearing-aid? There are signs in our culture of greater openness about and willingness to share experiences, feelings and a greater acknowledgement of our need for recognition, acceptance and affirmation.

Fourth, with pluralism, postmodernity and a widespread erosion of confidence in claims to certainty about metanarratives, perhaps education will begin to do justice to the diversity of ways of knowing, focussing not only cognitive, rational and conceptual knowledge, but also aesthetic, symbolic/gestural, embodied, kinaesthetic and spiritual knowledge.

Fifth, in acknowledging much greater access to and democratisation of knowledge – with multiple sources of information – Christian educational institutions should welcome and adjust to the ensuing distributed nature of authority. Centralisation and concentration of authority, with associated pressures toward conformity and compliance, even though marked features of the Church in recent centuries, do not fit well with the Christian mission to make mature, responsible and committed disciples.

Sixth, if in the past a strong emphasis in Christian education has been to pass on a body of content (scripture, doctrine, moral precepts), and if, in more recent times students have been encouraged to interrogate their own experience, in the light of current cultural developments in our communication environment, it is now necessary to give priority to equipping students to interpret and critique the culture, its assumptions and values, the habits it promotes, attentive to what it privileges and what it neglects, aware of how it frames our sense of identity, relationships, belonging and expectations.

Catholic teachers need to reflect carefully on the rapidly changing context brought about by Floridi's fourth revolution and its as-yet-unclear implications for our sense of identity, relationships, belonging, our thinking, valuing and imagining, our memory, hopes and constraints. Being immersed in a culture always entails being subject to unconscious codes that are difficult to discern, being complicit in hidden conflicts that can easily remain outside our consciousness, and being prompted to be creative with the resources available to us.[78] Integral to the challenge of interpreting the culture and induction into a Christian perspective, there needs to a recognition that both worlds, that of our contemporary culture and the world of Jesus, do not appear before us transparently, nakedly, obviously or simply in some unfiltered manner; they come to us via multiple mediations. The complex role of communication technologies in mediating to us our culture has already been apparent in this chapter.

Students, at all levels in education, need guidance in how to understand the technology and the social and cultural effects of new modes of communication. They should be challenged to become alert to what they are doing with the technology and to be discerning as to what it is doing to them. For example, is their use of search engines having the effect of enclosing them in a bubble which reinforces their prejudices and prior interests and assumptions? The data collected about us by Google and Amazon (and similar multinational companies) constructs a profile (of which we are unaware) of the sites we have visited, the purchases we have made, the searches we have conducted and they then serve up for us, when we search again, choices that are already sifted for us – usually ones we are quite happy to accept without questioning. Does this unduly restrict our encounters with items, perspectives, ideas and people that differ from us? Questioning the ethics of the uses we make of the Web should be part of the curriculum, just as should questioning our treatment of the environment. For example, what are good and bad uses of social networks such as Facebook? How can we protect ourselves against abuses? When we are online, do we conduct ourselves with care, courtesy, respect and sensitivity to how our communications are received when these are not face-to-face?

Students in Religious Education in schools and in Theology at university might be prompted to reflect on the presence of religious groups on the Web, on how religious faith is expressed there, and on both the opportunities and the limitations of communicating the Gospel via online communication. Teachers – of all academic disciplines – should monitor their own classroom use of communication media and question if valuable traditional skills and habits in thinking, speaking, reading and writing are being undermined. To what extent is there a place in students' educational experience for silence, reflection, patient waiting, concentrated attention, for personal interaction and collaboration in learning, for spending extended periods of time with people and with topics to ensure real familiarity and depth of engagement?

***

In Psalm 115, verses 4 and 8 warn us: 'Their idols are silver and gold, the work of human hands. ... Those who make them are like them; so are all who trust in them.' The two thinkers who have been the central figures in this chapter alert us to the need to be very conscious of the nature and the effects, the possibilities and limitations, of the communication media we employ or in which we are immersed. These technological media are part of the environment in which we swim, alongside our biophysical and our symbolic environment; all three aspects of this environment interact in complex ways.[79] Our religious faith and its expression cannot help but be affected by this triple environment. As Michael Warren points out: 'When our practice of religious language ignores the material conditions of our seeing, that language practice colludes in enabling the conditions of our seeing to go unnoticed.'[80] When this happens, it becomes harder to discern which aspects of our faith have become distorted by the fruits of our own labours, which are of the essence and which are peripheral; which belong to another age and which need re-interpretation or re-vitalising today. The Christian communications expert Peter Horsfield, in reviewing Christianity's changing relationship with and use of the media of communication over the past two thousand years, having noted how the faith is affected and changed by changes in the media environment, concludes by pointing out 'the challenges and opportunities presented to Christianity today by new media and the new media industries are not unique in Christian history' but he then specifies a neuralgic feature of our current landscape: 'the media challenge being faced by Christianity today is that the media structures and practices that have supported its historic organisation and authority have shifted, and social organisation is taking place and authority is being ascribed in different ways. One of the problems that many Christian leaders have in dealing with this shift constructively is that they are unable to see the media-specific nature of their religious authority and are therefore unable to facilitate, if they wanted to do so, the transfer of their authority to something more appropriate for the new situation'.[81] It would be wise for Christian leaders and teachers to learn from McLuhan and Ong – and those who carry forward their work – how to read our communication environment, together with its associated habits of attention and sensibility, so that we can continue to take our living tradition forward, arming our fidelity with cultural discernment and imagination.

ENDNOTES

1   Walter J. Ong, *Language as Hermeneutic. A Primer on the Word and Digitization*, edited by Thomas D. Zlatic and Sara van den Berg, Ithaca and London: Cornell University Press, 2017, p. 6.

2   Sven Birkerts, *The Gutenberg Elegies,* New York: Faber and Faber, 2006, p. xiii.

3   George Gerbner cited by Michael Warren, 'Storytellers Shape Spiritual Values', Media & Values, Issue 57, Winter 1992; accessed on February 25 2022 from media.it.org/reading-room/storytellers-shape-spiritual-values.

4   Alan C. Purves, *The Web of Text and the Web of God,* New York: The Guilford Press, 1998, p.112.

5   Luciano Floridi, *The Fourth Revolution*, Oxford: Oxford University Press, 2014, p. 90.

6   Floridi, *Fourth Revolution*, p. 93.

7   Ibid., p. 94.

8   Ibid., p. vi.

9   Ibid., p. 48.

10 Ibid., p. 53.

11 Trevin Wax, *This is Our Time: Everyday Myths in Light of the Gospel*, Nashville, TN: B & H Books, 2017, p. 20.

12 Wax, *This is Our Time*, pp. 109–10.

13 James Bridle, *New Dark Age: Technology and the End of the Future,* London: Verso, 2018.

14 Aric Sigman, *The Spoilt Generation: Why Restoring Authority Will Make Our Children and Society Happier* (London: Piatkus, 2009), p.115.

15 Pope Francis, *Laudato si'*, Rome: Libreria Editrice Vaticana, 2015, #107.

16 Antonio Spadaro, *Cybertheology: Thinking Christianity in the Era of the Internet*, translated by Maria Way, New York: Fordham University Press, 2014, pp. vii-viii.

17 W. Terrence Gordon, *Marshall McLuhan. Escape into Understanding*, New York: Basic Books, 1997, p. 138.

18 Anthony M. Wachs, *The New Science of Communication*. Pittsburgh, PN: Duquesne University Press, 2015, pp.2–3.

19 Neil Postman, *Amusing Ourselves to Death*, London: Methuen, 1987.

20 Gordon, *Marshall McLuhan*, p. 268.

21 Matie Molinaro, Corinne McLuhan & William Toye (eds) *Letters of Marshall McLuhan*, Toronto: Oxford University Press, 1987, p. 94.

22 Thomas J. Farrell, *Walter Ong's Contributions to Cultural Studies: The Phenomenology of the Word and I-Thou Communication, Revised Edition*, New York: Hampton Press, 2015, p. xxiv.

23   Ong, *Language as Hermeneutic*, p. 149.

24   Marshall McLuhan, *The Medium and the Light: Reflections on Religion*, edited by Eric McLuhan and Jacek Szklarek, Eugene, OR: Wipf & Stock, 2010, p. 70.

25   Marshall McLuhan, *Understanding Media*, London: Ark Paperbacks, 1987, p. 172.

26   Molinaro, McLuhan & Toye, *Letters of Marshall McLuhan*, p. 369.

27   Marshall McLuhan, *The Gutenberg Galaxy*, London: Routledge & Kegan Paul, 1962, p. 41.

28   McLuhan, *Understanding Media*, p. 20.

29   McLuhan, *The Medium and the Light*, pp. 162–3.

30   Molinaro, McLuhan & Toye, *Letters of Marshall McLuhan*, p. 385.

31   Gordon, *Marshall McLuhan*, p. 97.

32   McLuhan, *Understanding Media*, p. 195.

33   Neil Postman, *Teaching as a Conserving Activity*, New York: Dell Publishing, 1979, p.186.

34   Neil Postman, *The End of Education*, New York: Vintage Books/Random House, 1996, p. 192.

35   Michael Polanyi, *The Tacit Dimension*, Chicago: University of Chicago Press, 1966, p. 18.

36   Wachs, *The New Science of Communication*, p. 24.

37   Molinaro, McLuhan & Toye, *Letters of Marshall McLuhan*, p. 359.

38   Ibid., p. 360.

39   McLuhan, *The Medium and the Light*, pp. 52–3.

40   Marshall McLuhan and Eric McLuhan, *Laws of Media*, Toronto: University of Toronto Press, 1992.

41   Neil Postman, quoted by Lance Strate, *Media Ecology*, New York: Peter Lang, 2017, p. 33.

42   Walter J. Ong, *Orality and Literacy: The Technologizing of the Word*, London: Routledge, 1982, pp. 79-81.

43   Walter J. Ong, 'Realising Catholicism: Faith, Learning, and the Future,' University of Dayton Marianist Lecture, 1989, p. 15.

44   Walter J. Ong, *Faith and Contexts, Volume Four: Additional Studies and Essays 1947-1996*, edited by Thomas J. Farrell and Paul A. Soukup, Atlanta, GA: Scholars Press, 1999, p. 152.

45   Paul Soukup, 'In Commemoration: Walter Ong and the State of Theology', *Theological Studies*, Vol. 73, No. 4, (December 2012), p. 837.

46   Walter J. Ong, *The Presence of the Word*, New Haven: Yale University Press, 1967, p. 6.

47   Ong, *The Presence of the Word*, pp. 3-6.

48   Ibid., p. 175.

49   Ong, *Language as Hermeneutic*, p. 45.

50   Ibid., p. 55.

51   Ong, *Presence of the Word*, p. 117.

52   Ong, *Orality and Literacy*, p. 72.

53   Ong, *Presence of the Word*, p. 314.

54   Thomas D. Zlatic in Ong, *Language as Hermeneutic*, p. 151.

55   Ibid., p. 153.

56   Ibid., p. 156.

57   Jonathan Sterne, 'The Theology of Sound: A Critique of Orality', *Canadian Journal of Communication*, Vol. 36 (2011), pp. 207-25.

58   Nick Ripatrazone, 'A Catholic Media Trinity: Marshall McLuhan, Walter Ong and Andy Warhol', *America*, 27 December 2017. https://www.americamagazine.org/arts-culture/2017/12/27/catholic-media-trinity-marshall-mcluhan-walter-ong-and-andy-warhol; accessed 4 January 2018.

59   Gordon, *Marshall McLuhan*, p. 73.

60   Molinaro, McLuhan & Toye, *Letters of Marshall McLuhan*, p. 166.

61   Ibid., p. 180.

62   Gordon, *Marshall McLuhan*, p. 224.

63   Molinaro, McLuhan & Toye, *Letters of Marshall McLuhan*, p. 399.

64   McLuhan, *Medium and the Light*, p. 45.

65   Ibid., p. 143.

66   Thomas J. Farrell, 'Understanding Ong's Philosophical Thought', 2015, p. 4, https://conservancy.umn.edu/bitstream/handle/11299/187434/Farrell%20on%20Ong%20(2015-07-23).pdf?sequence=1&isAllowed=y; accessed on 21 January 2018.

67   Louis Lavelle, *La parole et l'écriture*, Paris: Le Félin, 1942/2005.

68   Walter J. Ong, *American Catholic Crossroads*, New York: Collier Books, 1958, p. 23.

69   Ong, *American Catholic Crossroads*, p. 24.

70   Ibid., pp. 94, 144.

71   Ong, 'The Knowledge Explosion in the Humanities' in Walter J. Ong, *Faith and Contexts, Volume Four*, edited by Thomas J Farrell and Paul A. Soukup. Atlanta, GS: Scholars Press, 1999, p.65.

72   Ong, *Presence of the Word*, p. 276 and p. 317.

73   Ong, *Orality and Literacy*, p. 75.

74   Walter J. Ong, 'Yeast: A Parable for Catholic Higher Education,' *America*, 7

April 1990, http://www.bc.edu/offices/mission; accessed December 2015.

75   Matthias Scharer & Bernd Jochen Hilberath, *The Practice of Communicative Theology*, New York: Crossroad Publishing Company, 2008, p. 21.

76   Kishore Mahbubani, book review of *Can Singapore Survive?*, *Times Literary Supplement* (London), 18 September 2015.

77   Neil Postman & Charles Weingartner, *Teaching as a Subversive Activity*, London: Penguin, 1971.

78   See Michael Paul Gallagher, 'University and Culture: Towards a Retrieval of Humanism', *Gregorianum*, 85.1 (2004), p. 161.

79   John Durham Peters, *The Marvelous Clouds*, Chicago: University of Chicago Press, 2015.

80   Michael Warren, *At This Time, In This Place*, Harrisburg, PN: Trinity Press International, 1999, p. 47.

81   Peter Horsfield, *From Jesus to the Internet*, Oxford: Wiley-Blackwell, 2015, p. 288.

CHAPTER EIGHT

Étienne Gilson: Putting Intelligence at God's Service

The French philosopher Étienne Gilson (1884–1978) is most famous for his many writings on the history of philosophy, particularly the thought of major Christian figures, such as Augustine, Bernard of Clairvaux, Bonaventure, Aquinas and Duns Scotus.[1] Much less known is the great importance he attached to Christian education. After a brief overview of his life and work, this chapter examines four themes in Gilson's educational writings. First, I comment on his reflections on adopting an historical perspective and on learning from the past. Second, Gilson has some wise insights to offer on the practice of teaching. Third, he makes some profound and illuminating observations on putting intelligence at God's service. Fourth, he poses a robust challenge to Christians with regard to how they engage with secular society and the State, not only over educational issues, but also with regard to the role of faith in the public domain.

Biographical overview

Gilson began teaching in the early years of the twentieth century and he was still in the classroom in the early 1970s. He taught in upper secondary schools between 1907 and 1913, and then secured a university post in Lille, Northern France. Called up for war in 1914, he served in the front lines at the battle of Verdun, where he was wounded and captured in 1916, remaining a prisoner of war until 1918. During those two years he 'studied St Bonaventure, lectured on the French philosopher Bergson, published an article on aesthetic judgements, learned to play tennis, directed an orchestra of men from the camp, perfected his English and German, and became fluent in Russian'.[2] This was a person who could read Aristotle, Virgil, Dante, Goethe, Shakespeare and Dostoyevsky; each in their original languages.

After the war, he secured university posts, first, in Strasbourg, soon afterwards in Paris, and by the end of the 1920s, in Toronto. During the summer of 1922 he went on a mercy mission in Russia, setting up 55 kitchens for starving children. From the early 1920s onwards, he was invited to give lectures at very many other universities – in Germany, Italy, Belgium, the United Kingdom, Canada, Sweden, in the United States and South America. In the years between the two world wars and beyond, he took part in ecumenical exchanges with English and German Protestants, and with Russian Orthodox and Jewish emigrés. After the Second World War, he became centrally involved in the writing of the United Nations charter (in 1945) and the French government invited him to play a major role in setting up UNESCO (United Nations Education, Scientific and Cultural Organisation) in 1946. From 1947–49 he served as a senator in the French upper chamber. At 80, he still retained his vitality, critical sense and intellectual curiosity.[3]

Mainly a historian of philosophy, Gilson also contributed to epistemology, metaphysics, social thought, aesthetics, philosophy of biology and linguistics. Education remained a constant interest and concern throughout his career. He engaged frequently in the social and political debates of his time and his country, always firmly and explicitly basing his interventions as a public intellectual on the foundations of his commitment to Christian faith and the teaching of the Church. His standing as a medievalist and as a philosopher led him to be invited to give the Gifford Lectures in Aberdeen, the Henry James Lectures at Harvard, the Powell Lectures at Bloomington, Indiana, and the Mellon Lectures in Washington DC. His first visit to North America was in 1926, to take part in an international congress in Montreal on Education and Citizenship.

He had the reputation of being a wonderful communicator in his lectures, having an acute, almost uncanny sense of the possibilities and the limits of what could be conveyed within the space of an hour. As a conference speaker, he was sparkling, and often attracted large audiences to hear his carefully crafted, sometimes mischievously playful and always penetrating arguments.

His writing is marked by erudition, clarity, precision, vigour, elegance and wit. Masterful works of exposition, informative and stimulating, flowed from his pen, year after year. He was a prolific writer on many major figures who developed various interpretations of Christian thinking. His special gift was to make these thinkers from long ago come across 'as real people with their own culture, personality, knowledge, ignorance, religious life, traditions, and innovations'[4] and he was brilliant at laying bare the first principles of a philosophical system. A writer of candour, he could be controversial, polemical, combative and pugnacious; equally capable of criticising both defenders and opponents of religious faith, where he thought they used specious arguments.

Gilson advocated a revitalised Christian humanism in education. The intellect was to be used in the service of truth and love. For him, the fundamental flaw in modern society was the separation of faith and reason, to the detriment of both. One should, in his view, distinguish faith and reason, and theology and philosophy, but not separate them. Gilson models how Christian faith can play a constitutive and regulative role in the way of life, virtues, intellectual habits, interests and deployment of energy of the Christian thinker and educator. Faith was never for him an embarrassment, something to be hidden or played down in his teaching or writing.

Historical perspective

Gilson was deeply committed to the need for a well-founded historical perspective to be brought to the study of major thinkers and topics. He played a major role in the revival of interest in medieval intellectual history in the twentieth century. He was responsible for launching (in 1926) a journal to promote and publish research in medieval thought – *Archives d'histoire doctrinale et littéraire du moyen âge*. Often he found himself fighting on two fronts with regard to his historical work. In the fiercely anti-clerical environment of the university in France, he encountered a prevailing assumption that little of philosophical worth had appeared in the years between the end of the ancient world and the beginnings of modernity. He seized on this gap and made it his life's work to demonstrate the richness, sophistication and significance of the philosophical and theological thought of a range of medieval figures, from the fifth to the fourteenth century, all of whom had been profoundly influenced by their Christian faith. He engaged rigorously with their texts, setting them in the context of the intellectual debates and the culture in which they arose. And, at the same time, he battled against Catholic neo-Thomists because they deployed concepts supposedly drawn from Thomas Aquinas, but did so in a manner that was divorced from the original texts and contexts. In other words, they were misrepresenting and thus being untrue to the real Thomas because they failed to attend to the historical evidence of the Dominican's thinking and they misinterpreted the spirit that animated his writings.

Getting behind the various specific arguments of a thinker to this underlying spirit that guides and pervades their thought – this was Gilson's approach to investigating and conveying a writer's works. 'Gilson's way of doing the history of philosophy is to first penetrate to the single insight, image or inner truth of reality that guides the philosopher and then try to reproduce this same experience for his students or readers in his works.'[5] He strongly emphasises the need for historical perspective – to enable students to see what the philosophers (they were reading) saw (from their point of view), to enable them to apply the principles of these philosophers to the students' own (and different) world, and, above all, so that students could learn to philosophise authentically for themselves.

It must be admitted that Gilson's method of developing historical perspective in his students seems, in some respects, old-fashioned today. He faced criticism in his lifetime, first, for his neglect of social history and second, for his particularly sympathetic exposition of the mentality of the medieval figures under scrutiny. Was he sufficiently detached from their worldview? Was he too passionately engaged? Did he over-emphasise intellectual history? Was his use of history a covert form of apologetics? However, although he believed that total detachment is impossible for a scholar, he was very conscious of the need to be vigilant in ensuring that the passion that incites the historian to study the facts as provided by the evidence should neither ignore nor distort that evidence.

If earlier in his teaching career Gilson strove to combine sympathetic engagement and scrupulously objective examination in his teaching of the history of philosophy, he had the opportunity from the late 1920s onwards to establish a centre that allowed greater scope for his more apologetic commitments in scholarship and teaching. This was the Pontifical Institute of Medieval Studies (PIMS), based at St Michael's (Catholic) College in the University of Toronto. This institute was founded in order to pass on a Christian philosophical way of life, one that displayed many of the features of the medieval mentality he had taught and written about with such renown in France. PIMS was intended 'to learn the medieval way of seeking truth in the light of Christian revelation'.[6] The curriculum at this institute would be multidisciplinary and holistic: it would include philosophy, theology, art, architecture, liturgy and literature. Gilson wanted graduates from this Institute to be able to locate their understanding of the thought of medieval writers within the context of the social and political events of that era, the canon and civil law that governed or restricted their lives, their liturgical experience and even the art and architecture that both illustrated and shaped their view of the world.[7]

In a recent doctoral thesis, Ronald Hurl shows that, for Gilson, PIMS was two things. 'First, it was a school of philosophy to foster an intellectual way of life much like Plato's Academy, Aristotle's Lyceum, Justin Martyr's philosophical school in Rome, St Clement's, Origen's Catechetical School of Alexandria, and Augustine's monastic school of philosophy. Second, it was also a place dedicated to preserving Western culture much like the Northumbrian monastery of Bede the Venerable (*c.*672–735) and the Palatine court of Charlemagne headed by Alcuin of York (735–804).'[8] Furthermore, it was important for Gilson, as the first Director of PIMS, that the education given there was formational, not merely instruction; that is, it must develop the inner life and culture of students and scholars, not merely convey knowledge and skills.[9] While not being narrowly confessional in its coverage (which included Jewish and Muslim literature), the educational vision at PIMS was explicitly inspired by Christian faith. Gilson argued that bringing into play an historical perspective is the only way to properly engage modern problems and revive the Christian philosophical life in a creative fashion.

Teaching

Gilson was a famous and frequently sought-after lecturer; and he inspired many students as a teacher, mentor and scholar, who themselves went on to have glittering academic careers. Hurl notes that Harvard University loved Gilson's popular teaching style and wanted him to train the other teachers there how to teach.[10]

One can draw five valuable lessons from Gilson's observations about teaching. First, he had a very high regard for teaching. As he believed that the teacher is a servant of truth and that the intellect participates in the divine light, he considered the vocation of teacher to be one of collaborating in a divine work; that of assisting in the growth of human persons in the sight of God. Such work had two components: contemplation and action. 'Teaching consists in communicating to others a truth meditated beforehand. It demands of necessity both the reflection of the contemplative in order to discover the truth, and the activity of the professor in order to communicate his findings to others. ... Teaching is the outward expression of inward contemplation'.[11] Drawing from Aquinas, he wrote, 'to act in view of imparting to others the fruit of contemplation is nobler than contemplation alone'.[12]

Second, teachers cannot do the thinking of their students for them; they must get people to think for themselves. 'There is no transfusion of learning in the sense that there are transfusions of blood. We can give our own blood to others; we cannot give them our own learning.'[13] By offering their students the example of a person patiently and doggedly seeking truth, the pains to be taken and the excitement and joy of this search, they can stimulate others to do the same. Shrewdly, he warned that what students actually learn from their teachers is often rather different from what their teachers hope they are learning.[14] Nevertheless, the task of a teacher is to galvanise the student to engage in the effort; to subject him or herself to the disciplines of learning. To obtain this effort and engagement by students is 'the highest and noblest part in the work of the teacher. It is also by far the most difficult one'.[15] However, it should be noted that, while Gilson thought that 'The proper effect of the act of teaching is to cause a personal discovery in the mind of the pupil',[16] he was very clear also that the effort involved in the ownership and internalisation of truth did not make that truth merely a subjective construction. 'We have so often thought, and written, and taught our students that the *discovery* of truth is a personal affair, that we have come either to think, or to make them believe, that truth itself is a personal affair'.[17] For him, to attain truth is to be in touch with objective reality; something valid universally, not just applicable to an individual.

Third, he emphasised the personal nature of the teacher-pupil relationship, one that is 'more intimate than that of the physician to patient, because it does not obtain between a mind and a body, but between two minds'.[18] Hopefully, this distinction would be less applicable today, when a more holistic approach to doctor-patient relations is standard. Given his understanding of teaching as oriented to the journey towards truth, this relationship called for 'a spiritual affinity between master and disciple,' such that both teachers and students 'wish to walk down the same road'.[19] Yet this affinity could not ignore that 'the very act of teaching implies the admission of a certain inequality, not indeed in nature, nor even in intellectual ability, but at least in knowledge'.[20] At least during the pedagogical process, if not outside it, a certain asymmetry exists between teacher and pupil. Some forms of affection and friendliness by teachers might prevent pupils from making the necessary effort to wrestle with the demands made upon them, even though sympathy and encouragement for pupils provide important support for learning.

Fourth, Gilson thought that the process of teaching gives teachers new opportunities to learn themselves; it was not simply sharing the fruits of their earlier acts of contemplation, a communication of a truth they had previously discovered, but a prompt for their further learning and their deeper appreciation of the implications of what was being taught. 'The real teaching begins when you are beginning to teach yourself, that is to say, to realise the meaning of what you have been taught'.[21]

Finally, Gilson was wise enough to point out that teachers should not expect from many of their pupils a profound appreciation of the efforts put in on their behalf. 'However heavily we load our programmes, and however widely we may diversify them in order to answer the future needs of all our pupils, many of them will feel later on that they have been taught many things they did not need to know, whereas what they did need to know has never been taught to them in school'.[22] Idealism on the part of teachers, while necessary, must be matched by realism about how their work might be assessed by their students. Very often any rewards in teaching must come from the sense of exercising a worthwhile vocation, an act of loving service.

The intelligence at God's service

Gilson had great respect for intellectual work. It was a central feature of his Christian discipleship. Yet he acknowledged that it also carried the risk of deflecting us from our relationship to God and indeed, slipping into idolatry. 'Either we will serve him in spirit and in truth, or we shall enslave ourselves ceaselessly, more and more, to the monstrous idol which we have made with our own hands to our own image and likeness'.[23] When worship is neglected, the rest of human endeavours will be undermined and then Christians stop being salt and light to the world. 'Humanity out of proportion to God finds itself out of proportion to everything'.[24]

He knew that some Christians throughout history had distrusted any reliance on rational speculation. 'In our day, as in the Middle Ages,' [it may be felt that] 'science swells up; intellectual curiosity, because it tends to engage all the activities of the mind, risks cooling our taste for interior progress. ... Whoever wants to make of reason the whole of the mind ruins the mind, and if a certain antirationalism still exists today, the responsibility for it is incumbent as much on those who misapprehend reason by excess than on those who may misapprehend it by default'.[25] Three comments are in order to show how Gilson thought that the intelligence could be safeguarded so that it could act in God's service.

First, he insisted on the ascetic nature of intellectual work and the importance of a close relationship between intellectual and moral virtues. Scholarly investigation 'requires a painful effort to make the choice of a specific form of being'.[26] Here he refers to the cost of following a vocation. 'Servitude is the necessary path to being and emancipation'; in submitting to an exterior discipline 'we agree to benefit from the moral experience of all humanity'.[27] 'A true scholar is a man [sic] whose intellectual life is part and parcel of his moral life. ... Moral honesty is, at the bottom, a scrupulous respect for the rules of justice; intellectual honesty is a scrupulous respect for truth'.[28] Gilson uses the word 'hygiene' to describe the positive value of being subject to the asceticism that is part of artistic, scholarly and religious endeavour. 'Just as art is hygiene for our sensibility, morality is hygiene for the will. ... Above art and morality, and encompassing them, stands religion, the superior hygiene of the personality.'[29]

Second, he considered that the intellectual light that could dawn in humanity, both as the fruit of our own efforts to seek truth and from the example and promptings of others, constituted in a special way the presence of something divine in us. Ultimately, all truth comes from God, even if we fail to acknowledge God as the source. Thus, for Gilson, to educate is to play a role in the growth of something divine within humanity.

Third, Gilson uses a very interesting refrain: *'piety never dispenses with technique.'*[30] In an essay entitled 'The Intelligence in the Service of Christ the King' he explains how both piety and technique are required in deploying intelligence for the sake of Christ. 'For technique is that without which even the most lively piety is incapable of using nature for God. To serve God by science or art, it is necessary to begin by practicing them *as if* these disciplines were in themselves their own ends. ... It is impossible to place the intelligence at the service of God without respecting integrally the rights of the intelligence: otherwise it would not be the intelligence that is put at His service; but still more is it impossible to do so without respecting the rights of God: otherwise it is no longer at His service that the intelligence is placed.'[31] Having holy intentions to serve God is insufficient if we have the capacity but lack the discipline to ensure that our efforts are carried out competently. Becoming competent in the relevant disciplines is part of our religious duty if our service is to be rightly directed and properly exercised, and if our work is to honour God. If Christians wish to serve God, using the talents they have been given, they should also be well-informed on what the Church teaches about the nature and ends of the social order (if they are politicians), or about the ends and means of education (if they are teachers), or knowledgeable about the Christian understanding of the human person (if they are in medicine).

Christians in society

In addition to his main work as a university professor, Gilson exercised an important role as a public intellectual concerned about the political choices of his era. He regularly engaged in debates about the place of the Church and the responsibilities of Christians in a secular society; especially with regard to political parties, education, international relations, European reconstruction, and through his advocacy of a liberal interpretation of secularity that is not hostile to religious faith. For an overview of his thinking about how Christians should relate to the political and social world, see the series of lectures he gave in 1952.[32] He protested against anti-Semitism, warned against excessive nationalism and acted as a faithful yet also critical friend to the Catholic Church. The focus here is on Gilson's views on how Christians should relate to the State and, as a major subset of this, his defence of Christian education against incursions from it.

The Christian of any era has to live in the world of their time and work out the relation of their faith to that era. 'Nothing is less modern than the crisis of relations between Christianity and the modern world,'[33] he wrote in 1946. He rejected communism, fascism and any subordination of politics to economics or of ethics and spirituality to politics. He walked a path that avoided both modernism (which conceded too much to the assumptions of modern culture) and integralism (which set Christians apart and in hostility to that culture). Key themes in his public interventions were the need for constructive engagement in society by Christians, freedom from State control in the expression and conduct of their faith, developing a renewed Christian humanism, and the primacy of worship as the context for right thinking and action. He also stressed the importance of Christian schools for the healthy future of the Church, called them to offer serious Christian teaching by teachers who have experienced appropriate Christian teacher training and formation that fits them to serve as authentic Christian educators.

If the role of the State is to promote the common good and secure the temporal goods of the people, it is the Church's role to help people respond to their supernatural call from God to share in the divine life. The State, while claiming to be neutral in matters of religion, often slips from neutrality into being an adversary, seeking to prevent religious believers from expressing their faith in the public domain. Some secularists claim that they only wish to constrain religion that is abusive, dogmatic and fanatical – in other words, the deformations and depravities of religion; but this leads to a situation where they alone claim to know what true religion is, and where those who wish to follow a religion must be instructed by those who practice no religion themselves.[34]

An important distinction is made by Gilson between the world and nature; these are not to be confused in his view. The Christian is called simultaneously to negate the world but to affirm nature. 'The "world" is not nature; it is nature seeking to be independent of God, to become something autonomous, self-contained and self-sufficient. Christians must avoid two dangers here: either accepting the world in affirming nature, or denying nature in affirming super-nature.'[35]

He pointed out that it would not be sufficient to deepen their own faith (vital though this was); further than that, it was necessary to understand social realities and assumptions, and the strengths and weaknesses of society, if there was to be any hope of acting effectively within it and to be in a position to influence it.[36] In social and political engagement, the task is to seek to ensure that the conditions required for the full development of religious life are assured.[37] In order to create a climate that is favourable to Christian works, and which enhances their fruitfulness, Christians must assist in the development of an informed and self-aware Christian public opinion.[38] To carry out such a task of developing a Christian public opinion there needs to be unity among Christians and the capacity to organise themselves to work together. Nothing is further from Gilson's mind than a retreat from society or abstention from social engagement, just because it is contaminated by false ideas and values.[39]

As for his defence of Christian education, Gilson begins by clarifying what he means by the liberal State and then offers a succinct definition of Christian education. 'By liberal State, we mean any State which does not set itself up as the ultimate end of its citizens. By Christian education, we mean the kind of education which is given in schools in which the whole life of both teachers and pupils is informed by the love of Christ.'[40] Then he calls his fellow believers to work towards a new 'Catholic order'. This call meant for him neither a restoration of a previous Catholic style of regime, where Church and State operated hand-in-glove, nor the segregation of Catholics as a form of interior secession or counter-society; rather, he meant putting in order or restoring to internal harmony a currently fragmented Catholicism in France. One might describe this as a rejuvenated form of Christian presence, in the world: plural, lay-led (but informed by a teaching Church) and inspired by the Gospel.[41]

Gilson claims that, for the first time in history since the end of the classical period, the western world 'has begun not only to reject Christian faith, but even to refuse to live on the intellectual and moral capital that Christianity had accumulated for it'.[42] He sees a close resemblance between the situation around him in France in the 1930s and that of the first Christians who struggled for their faith in a Roman Empire whose forces were ranged against them. Moral disorder is not something new; but what is different now is that, so acclimatised have people become to prevailing forms of paganism, they do not even realise that they are living in the midst of moral disorder. If there is any truth in this, then Christians need to re-think how they set about fostering the conditions for upholding, sharing and deepening their faith. And of course that includes what goes on in their schools.

Gilson advocates a Church free from the State. Even State protection for the Church, however desirable some think this would be, would be a temptation and would not lead to the Christianisation of society. The separation of Church and State offers a fine opportunity for a renewal within Christianity. In seeking to avoid either privilege for the Church or persecution of it, Gilson does two things. First he asks from unbelievers for a level playing field for Christians who should be allowed to contribute to the common good with the resources at their disposal. Then he warns Christians that, in asking for equal treatment, they must show themselves worthy of it.[43] They have to be as professionally competent as their secular counterparts. Gilson does not ask for favours for Christian schools, simply for State support proportional to the services these schools offer to society. However, he counsels his readers that they should be aware that the State will seek to domesticate the Church when it pays for her services; it will try to restrain and control the scope of Christian educators to provide Christian education.

***

Without doubt, some of Gilson's ideas remain contentious. Yet he continues to offer Christian educators a valuable example of how they can understand and live out their vocation: putting their gifts at God's service, combining love of truth with care for students, and drawing on a well-informed historical perspective that is receptive to the wisdom of the past as a resource for addressing the needs of the present. Above all, for teachers in Catholic schools and universities, he models how to go about the task of holding together and, ideally, integrating, in a manner that is mutually reinforcing, the life of faith, professional competence, intellectual rigour and engagement in the world.

ENDNOTES

1   For example, Étienne Gilson, *History of Christian Philosophy in the Middle Ages*, London: Sheed and Ward, 1995.

2   Richard J. Fafara, *Étienne Gilson. Formation and Accomplishment*, Toronto: Pontifical Institute of Medieval Studies, 2018.

3   Florian Michel, *Étienne Gilson*, Paris: Vrin, 2018, p. 299.

4   Fafara, *Étienne Gilson*, p. 15.

5   Ronald H. Hurl, *Ars Christiane Philosophandi: Étienne Gilson's Concrete Approach to the Christian Love of Wisdom*, PhD thesis, Catholic University of America, Washington, D.C., 2016, p. 243.

6   Hurl, *Ars Christiane Philosophandi*, p. 7.

7   James K. Farge, 'Why and How Gilson's Institute of Medieval Studies was Different from Other Medieval Programs', *Studia Gilsonia*, 10, no.4 (October-December 2021), pp.775 – 786.

8   Hurl, *Ars Christiane Philosophandi*, pp. 358-9.

9   Ibid., pp. 409-410; 425.

10 Ibid., p. 416.

11 Étienne Gilson, *A Gilson Reader: Selections from the Writings of Étienne Gilson*, edited by Anton C. Pegis, New York: Doubleday/Image, 1957, p. 224.

12 Gilson, *Gilson Reader*, p. 311.

13 Ibid., p. 307.

14 Étienne Gilson, *History of Philosophy and Philosophical Education*, Milwaukee: Marquette University Press, 1948, p. 10.

15 Gilson, *Gilson Reader*, p. 303.

16 Ibid., p. 306.

17 Étienne Gilson, *Un Philosophe dans la Cité*. Oeuvres completes. Tome 1. Edited by Florian Michel, Paris: Vrin, 2019, p. 329.

18 Gilson, *Gilson Reader*, p. 306.

19 Gilson, *History of Philosophy*, p. 22.

20 Gilson, *Gilson Reader*, p. 302.

21 Gilson, *Philosophe dans la Cité*, p. 200.

22 Gilson, *Gilson Reader*, pp. 308–9.

23 Étienne Gilson, 'The Terrors of the Year Two Thousand,' lecture at St Michael's College, University of Toronto, 1948, p.18. Reprinted 1984.

24 Francesca Aran Murphy, *Art and Intellect in the Philosophy of Étienne Gilson*, Columbia, Missouri: University of Missouri Press, 2004, p. 272.

25 Étienne Gilson, 'Essay on the Interior Life,' *Revue philosophique de la France et de l'étranger* 89, (1920): 23–78, pp. 500, 524. Republished as Appendix to Alex Yeung, *Imago Dei Creatoris - Étienne Gilson's 'Essay on the Interior Life' and Its Seminal Influence,* PhD thesis, 2011, Rome: Ateneo Pontificio Regina Apostolorum.

26 Gilson, *Interior Life*, p. 504.

27 Ibid., p. 521.

28 Gilson, *Gilson Reader*, p. 26.

29 Gilson, *Interior Life*, pp. 519, 520.

30 Gilson, *Gilson Reader*, p. 40.

31 Ibid., pp. 40-41.

32 Étienne Gilson, *The Metamorphoses of the City of God,* translated by James G. Colbert, Washington, DC: Catholic University of America Press, 2020.

33 Michel, *Étienne Gilson*, p. 32.

34 Gilson, *Philosophe dans la Cité*, pp. 550, 556.

35 Ibid., pp. 668-71.

36 Étienne Gilson, *Pour un Ordre Catholique,* Paris: Parole et Silence, 2013, p. 26 (originally Paris: Desclée de Brouwer, 1934).

37 Gilson, *Pour un Ordre Catholique,* p. 28.

38 Ibid., p. 35.

39 Ibid., p. 36.

40 Étienne Gilson, 'The Breakdown of Morals and Christian Education' lecture at St Michael's College, University of Toronto, 2 February 1952. https://www.catholiceducation.org/en/education/catholic-contributions/the-breakdown-of-morals-and-christian-education.html; accessed on 18 April 2020.

41 Gilson, *Philosophe dans la Cité,* p. 15.

42 Gilson, *Pour un Ordre Catholique*, p. 162.

43 Ibid., p. 71.

Conclusion

It would be an overstatement to claim that each of the figures whose life and writings have been presented in this book were all singing the same tune, or that their respective messages were merely echoes of each other. There are obvious differences between them due to differences in their historical and cultural context, their personal location and upbringing, their personality and special skill set, the resources available to them, the company they kept and the challenges they faced. Nevertheless, it is possible to note common themes which surface again and again in their teaching. Among these, the following deserve a mention.

First, there is the interconnectedness of all aspects of creation, each of which has God as its author and in each of which God is at work. Second, Christ is the key to understanding creation and God's purposes in it, as well as showing the character of God and what human beings can be like if in communion with God, living according to the pattern of Christ and by the power of the Holy Spirit. Third, they believed that we can only properly understand any creature or aspect of creation if we take into account its relationship to God. Fourth, their Christian anthropology depicts men and women as being made in the image of God and invited to grow into God's likeness by aligning themselves with God's purposes, a process which calls for integration of all aspects of our nature: physical, emotional, psychological, intellectual, moral, social, cultural and spiritual. Fifth, each of the witnesses we have considered in the preceding chapters both outlined in their writing and exemplified through their practice the necessary moral virtues and teacher qualities that render Christian life attractive, and that make Christian education credible, winsome and life-enhancing.

As Christian educators, the men and women who have been examined here operated in diverse contexts and for diverse groups. Therefore the form or genre of their teaching took different shapes according to the situation of those they sought to reach and influence. An important factor in my selection of key exponents of the art of Christian education in the Catholic tradition was to make evident the very broad scope of Christian education and the wide range of 'students' being addressed, both in Part One, which covered earlier centuries of the Church's history, and in Part Two, which has as its focus Catholic educators from the twentieth century.

As for Part One, Maximus shared his understanding of Christian faith with fellow monks, secular rulers and leading figures in the Church, doing so in his letters and through his writings. In him we find a complex but fully integrated worldview where Christ reveals the mysteries of God and how they all cohere together. Christian doctrine and its implications for spiritual life were the focus of his concern. Hildegard, who received a much more informal education than all the other figures treated in this book, conveyed her message via her many letters but mainly in her role as abbess and founder of Benedictine communities. Her principal audience was women and she gave much attention to the nature and needs of a community of women religious, including both their physical and psychological wellbeing, as well as their spiritual development. Externally to the community for which she was responsible, a major concern for her was the laxity and shortcomings of the clergy, and the need for reform in the Church if heresy was to be avoided and authentic Gospel living was to be embraced. Thus, her teaching took on a prophetic tone. In contrast, Bonaventure shared some of Hildegard's concerns in his role as spiritual leader of the emerging Franciscan order, but, unlike her, he also studied to a very high level and he went on to exercise a significant teaching role at the university in Paris, lecturing and writing major theological treatises which exerted considerable influence throughout Europe.

With regard to Part Two, as a lay woman, Edith Stein had considerable teaching experience in a modern secondary school. She also taught in higher education, with a special focus on the formation, initial and ongoing education of teachers. In later years a prime target group for her reflections was the Carmelite community she had joined. One also comes across many of her insights into teaching in the prolific correspondence she kept up with the numerous people who depended on her for advice. As with Hildegard, Stein gave special attention to the role of women, not only in religious life, or in the home, but also in society and in professional life. Elizabeth Jennings was neither a member of a religious order, nor an academic. Her teaching was not carried out in educational institutions; instead it was communicated in her poetry and, to a lesser extent, her writings about literature. If the sacramental perspective is a vital element in a Catholic worldview, Jennings' poetry and other writings eminently demonstrate how that perspective lights up nature, art, human experience and liturgical seasons. Paulo Freire devoted his whole life to education, principally concerned to revitalise adult education in his own teaching, his university lectures on education, as an educational policy maker and as an international consultant. He bridged the gap that often exists between, on the one hand, promoting authentic personal relationships which display respect for, affirm the dignity of and empower autonomy and agency among learners, and, on the other hand, committed political engagement in aid of liberation of those he wished to serve. As with Hildegard, Freire was prophetic in tone and role. Marshall McLuhan and Walter Ong spent their careers working as university lecturers. Both addressed technological change and its effects on education, the Church, social life and culture. As a result, they alerted their readers and their students to the sights and sounds, the images and media that are pervasive in modern society; in doing so, they challenged their students and the public at large to be much more discerning about what they were assimilating and the effects, often unconscious, on their assumptions, outlook, priorities and values. Étienne Gilson demonstrated in his life and work the harmony between faith and reason, and he modelled how to combine personal commitment to Christian discipleship with high-calibre professional and academic rigour. In his public engagement on behalf of the cause of Christian education (illuminated by the Catholic intellectual and spiritual tradition) he re-energised much Catholic scholarship, championed resistance to secularising forces that would empty education of its Christian legacy, and challenged Catholics to improve the quality of their educational provision.

There are other features held in common by these lights for our path. I pick out six here for consideration, and readers are invited to reflect on the bearing of these in their own life and work.

First, all of them were conscious of inheriting a legacy from the Christian intellectual and spiritual tradition passed on to them by the faithful from previous generations. What had been received from the past constituted for each of them a precious resource which offered a reliable foundation and framework for the tasks facing them. What had been inherited needed to be assimilated, internalised, owned, enacted, shared and re-invested in ways that responded to the tradition with creative fidelity.

Second, both the need and the scope for grateful giving back to others what had been received would be both facilitated and restricted according to the opportunities and limitations of their cultural context, personal location and particular gifts. Only some things, not everything desirable, could be achieved. Therefore prioritising was incumbent on each of them. That required careful discernment of their gifts and how these could be applied in the situations they faced.

This leads into a third common feature: they all possessed a strong sense of vocation, of hearing a call from God that spoke to them, not only of where God wanted them to be, who God wanted them to serve, what God expected them to do and how God wanted them carry this out, but, above all, a conviction about who God wanted them to be. When one senses that God is calling one in this way, one experiences a combination of God's demandingness (such that 'I can't *not* do this; I would be untrue to myself, inauthentic and lost if I refused') and divine affirmation (hearing internally the words 'you have my mandate for this, my support and my confidence that you have it in you to do it, to my satisfaction at least'). As the storyteller George MacDonald put it: 'Every one of us is something that the other is not, and therefore knows something – maybe without knowing that they know it – which no one else knows; and it is everyone's task, as one of the kingdom of light and an inheritor of it all, to give their portion to the rest'.[1] Clarity and stability in one's vocation has the benefit of providing not only orientation (one knows in what direction to look; one's horizon does not constantly shift with every passing wind or storm), but also centredness.

> Whatever we want at the centre of ourselves shapes the environment around us. Purity of heart and singleness of purpose are opposite sides of the same coin. Everybody is centred single-mindedly on something: on family, on work, on leisure, on money, on something! The only difference is that those who are pure of heart in the classical sense are centred on the 'ultimates' of life, on God, goodness, love, justice and wholeness of heart.[2]

Teachers who are centred on what is ultimately important and life-giving possess an internal compass which enables them to find a way forward even in the midst of complex situations and ambiguous circumstances. Nurturing a sense of vocation should assist educators in maintaining a humble confidence in using their gifts. It can be salutary for teachers and academics to ask themselves occasionally: what is the good I hope to do for my students through my work?

Fourth, the people examined in these pages found themselves having to address challenges and to face threats that presented major obstacles to the exercise of their roles. Maximus experienced the wrath of the Emperor, leading to banishment and then mutilation. Hildegard was dismayed by the shortcomings of many of the clergy and the distortions of the faith advocated by heretics. She also battled lifelong and debilitating physical ailments as well as criticisms of some of her initiatives. Bonaventure had to steer a middle path between alternative and sometimes extreme interpretations of the Franciscan charism, as well as deal with suspicion and often resentment from secular priests on the university faculty about the growing influence of the still relatively new mendicant orders. Edith Stein faced wearying and painful opposition within her family when she converted from Judaism to Christianity. Then as a woman, she encountered resistance from university authorities and a refusal to allow her the academic post her qualifications and ability deserved. Above, all, however, because of her Jewish descent, she was the victim of the poisonous and ultimately deadly anti-Semitism of her time. Elizabeth Jennings suffered from both physical and psychological problems for much of her life, she went through periods of depression and hospitalisation, even attempting to take her own life. Paulo Freire experienced imprisonment and exile as a result of his efforts to reform education in Brazil, rarely received due recognition from his church and encountered suspicion on account of his use of Marxist themes in his critique of damaging approaches to education. It is probably fair to say that McLuhan and Ong had things considerably easier than any of the men and women just mentioned, but they too went through moments of self-doubt and experienced misunderstanding of what they were attempting to communicate. Gilson battled for a space for Catholic education that resisted the forces of both communism and fascism which would both destroy Christian culture. He combatted the sceptical rationalism that prevailed in the university context of his time, not only by exposing its philosophical incoherence, but also by pointing out its damaging social consequences. And he played an important part in opening up a more authentic interpretation of the thought of that guiding light of Catholic educators, St Thomas Aquinas –

at a time when such an approach was still highly suspect in some Church circles.

Fifth, in the face of such opposition, and in response to the trials undergone, each of our 'lights' displayed endurance, perseverance and unflagging trust in God. They were committed to the long haul, regardless of whether this was accompanied by any sense of achievement or success. They would have signed up to the wise observation: 'Know that what we have to endure is as important as what we can do.'[3] As teachers, it is likely that we will at various times experience many types of obstacles. These might include periods when we lack inspiration, or when we meet indifference from our students in response to our self-giving. At other times we can encounter resistance from colleagues to proposals we put forward, as well as misunderstanding of our purposes, methods or priorities from some parents. Unsympathetic bosses and modes of evaluation that slip into surveillance that feels intrusive, even demeaning, can undermine our enthusiasm for our work. We can feel bewilderment at the pace of change when that seems to us to distort, obstruct or undermine our own commitment to what is needed; or we become frustrated with the slowness of those changes we deem to be necessary. Whatever our particular educational context, we can be sure that endurance, perseverance and trust will also be asked of us. If we are to survive beyond the most difficult moments, it will be necessary for us to find resources and practices that contribute towards healing and personal renewal in order that we can continue to carry out our role in the right spirit; we need to beware becoming overstretched, tired, or even risking burnout. When that happens, we are more liable to make mistakes, to lose heart, to feel dismayed by set-backs and shortcomings. Self-knowledge must include awareness of our limitations and needs, as well as of the gifts we ought to be sharing. Often we can only sow seeds, then let God bring them to harvest. Fortunately, God is not in a hurry and God's timetable runs differently from ours. Our loving presence, rather than our productivity, our availability rather than our ability, this is what God asks of us.

A sixth feature, shared by the witnesses brought forward for our attention, is their assumption that there should be no sharp separation between three dimensions of a Christian educator's role, dimensions that too often are treated in isolation from one another: the spiritual, the intellectual and the professional or practical. There is a danger that spiritual considerations are kept apart, not only from everyday concerns about sex and shopping, household management and financial investment, physical exercise, entertainment and leisure, but also from the murky world of voting and politics, leadership and policy-making, the exercise of power and influence, as well as from academic questions about the types, sources, reliability and modes of evaluation of knowledge, and the merits of different approaches to pedagogy. Too sharp a separation between spiritual, intellectual and practical considerations leaves the spiritual in an ideal realm that lacks connection with either rationality or the practical demands made on professional educators. It also threatens to deploy intellectual concerns in a narrowly objective cognitive manner that fails to attend to the subjective and spiritual roots of the knower, and thus to remove theory from the reality experienced on the ground. The spiritual writer Evelyn Underhill noted a century ago that:

> The distinction between the spiritual life and the everyday things of life is false. We cannot divide them. One affects the other all the time. ... The spiritual life is simply a life in which all that we do comes from the centre, where we are anchored in God; a life soaked through and through by a sense of his reality and claim, and self-given to the great movement of his will.[4]

God is not to be removed to a safe sacred space that is uncontaminated by mundane concerns. As a contemporary spiritual writer observes, 'The way to know if God is being born in the messy stable of your life is if God revolutionises the way you think, the way you act and the way you treat other people'.[5] Thus the spiritual has to touch down into, or be incarnated in the quality of our intellectual operations, our professional tasks and in our relationships.

Let me close my extended appreciation of and commentary on

the men and women proposed as lights for the path of teachers in Catholic schools and universities with the following prayer:

> As I journey on alone, grant me:
> the eyes to see the adventure unfolding before me,
> when all I can see is the death of my hopes;
> the ears to hear Your whisper in the silence, calling me on,
> when all I can hear is the echo of my own small voice;
> the courage to believe in Your promise for my future,
> when all that seems real are the mistakes of my past.
> Be my constant companion every step of the way
> And, when aloneness turns to loneliness,
> Grant me the comfort of knowing that
> Underneath are the everlasting arms.[6]

ENDNOTES

1   George MacDonald, quoted by Northumbria Community Trust, *Celtic Daily Prayer. Book Two,* London: William Collins 2015, pp. 1476–7.

2   Joan Chittister, quoted by Northumbria Community Trust, *Celtic Daily Prayer. Book Two,* London: William Collins p. 1165.

3   Roland Walls and the Community of the Transfiguration, quoted by Northumbria Community Trust, *Celtic Daily Prayer. Book Two,* London: William Collins p. 1409.

4   Evelyn Underhill, *The Spiritual Life,* London and Oxford: Mowbray, Underhill, 1984, pp. 31–2.

5   Mark Oakley, *By Way of the Heart,* Norwich: Canterbury Press, 2019, p. 135.

6   Northumbrian Community Trust, *Celtic Daily Prayer. Book Two,* London: William Collins, 2015, p. 1026.

Questions for Personal Reflection or Group Discussion

1. Is there anything in the chapter that reinforces or affirms the beliefs you already held before reading this book?
2. What, if anything, in the chapter strikes you as unfamiliar, strange or difficult to grasp and which might be worth investigating, following up or further reflection (perhaps with the help of others)?
3. Does the worldview and faith of the person who is the focus of the chapter differ in any way from your own in content or emphasis? If so, how?
4. Which ideas in the chapter seem most fertile for and relevant to your own educational context? Which notions seem to you to be not applicable to or which could not be put into practice in your teaching? What are the major obstacles or challenges in your educational context to applying the beliefs and practices of the person who is the subject of this chapter?
5. If you were asked to identify ONE key point from the chapter which you hope will guide or inspire your own practice as an educator in a Catholic school or university, what would you select?